This beautiful creature has always m. When I Googled it for info, I found out many cultures associate the butterfly with our soul and that Christianity sees it as a symbol of resurrection. Many see it representing endurance, change, hope, and life. It is a spiritual symbol for life after death because of its metamorphosis, or transformation, from a caterpillar that crawls on the ground to a beautiful, almost-ethereal creature that flies through the air.

Five things to learn from the butterfly (technical information from Christian Devereaux, PhD, LCAT, LMHC, BC-DMT) when I Googled *butterfly*:

- If nothing changes, nothing changes. Metamorphosis has four stages, and each stage is dependent on the other. Change is sometimes painful but necessary. If no change occurs, then the butterfly cannot fly!
- Everything we are taking in will be fuel and nourishment for our new form. The first stage is the feeding stage. The caterpillar must eat and eat to fill itself with nourishment to be stored and used later as an adult. Trust that the process is nourishing one's future form, even if the experiences are particularly challenging.
- Shedding of old patterns is necessary. The caterpillar splits and sheds its skin four to five times, needed to occur more than once.
- Solitude provides space and time for internalization. After the caterpillar is full-grown and stops eating, it becomes a chrysalis, at which point it suspends itself under a branch, hides in the leaves, or buries itself underground. During times of transition, we may need to go underground as well for our own emotional and personal transition. It may look

like nothing is going on, but big changes are happening. The special cells are growing rapidly. They will become legs, wings, eyes, and other parts of the adult butterfly. This takes a week, a month, or even longer.

- Sometimes a breaking down must occur in order for restructuring to begin. The last stage of the caterpillar actually means the body is required to break down its parts or liquefy in order to come into another form (melting into the process) where one can feel for a period like one is holding on to nothing. We may not consciously identify what is happening, but the body can sense the changes and has a range of emotional reactions.

By reflecting on these five lessons, we can learn from the movements of metamorphosis that may lead us to satisfying transformation into new forms.

I heard a story about a scientist who observed the challenge the chrysalis was having, straining and trying to free itself from the hard cocoon and took mercy on the butterfly trying to emerge and clipped the edge to free the butterfly. The beautiful butterfly came out, wobbled, and fell over, then died. The lesson could be that it is essential to go through the painful process of spiritual birth to become a beautiful creation to fly! Read 2 Corinthians 5:17–21, Galatians 2:20, Isaiah 43:18–19, Colossians 3:9–10, Ephesians 2:10, Ezekiel 11:19–20, Romans 6:1–23, 2 Peter 1:4, Ephesians 4:22–24, John 3:16, and Acts 2:38–39.

# Dedication

I dedicate this book to the awesome Creator, God of the Universe, who encouraged me through the Holy Spirit to pen these words to encourage others, to remind them they can have a home with Him after this earth existence and how to get there, along with how to survive the challenges of this world! Father God, with my Savior and Lord, Jesus, and my Teacher/Friend, the Holy Spirit, have inspired, taught, and directed me in this effort. What a journey we have had! Reading the Word and allowing the Holy Spirit to teach and heal me and others has been my focus. Along the way, God has provided loving people like my husband, parents, family, extended family, a myriad of friends and then used the challenges of circumstances and people to hone me and teach me to be an overcomer. My wonderful spiritual books have me perusing their treasures, and there are many being opened at one time to gain the true lesson for me to learn. I celebrate you, God, for who you are and what you mean in my life and the lives of those who allow you to be the most important focus in theirs. Thank you for being the Potter, taking my sins, my bad choices, my thoughtless shortcomings, and everything that does not glorify you, to spend the time with me to mold me and help me become more like you, Lord.

My generous and loving husband has given me the freedom to be me and encouraged my efforts to pen this endeavor. What a blessing he has been to my life and my spiritual growth! Thank you, Jim, for your thoughtfulness, support, and unconditional love!

I do not believe I have ever been able to convey adequately to my children what they (and their extended families, the grandchildren and spouses) have meant to my life. My fantasies as a child were filled by having a family to love. My children, Gregory, Julie, and James, have offered so many gifts to me in this life. They are so cherished and a vital part of my life, and I am so thankful for these life experiences through them. Often they were the teachers, perhaps unknowingly, but a vital part of my growth and spiritual relationship. I thank the Lord for my parents and stepparent. Mother was God's thread of love (flowing through her) to enrich me, and I miss her so much. Every person that I have come in contact with during this life journey has taught me something if I allowed it, because the Lord promises He can turn something good into everything for those who love the Lord and are called according to His purpose (loosely translated from Romans 8:28). I am so genuinely thankful for all my family and friends who have loved, inspired, encouraged, and helped me through some pretty tough times and offered support of all kinds to my life. I am thankful for the challenges I have encountered, for they are important teachers when I allow the Lord to use them to perfect His mighty work for my growth. Praise you, God, for your loving faithfulness and mercy with grace toward me. I do believe we carry with us some of the qualities of those who touch our lives.

Blessings,
Patti Grace

# Contents

Foreword 9

Preface: Why This Book? 13

Acknowledgments 17

About the Author 21

Chapter 1: What to Expect to Receive from This Fellowship 25

Chapter 2: Knowing God: The Godhead, the Trinity 41

Chapter 3: What Voices Are You Listening To? 59

Chapter 4: Watch Your Words 67

Chapter 5: Taking Care of the Temple That Houses the Holy Spirit 79

Chapter 6: The Facts of Life 117

Chapter 7: Ways to Develop Intimacy with the Holy Spirit: Remembering Your First Love 135

Chapter 8: Weapons Provided for a Believer: Spiritual Warfare 163

Chapter 9: Crying Out to God: And Some of God's Responses 177

Chapter 10: The Fruit of the Spirit: So How Far Have You Come in Your Walk? 187

Chapter 11: About Prayers 191

Chapter 12: Final Remarks 199

Chapter 13: Extra Goodies: A Collection of Inspirations to Uplift You (From Family and Friends) 203

## Foreword

I have recently gotten to know Patti very well through Bible study and the struggles that have hit her in recent times. She is a walking miracle after what she has come through in her health. I trust her knowledge on the Holy Spirit to be a very thought-provoking read and one that will cause growth to happen, because I know the Hand of the Lord is on her. Patti, God bless you as you share who the Holy Spirit is!

—Pastor William Cole
Current pastor of Christ Centered Church

\*\*\*\*\*

Patti and I have been Christian friends for many years. We have worshiped together, prayed together, and cried together. She has been such an inspiration to me due to her kind heart, thoughtfulness for others, and deep relationship with the Lord. Patti has helped me grow deeper in my faith, and I've seen the Lord work in her life, especially during the time when we almost lost her in 2019 to a terrible aneurysm. But our God healed her as she had to finish this book in hopes to bring others closer to Him. We call each other our Prayer Warrior. The one thing that I know for sure is, when I need someone to pray for me, she is who I call, as she has a direct line to God Almighty. This book, I know in my heart, was inspired by our Heavenly Father as Patti listened quietly and closely to His direction and inspiration.

—Judith Courtney
Sister for Christ

"Be still and know that I am God."
—Psalm 46:10

(Judith has a music ministry that honors God and lifts up His people. She writes her own music, and wow, does it bless your heart when she ministers! She has been such a wonderful blessing and inspiration in my life!)

*****

God has led you to this very practical account of my dear friend's spiritual journey and the truths that have transformed her life. You must be ready to know what Patti has written. This book will answer many of your questions about our Heavenly Father. Patti's winsome personality shines through this work of love and devotion. Enjoy it, but be prepared; God and Patti are collaborating together to call you to your rightful place of disciple, missionary, and follower of Christ.

My friendship with Patti covers a great many years, a couple of which we were serving on the staff of Calvary Baptist Church in Central Kentucky. Our conversations were permeated with observations and testimonies about what we saw God doing. I am so thankful to know her and to see how God uses broken people and broken paths to lead us back to Him.

—Chris Brummett
Minister of Adult Outreach
Calvary Baptist

(Chris and I worked together and initiated the Divorce Care Class offered at Calvary Baptist.)

*****

*Fellowship* is a word we use often in the church. In the mind of many, one immediately jumps to potluck meals and times around the table, socializing. While this is certainly an aspect of fellowship, true fellowship goes much deeper. The pages that follow will open the windows of heaven and provide personal insight into the various aspects of drawing close to God. Fellowship is intimacy with our Lord, and we will experience an up-close and personal account of what that looks like through the lens of one who practices genuine fellowship.

I have known Patti for a number of years now and had the privilege of being her Pastor while she was on staff at our church as a Ministry Assistant. Patti truly walks the walk and talks the talk. She models faith, joy, and consistency while maintaining a deep relationship with God. It is with much joy I commend this outstanding personal reflection on true fellowship and am confident it will strengthen and encourage many in their walk with the Lord.

—Doug Wesley
former Senior Pastor
Calvary Baptist Church
Danville, Kentucky

*****

What I know about Patti is that she *loves* God. She is an overcomer, a survivor, and a thriver, deflecting the enemy's attacks at every turn. She is driven to get the messages she has been given and the testimonies of her life story in the hands and hearts of every soul that she can. And there's no doubt that Patti has lived an extraordinary and miraculous life and humbly shares it here.

Unconditional *love*! Like Patti's, my underlying message is always unconditional love to love and to be loved—as God loves, without judgment, no strings. If God is love, He can't be *not* love! It must start with gratitude and to be complete, requires forgiveness. Love God, love ourselves, and love others. (And the harder they are to love, the more they need it!)

—Charla Anderson

(Charla has been active on Radio and TV. Her published book *Candy Bar Hugs: It Doesn't Take Much to Make a Difference!* offers stories of serving the person right in front of you as a child of the Most High God, which of course she is! She believes that is our purpose. Charla Anderson has two forthcoming books, *Split-Second Transformation: Change Your Words, Change Your Life* and *Outrageously Courageous: Bold Faith, No Fear.* I have thoroughly enjoyed her *Candy Bar Hugs: It Does Not Take Much to Make a Difference!* So I am sure you will want to read her two new offerings.)

## Preface

Life is a treasure hunt! The thrill of discovery spurs me onward to experience joy as the Lord reveals His mysteries to me. Have you ever wondered why God created man, anyway? Could it be God created mankind in His image to fellowship and for us to worship and enjoy Him forever? We know He desires us to worship Him and glorify Him, but He wants it to be out of love that we do, not because we are robots that were programmed to do so. God gave us everything we need to acquire His nature and to become like Him more than anything else He created. He gave us an incredible brain to make a choice to love Him or not to love Him. He gave us free will which was different from the other physical things He created on earth! As we make our choices on this earth, we can choose to do things our way or the way the world does things, or we can seek the Creator and learn to do things His way and apprentice ourselves to the Great I Am! In order to know Him more intimately, I needed to spend time with Him, learning His Word, listening to that "Still Small Voice," and learning more about His personality so I could become more like my Creator. Like any relationship, I would talk, ask questions, and listen for His answer. He does communicate with us. I have heard people say, "I wish I could know God better." This book shares some of the ways we fellowship with Him. As you seek Him, He will respond to you personally as well. Has the thought ever occurred to you that we are actually made in His Image!

As the book evolved, it became apparent that I should share the essence of what the Lord had already shown to others for time as we know it is running out here in this era in God's plan. Often during quiet times with the Lord, in my spirit these words flowed: "Look up, for your redemption draws nigh." It seems as if it is for everyone, not just me. So I felt an urgency to learn as quickly as I could the wisdom that many others had discovered in their walks with the Lord, so it was unnecessary to duplicate that message. Please understand the focus of this sharing is not to elevate the messenger but the Mighty Lord God who gives it to those who ask for His Wisdom. The servants who receive the message do not need that elevation because the Lord should receive all the credit for His Word, and He should be thanked for allowing us to be the vessel to share. Everyone can receive from the Lord, if one makes oneself available to listen, and makes time to hear! Love is the essence of the Presence of God!

"Walking in the garden in the cool of the evening as Adam and Eve did with the Lord" has always been a desire of mine. With this thought in mind, my journey began to learn more about the Lord and what was in His heart. The words in this book would not be available without the help of my family, church family, and friends who come to me sharing and seeking encouragement, asking for prayer and determining the perfect will of God in our lives and discovering the joy of a personal relationship with our Creator! My daughter, Julie, gave me a book, *Jesus Calling* by Sarah Young, that inspired the direction of this endeavor. As I read the daily devotional, I would pause and remember the scripture so often impressing my mind, "Be still and know I am God!" In that stillness, I almost "heard" a response to my prayers, praise, and thanksgiving—the words seemed to flow on their own on to a journal I kept, and now I believe the Lord is leading me to share with others this amazing experience to bless you, the reader, as it blessed me. Reading it over and over, I felt a closeness with the Lord, as if we were "walking in the garden together." I left the dates in because they could have some special meaning to you. When you read the words, put your name in the place of mine and see how the Lord will speak to you, dear reader.

I love the Word, and my desire is that the Lord bless all who read this book! My hope is that it will produce a hunger within to know the Holy Spirit so a personal relationship with Jesus Christ will be the result. I am prayerful that what the Lord has inspired me to write can bring the unsaved to the Lord and minister to believers to be encouraged that the Lord can use anyone to spread the good news of Salvation. Reading the book will assure that fellowshipping with the Holy Spirit is for everyone. I am only a seed sower, and with the mighty power of the Holy Spirit, those seeds will fall on fertile ground! My heart's desire is to walk with God and that my ways please the Lord!

My prayer for you, dear reader, is this: May this book inspire you and challenge you, but may you know the Father, the Son, and the Holy Spirit more intimately when you finish reading it. May you be focused on God's Word, the scriptures, and test all influences by God's truth and not believe the lies of the adversary and the world. Most of all, may you develop an active dialogue with our incredible God as you take the time and allow Him to be the main focus in your life, the God He wants to be! May you take this a step further and go into all the world with the Great Commission and be the instrument the Lord intended you to be to spread the gospel and help get the good news to a hurting world that so desperately needs it!

Blessings,
Patti Grace

# Acknowledgments

To begin with, let me acknowledge what David began to learn as a shepherd boy in Psalms 23 (but I am still learning): "The Lord is my Shepherd, I shall not want!" O gracious God, thank you for your loving care for me as I walk through this life. Help me share what you are teaching me with others so they may feel the joy you impart to me as I allow more of you in my life daily. You have blessed me with relationships and people to love and be loved by on this walk. We are a sum total of all the people and situations we experience in this lifetime, and each thing helps us grow and increase our worth in the Kingdom when we allow you to turn it into good because we know you love us, and we are called to your purpose (Rom. 8:28). (Keeping in mind every teaching must align with the Word and the Holy Spirit, for they are the true teachers. Always testing what is heard and read with the Scripture keeps one on the true path the Lord has prepared for us.)

Lord, you blessed me with a family and friends to fulfill a loneliness (as an only child) I felt growing up. You gave me a loving and wise Mother and Dad to protect me and guide me. Perhaps all of us believe lies the adversary tries to impress on us, and you showed me your truth as I invited you to do in my life. You allowed me to experience a childhood dream of having my own family and three children, for which I am most grateful! The thrill of holding that first child, my son, Gregory, after my first son was a stillborn, opened my heart to embrace a totally new kind of love! This type of unconditional mother's love broadened my capacity to define the word love. Then five years later, my beautiful joy girl, Julie, was born! More love! I thought my world was complete. Death was hanging around, waiting with the entrance of each of the three children, but thank you, Lord. You showed up to strengthen me with each challenge! Then when I thought my family was complete, you brought another son, James, into my life because we needed him, and he needed us! You taught me about grafting a person into my family as you graft Gentiles into your Jewish family. You love us just the same as if you chose us in the beginning as the apple of your eye, and I love James the same as if I had birthed him! He also was there to help us grow and increase our capacity to love! You were there to pick up the pieces after my marriage ended and help me be the overcomer you designed me to be even though it took longer than it should have taken because I got in your way. I had a lot of wounds to heal, but that "balm of Gilead" was poured out for me. Then, I truly believe, because of my Mother's prayers, you showed me a new direction to bless my life with a man, my current husband, Jim, whom I had dated a few times in the summer before college. A fine man, but timing was not right. We went our separate ways, and then forty-five years later, a reunion! This blessing has allowed me to be my own person and follow your calling for me. Thank you, Lord, for seeing what I needed even when I did not see it at first, but you knew! This loving home environment comforts and nourishes the task you have called me to do!

My teenage and adult lives experienced a myriad of geographical locations that were very difficult at times, but as I look back, dear Lord, you were there to comfort me when I allowed you. Friends I met along the way are too numerous to name all, many of whom are still my friends! They, however, made a profound impression on me. My friends often became my family when I was not near my parents. Bless you all and know what an integral part of my life you have become! I have learned and continue to learn about family as my family increases.

I learned to pray for spouses for my children and grandchildren; they came on the scene and blessed our family, for which I give thanks to you, Lord. There were two daughters-in-law, Jeanie and Tami, and one son-in-law, Christopher. You have blessed me with eight grandchildren, Jennifer, Ethan, Breanne, Tanner, Austin, Jordan,

Dylan, and Tristan, which was probably all you had planned for me, I thought, with grandsons-in-law, Philip and David. Then just last year the generations keep going, a delightful baby girl, Mackenzie! More love! With more excitement, this past year another grandson, Tanner, married Kalee, and the family continues! Now, in 2020 we just received another great-granddaughter from Jennifer named Emma Claire; she arrived in May 2020. More *joy*! And just announced, a male great-grandchild in November to look forward to from Bre!

Lord, You have dealt bountifully with me! (Ps. 13:6)

Throughout my journey with the Lord, many wonderful pastors and other Christians have been used to teach me, import wisdom to my walk, and encourage me, then challenge me to grow and soar to new heights! I could write a whole chapter on that! Teachings I have received from my pastors and others people called by the Lord to preach and teach His Word are too numerous to name. Thank you all for your knowledge and the ways you responded to God's call on your lives to help us all grow in Him! I would, however, need to mention a few from several different denominations. I joined the Christian Church in California (and cannot remember my pastor's name), my pastor Richard Freeman from my time in Waco, Texas; my pastor Mark Wyatt from north of Dallas; my pastor Doug Wesley from Danville, Kentucky; my pastors here in Lexington, Tommy Howard and Willie Cole along with Ben Moore, who mentored me in a small group. Also, my walk has been enriched by many men and women of God who use the airways, books, live meetings, and tapes or CDs for the Great Commission as Jesus instructed us to do. Since the focus is on the Lord and what He provided, I will not mention all the vital teaching from these many sources, but thank you, Lord, for providing them to help me know more of you and your will in my life! They have blessed my lives as I learned your truth through your teachings to them! As we do not forsake the assembling ourselves together (Heb. 10:25), you are showing us your whole truth as we bring what you teach us individually for us to encourage, help, and learn, discovering how it fits into your big picture. You have been there for me, past, present, and I can rejoice knowing you will be with me always as Savior and Lord of my life, dear God, and in the future, as I am part of the Bride of Christ to live with you forever!

## About the Author

The splendor of the woods lured me to investigate the mysteries of the Appalachian Mountains of Virginia during childhood. The crunch of the colorful leaves under my feet and the smell of the mint along the creek while watching the tadpoles and crawdads wiggle in the shallow water brought lovely memories of the house where I was born and loved to play with my cousin, Linda. Always interested in discovering my mountain roots, I played, picnicked, and enjoyed family with a Mother and Father who gave me love as a good beginning. As the seasons unfolded and the lovely flowering trees exploded into vivid color everywhere, the culture embedded itself in my activities. Relatives were nearby and very important; aunts, uncles, and cousins were close and an integral part of my childhood. Three first cousins, Shelby, Christine, and Linda were close like sisters. My maternal grandfather was an elder/preacher in the Old Regular Baptist Church and followed in Jesus's steps as a carpenter. My maternal grandmother left me a blessed legacy of prayer and praise, knowing the Lord personally and desirous to have her children and grandchildren follow her glorious walk to Heaven and go to be there with her. My paternal grandmother's love flowed out to all who knew her. I was blessed to have great friends throughout my life starting in Pound with one who almost had my name, Patricia Ann Mullins with the same maiden last name who remained friends by reconnecting later in life in Kentucky. Mine was Patricia Grace Mullins.

My father, Roy, an electrician in and around the coal mines had a buddy who was killed in a mine accident. My mother, Bertha Ellen, had a prophetic dream which kept my father home from work that day, and she decided it was time to move to another environment and into the construction business. The family relocated to Ohio, then Maryland, then New Jersey, where I met my longtime friend, Margaret, and finally Lexington, Kentucky. I attended high school in three different states graduating from Lafayette High School then on to the University of Kentucky. After college, California was home where I was employed by Douglas Aircraft Company and then IBM as a Computer Analysist. There I met a coworker whom I married and later eagerly awaited a son, Gregory. A move to Texas came along with the birth of a delightful daughter, Julie, and also an unexpected but welcomed son, James, was adopted. When Greg was born, my family joined a church in California, and I began my spiritual awakening and spiritual growth but moved soon after and did not get baptized until moving to Waco, Texas. A hunger to learn the Word and grow while fellowshipping with other believers made the church a vital part of my day to day life.

Moving again, this time to Dallas ushered in a most difficult time in my life. I thought I would get married and be married the rest of my life to one husband, but the difficulties encountered snapped me back to reality to deal with a new life. I reentered the work world after being out of it for many years and raised three children as a single parent. Gregory was nine, Julie was four, and James was twelve. I certainly learned why the Lord gave two parents to a child! It felt like trying harder than I was able and never quite achieving my goals. It was truly impossible to be a bread winner and meet all the needs of the growing, changing children while all the while suffering the grieving that came with the death of a marriage/dream I had wrapped my head around for many years! Feeling such a loss and trying to heal and give the children what they needed was almost an impossible task; however, the Lord was always there with His Hand reached out and pulled me up when I felt short of my expectations. I met another longtime friend, Elaine, with whom I studied the Word and grew spiritually with. On weekends, she and I sat down, evaluated our talents, prayed for the Lord to use those talents, and opened a wedding planning, party, and catering business to supplement our income. We engaged both families to help. I worked not only that job but many other money-making efforts such as Mystery Shopping, Focus groups, etc., helping to add dollars to the family's growing budget.

Finally, after opening a brick and mortar shop in an office building, we began a ministry with newsletter handouts, daily prayers as customers requested, filling needs and operating in a quiet ministry. With the food left from the business on Fridays, three other women, Elaine, Pam, Judith (and her daughter, Allison) and I began a street ministry in downtown Dallas, feeding the homeless, giving them encouragement, prayer, personal items, and the Word, filling needs, and offering them Bibles. Elaine had taught the Bible in a high school (at a time when that was allowed), and together, we conducted Bible studies in nursing homes, assisted living and retirement homes, mostly ministering to the elderly.

In 1966, my Dad died while I was living in California. Mother stayed in Kentucky, married again, and made her home in Harrodsburg, Kentucky. When Mother became ill, I prayed about returning to the Lexington area and felt peaceful about the timing. I was an only child and felt that Mother needed me. (My children were settled and happy now with lives of their own.) Mother and her husband, Jim Rhodes, welcomed me to live with them at Lake Herrington, just south of Lexington.*

Through a ministry at Calvary Baptist Church in Danville, one

---

* Here is a footnote to the story... After I returned to Kentucky and was living at the lake with Mother, Mother told me she had been praying that the Lord would bring me back to be with her and that He would also bring me someone to love and be loved by before she left this earth. I said, "Mother, do you mean Jim [my present husband]?"

Mother said, "Yes, and he is better than I prayed for."_____

That opened the door for the wonderful life together which was an answer to Mother's prayers (and a longtime family friend, Ginny Lou, who had been praying for us), and it meant a second chance for Jim and me! God is so good!

of the pastors and I set up a Divorce Care Class. I facilitated the class, and there, my present husband, Jim (whom I had dated a few times during college as a freshman and he a senior) attended the class. God gave us a second chance and blessed me with a precious man to love. We developed a friendship, married, and presently are very involved at Christ Centered Church in Lexington, Kentucky. A couple years ago, we conducted a Bible Study/worship service for the residents of the Villa, an assisted living facility in Lexington. Together, we volunteered for hospice for a season and now are very active in the YMCA to help stay healthy physically, mentally, and spiritually. We have both been on the YMCA Board and work toward encouraging the seniors to fellowship and keep healthy with a good quality of life.

Our lives have been enriched with eight grandchildren and two great-granddaughters along with wonderful spouses for the three children. All live in the Dallas-Fort Worth area except for a one grandchild who lives in New York City. Another great-grandchild, a boy is due in November.

### What to Expect to Receive from This Fellowship

As we begin our journey together, dear readers, may I share with you the greatest truth I have discovered walking along the road my many years, in my day-to-day living, a statement so profound it has changed the most resistant heart! Sometimes the simplest words are the most life changing!

God loves you!

Whether you feel or have experienced it personally, this is a *truth* that God built His creation on, and He reaches out to you, individually, to impart truth to you, in many ways! God wants us to internalize that statement, not just once, but daily, in a moment-to-moment, intimate interchange of fellowship. He promises us He will never leave nor forsake us (Heb. 13:5).

God is love!

Everything He did for us in the beginning was love. Have you wondered why God created us, anyway? We were created out of His love to fellowship and glorify Him, but He had angels to glorify Him, so it had to be even more than that. Genesis 2 tells us that the Lord created the garden, and verse 5 tells us there was not a man to till the ground. So we were necessary for that job to be done. Did we even know that or realize that fact?

He desired our returned love so much He designed us with the most precious gift, free will, to choose whether we would return that love or not. He did not want to create a robot that was forced to love but showed us the most awesome kind of His love to spark a desire to return to Him, in love, and experience all He has to offer us, not just once, but as the most desirable interchange of love one can imagine! Perhaps a little of this comes out in our desire to be parents and have something to love and be loved by! Of course, a parent does not desire to be worshiped (hopefully), but something inside us must be reaching out to follow the instructions of our Creator to be fruitful and multiply and fill the earth and subdue it and have dominion (Gen. 1:28). God also wanted to fellowship with His creation. He walked in the Garden in the cool of the evening with His creations to fellowship with them and teach them His ways, the correct ways to enjoy the life He had given them.

Sid Roth (Jewish evangelist) told about his friend and well-known prophet Bob Jones, who shared a powerful experience from several decades ago of being transported in the spirit to heaven. Jesus sent him back to earth with this message for The Body: "Did you learn to love?" Could this be the *main* purpose of our life here? Could our main goal of life be walking in love? Your life is a precious gift from God, and perhaps the Holy Spirit is trying to tell us what we do with it is our gift to God. When Jesus was asked by the religious leaders of the day, trying to trick Him, "What is the greatest commandment?" He replied, "You should love the Lord your God with all you heart, soul, and mind, and your neighbor as yourself." (Not more than or less than yourself.) However, I heard Andrew Womack (Bible teacher) this week discuss the true meaning of love in this passage, and it was to love with the kind of love God has. Jesus loved us so much He gave His life for us! That really puts love in a different realm than we have been used to thinking about it (Matt. 22:35–40; Mark 12:28–34).

### Do You Want to Know the Secret of an Abundant Life?

On the morning of June 1, 2019, in the twilight, before the cares of the world closed in, as my mind was tuned to spiritual things, some thoughts formed. As I was lying there, praising, thanking, and worshipping God, as I was bringing my prayer requests for others and myself to the throne of God, Matthew 22:36 came to mind. When the Pharisees were trying to trick Jesus to tell them the most important commandment, He stated, "You shall love the Lord your God with all your heart, soul, and mind...and your neighbor as yourself...on these two commandments hang all the law and the prophets." Then

I heard, in my spirit, of course, "This is the secret of an abundant life!" Wow, as the thought lingered, it was impressed in my spirit, "If a person seeks God, He will be found!" Becoming one with Jesus through the Holy Spirit gives one access to the Mind of Christ, and learning His perfect will in one's life brings about a touch of heaven on earth! Remember, God is always seeking us!

God's perfect will for us is far greater than anything we can imagine! As we accept Jesus as our personal Savior and ask Him to be Lord of our lives, we learn to trust and love the Savior for who He is and what He has done for us. Putting Him first in our lives and dying to self is called crucifying self. Since we are a triune being, it takes commitment and our willingness to work in all parts of our spirit, soul, and body. Then, when we truly learn to love the Lord, His love helps us love others, not more than or less than, but as ourselves. What a wonderful truth for us to develop in our walk and journey with Him! If everyone would operate this way, what an incredible world it would be!

*Love* is a word we throw around so much it has a watered-down version of the original kind of love the Lord pours out to us. We say we love something every day. Sprinkled throughout scripture are examples of God's kind of love. John 1:1 tells us, "In the beginning was the Word, and the Word was with God, and the Word was God." Verse 12 states, "But to all who received Him, who believed in His name, He gave power to become children of God; who were born, not of blood nor of the will of the flesh nor of the will of man, but of God!" Verse 14 says, "And the Word became flesh and dwelt among us, full of grace and truth; we have beheld His Glory, glory as of the only Son from the Father." John 3:16 says, "For God so loved the world that He gave His only begotten Son that whoever believed in Him shall have everlasting life."

God wants you to experience His love and reach out to Him, drawing Him closer with your desire to know Him intimately. Genesis

1:1 states, "In the beginning God created the heavens and the earth," everything His creation would need or ever want. In Genesis 1:26, God said, "Let us make man in our image, after our likeness, and let them have dominion over the fish of the sea, and over the birds of the air, and over the cattle, and over all the earth, and over every creeping thing that creeps upon the earth." Verses 27 and 28 state, "So God created man in His own, in the image of God He created him, male and female He created them." And God blessed them, and God said to them, "Be fruitful and multiply, and fill the earth and subdue it; and have dominion over the fish of the sea and over the birds of the air over every living thing that moves upon the earth."

In Genesis 2:15, God took the man and put him in the Garden of Eden to till it and keep it. And the Lord God commanded the man, saying, "You may freely eat of every tree of the garden, but of the tree of the knowledge of good and evil you shall not eat, for the day you eat of it, you shall die." After the Lord made all of creation, He said, "It is good." However, after making man, He said, "It is not good that man should be alone." So the Lord formed every beast of the field and every bird of the air and brought them to the man to name. Then God created the woman. They lived in a lush garden surrounded by beauty beyond imagination! They were given dominion over everything He created and lacked for nothing! They were to rule and procreate to fill the earth and were told they could eat of all the fruit of garden with only one restriction, the Tree of the Knowledge of Good and Evil. When Adam and Eve disobeyed in the garden, this Omnipotent (all-knowing) God had a plan to bring mankind back to Him, in love. He would send His only Son to pay for the sin that had been introduced in the Garden! Adam and Eve were created perfect, with a free will to choose what they wanted. Our loving God, who had breathed His very breath into them, knew they would disobey, and desiring their fellowship so much, He already had a plan to bring them back to Him. They were the gods of this earth who had been given everything they needed, until they gave their dominion to a subtle deceiver coming to them as a serpent who tricked them by making them think God had withheld something from them. Satan deceived them with Words! Read Chapter 3 of Genesis for yourself and see how he tricked them so you will know his way when he tries to trick you with his beguiling words!

Mankind lost dominion over the earth and all creation the Lord had given them that day. God put a curse on the serpent to crawl in the dirt in verse 14, and in verse 15 on the woman for pain in childbearing and that the man should rule over her, and on the man he cursed the ground and forced him to tend it by the sweat of his brow. The first blood sacrifice was introduced on earth after Adam and Eve disobeyed and ate of the Tree of the Knowledge of Good and of Evil, discovering they were naked and ashamed, so they covered themselves in fig leaves. Verse 21 shows how the Lord God made garments of skin and clothed them. The first blood sacrifice! But God had a plan! In verse 15, the Plan of Salvation (Matt. 1:18). God so loved the world! His Son, Jesus, would be born and fulfill the Promise of Genesis 3:15 and restore that intimate fellowship with God's children and again be able to walk in the garden in the cool of the evening with His creation. Jesus was the plan to break the curse and restore to mankind what he had been seduced to give away to satan. Jesus came to restore dominion of the earth to mankind, and even though satan has been defeated, he still tried to be powerful with his lies and deception! He only has the power we give him. He still talks to us as he did Adam and Eve and tries to deceive, makes us fearful, and lies about everything. But his influence is in our mind, and the battle is between our ears! DO not see satan behind every rock, for he is a very real presence, but Jesus showed us during His temptation in the wilderness to quote scripture out loud to him. Matthew 4:1 tells us Jesus was led into the wilderness and allowed to be tempted of the devil and went without food for forty days. At each temptation, Jesus quoted out loud a scripture to the devil after the words "It is written." Jesus did it all, and we now can be restored to an intimate relationship with God because when He ascended into heaven, He sent the Comforter to live inside us, providing a channel available every minute of every day to reach The Mighty God, for those who love the Lord and desire to be His followers.

Perhaps you say, "How can that be?" We perhaps do not think about the creation from the Lord's perspective. We have been created as a triune being, a soul, which is mind, will, and emotions, that lives in a body, and the very breath of the Lord (which is the Holy Spirit) breathed into us to bring us life! In the Garden, the fellowship with God's creation of mankind resulted in direct fellowship with Adam and Eve in the cool of the evening, walking in the Garden. Fellowship was ended after disobedience entered the Garden. In the Old Testament, only the Priests were allowed to commune with God, and they were responsible for informing the people of God's will and His directions. Fellowship with the Lord did not return until Jesus came to the earth to be the ultimate sacrifice for our sins. A small number of people were able to fellowship with Jesus on earth during His lifetime, but only those immediately around Him. So when did fellowship become available to God's creation again? It was a long time coming, but God had a plan!

When Jesus gave Himself on the cross as the sacrificial lamb for sin, He did not leave His followers without a plan or a hope. (You may ask, "Why did Jesus have to be the sacrifice for sin?" That will be addressed later, separately.) Satan was defeated on the cross, and his future was pronounced, but the final judgment of him and his demons will not be carried out until Jesus returns as Lord of Lords and King of Kings. Satan will be bound for a thousand years, and peace will be experienced on earth with the true fellowship that was intended in the Garden. The Great White Throne Judgment will carry out the final chapter of satan and his demons. Revelation

20:1 states that when Jesus returns, "An angel from heaven descends holding the key of the Abyss (the bottomless pit), and a great chain will be in his hand." Satan was bound for a thousand years, and the angel hurled him into the Abyss, closed and sealed it above him, so that he should no longer lead astray, deceive, and seduce the nations until the thousand years were at an end. (After the thousand years, he must be liberated for a short time.) Blessed are the believers who had stayed true to the Lord Jesus and were in the First Resurrection, those who had not taken the mark of the beast or paid homage to the beast or his statue during the Tribulation and those who had been beheaded for witnessing and testifying for the Word of God. These were judged according to their works. Joyfully, we should all desire to be in that First Resurrection as Jesus's own will be ministers of God and of Christ, and they shall rule along with Him a thousand years!

At the completion of the thousand years, satan will be released from his place of confinement and will go forth to deceive and seduce and lead astray the nations that are in the four quarters of the earth (Rev. 20:7). Then he will be hurled into the fiery lake of burning brimstone, where the beast and false prophet are, and they will be tormented day and night forever and ever (through the ages of the ages) (verse 10).

Then comes Jesus at the Great White Throne Judgment. This is the Resurrection you do not want to be a part of! The books in heaven were opened. Then the Book of Life was opened, and the dead were judged (sentenced) by what they had done in accordance with what was recorded in the books. Death and Hades were thrown into the lake of fire. This is the second death; if anyone's name was not recorded in the Book of Life, he was hurled into the lake of fire. Do you want your name recorded in the Lamb's Book of Life? I had fully intended to address this part of the Scripture later but felt compelled to not soft-soap anything—it is what it is! The Word does not lie. My reason for writing this book is to reach everyone I can with the

Gospel message and let those who have hearing ears and seeing eyes seek the truth of the good news and secure a place with Jesus for eternity. All the end-time signs are being displayed throughout the earth now. Earth is having birth pangs and trying to give birth to a new age. Very often in my quiet time and worshipping the Lord, I hear in my spirit the words "Look up, for your redemption draws nigh." I take this to mean time is getting short for all of us to face our world and future and choose now where we want to continue our existence after time of our journey here is finished.

The Apostle Paul mentioned a war going on inside of us (Rom. 7:14–25). It reminds me of the story about the two wolves inside of each human. One is present, full of evil, with hate, unforgiveness, negativity, worry, etc. The other is good, with the Fruit of the Spirit, love, peace, patience, etc. (Gal. 2:22). Which wolf will win? The answer, as you might have guessed is, it's the one you feed.

Luke 15:11 speaks about the Prodigal Son. Jesus spoke in parables to illustrate a story, and this one hits home to a lot of people. People behave like prodigals at some time in their lives until they learn the truth, and the Living Word tells us, "Know the truth and the truth will set you free" (John 8:32).

We were born into a world of sin, we live in a fallen world of sin, and when you die, you will have died in sin and will be separated from God. You will miss out on that incredible fellowship with Him that which He designed for you unless you make the choice to where you desire your life to continue after your earth journey. We were created to glorify Him and know Him intimately. Only you can make that personal choice for you! Make that choice wisely and decide where you want to end up after this short span of life on earth is finished. This is your choice to make for both now and forever. Do not miss the awesome gift the Lord has for you. Open that gift and be changed forever! Live now on earth with an eye to our real eternal home, seeking the Lord and finding Him on a daily basis. The exciting thing is that you can live on earth and experience some of the real joy of the Lord that will even be enhanced after we reside permanently with Him in heaven.

The theme of this book is to determine your true relationship with God, what do you want it to be, and through it and the testimonies of others, there will be suggestions of available ways to know Him both as Savior and Lord of your life. I can promise it will change your life for the better, for the Lord honors every effort we make to know Him, as He desires us to do. "Choose this day whom you will serve." (If you don't, you will choose by default, and the adversary will claim you for his own!) Joshua said, "As for me and my house, we will serve the Lord" (Josh. 24: 15).

Knowing Him as Savior comes first, of course, and you become a believer of the Lord Jesus Christ. Then after you become a believer, you grow in the knowledge and experience of Him as you make Him the Lord of your life. This is actually discipleship and is addressed in the meaning of the unusual scripture "Work out your own salvation with fear and trembling" (Phil. 2:12). (One translation says "With awe and reverence." This explains it a little better in today's terms.) This does not mean we can save ourselves, but as we submit ourselves to the Holy Spirit and experience more of Him in our lives, our spiritual muscles grow and we become more like our Lord in personality and intent. Stick with the scriptures from the Bible, and you will discover the answers you have been searching for in simple terms, layman to layman. For those of you who already call Jesus Lord of your life, you will become encouraged and lifted up to strengthen your spiritual muscles as you read of the experiences of others and see what the Lord is doing personally in the lives of so many types and ages of the believers who were willing to share what the Lord means in their lives. Please, always, in everything you read or hear, evaluate it through the Word of the Bible before accepting it as truth. The Holy Spirit gives us discernment as we grow in Him to know the truth, and the truth will set us free (John 8:32).

Adrian Rogers was preaching a sermon on television about the "Keys to a Happy Marriage and Healthy Relationships," and so many things in this world are a picture of spiritual principles to teach us how the Lord works in His Kingdom. Marriage is one of those. Our intimate relationship between the Lord and His bride (His believers) is a picture of a perfect marriage. With the next instructions from Adrian Rogers, try putting your relationship with your spouse in the equation, with Jesus Christ as the focal point of this marriage.

### Keys to Strengthen a Marriage (Or Relationship)

1. Make a decision to come to Jesus.
2. Depend on Christ in all things as this allows Him to come and live in you.
3. Devote to Christ and love others with a supernatural love.
4. Develop and grow. We are either growing toward Him or away from Him.
5. Discipline; *choose* what you see, hear, and do. Garbage in, garbage out. "Watch what you watch." The Word leads into discipleship, which is our daily walk with the Lord, being still and listening to Him, studying His Word, and spending quality time with the Lord, dying to self and growing our spiritual muscles by allowing more of the Holy Spirit to take over our will and make our decisions though His eyes.
6. Determination; making up your mind *before* you encounter situations that tempt you to follow the low road, like making a decision beforehand to say no to drugs, say no to bad choices and a bad environment.

So it is clear: we need to bring our "one flesh" to Him, make the Lord first in our lives, and together die to self and allow His divine plan to lead us as He unfolds it to us. Remember, God's plan is pure, and if a person fails, God is a forgiving God; He forgives again and again. With repentance comes forgiveness and another chance to do it right with the Lord. Adrian Rogers reminded us that the first miracle of the Lord was to turn water to wine at a wedding. He is still in the business of performing miracles so we can benefit from His love, His mercy, and His forgiveness.

Genesis 2:24 tells us we are to leave our father and mother and cleave to each other in a marriage. Exodus 20:14 tells us, "Thou shall not commit adultery." Jeremiah 2:9 says that Israel committed adultery with stone and tree and polluted the land. How weird is that? So, *adultery* can be expanded to mean more than sexual adultery. Adrian Rogers says *adultery* means to make impure, and surely in this Scripture, Israel was pictured as going after other gods made of stone and wood. Therefore, we need to evaluate our intent and guard our actions against anything that would border on adultery. When a Christian marries another Christian, there is a three-strand cord that binds all three together in a covenant. Remember, *love* is a decision we make.

In Exodus 21:2, the first Commandment tells us to have no other god before God, and the second one tells us to not make any graven images to bow down and worship. "I, your God, am a jealous God." Then He tells us a curse if we do, but also a blessing of showing steadfast love for those who love Him and keep His commandments.

## Worship

Worship was designed for our Creator, God. In His Word, Revelation 4:8, it states there are four living creatures to praise Him, saying, "Holy, holy, holy!" It must be vitally important for the purpose of those beings to have that reason for their existence, to praise God. The main difference on earth between marriage here and being the Bride of Christ is that we are designed to reverence (deep respect) our spouse, but true worship belongs only to the Lord. The scripture tells me He must be first before anything on earth—put Him first! Then through that proper focus, the Lord blesses us in our marriages and with our children and our jobs when the priorities are His way. When we endeavor to glorify the Lord first in our lives and expect Him to pour out His blessings to our family, He never disappoints. He wants our lives balanced, with the proper focus on giving to Caesar what is Caesar's and giving to God what belongs to God (Mark 12:17). Mankind is a spiritual being first, in a body, with soul (mind, will, and emotions). So let's get used to praising and worshipping God, for it looks like from the scripture we will be doing a tremendous amount of worship when we go be with the Lord after this earth "trip."

Singing Songs of Praise to the Lord
Exodus 15:1 states, "Then sang Moses and the children of Israel this song unto the Lord, and spoke, saying I will sing unto the Lord, for he hath triumphed gloriously: the horse and his rider hath He thrown into the sea." Psalm 40:3 says, "And He hath put a new son in my couth, even praise unto our God: many shall see it, and fear, and shall trust in the Lord." This new song must be God inspired because we know that the Psalms were used for worshipping God in being sung back to God, and many scriptures refer to musical instruments being used. Psalm 105:2 states, "Sing unto Him, sing psalms unto Him: talk of all His wondrous works."

Psalm 13:6 says, "I will sing praises unto the Lord, because He has dealt bountifully with me." This was a personal scripture I used to praise Him when our church in Waco had a study in the Psalms. My oil painting of my daughter and me, representing mother and child, honored the Lord because He brought me a long-sought-after daughter, which was pure joy for me (I almost named her Joy), and gave me the talent to paint the picture. Thank you, Lord! You may say I do not have a good voice for singing; perhaps we are to let go and allow that song to come out to bless the Lord anyway. The

Lord always cherishes our efforts. It could sound like honey to Him. Years ago, choirs, both secular and church ones, the Sweet Adelines (barbershop group), and singing for myself were very important to me, and my voice was pleasant, but today since I have not used it much, the vocal cords are not what they used to be. But I sing in church with a passion and really enjoy the worship in song. I sing to the Lord and feel it pleases Him, and that is a blessing to me.

King David was a man after God's own heart because he was repentant and cried out to the Lord for forgiveness when he sinned, and of course, the Lord forgave him. But I believe David's focus on worshipping the Lord had to mean a great deal to God. In 2 Samuel 2:6, David danced before the Lord with all his might, (and David was girded with a linen ephod with shouts, and the sound of the horn) then the Ark of the Lord (which represented God's presence) was brought up. (Here his wife, Michal, daughter of Saul, despised him for doing it.) David wrote many of the Psalms, and many were used in praise and worship. The first book of the Chronicles 16:9 states, "Sing praises to Him, tell of His wondrous works," and 1 Chronicles 13:7–8 talks about celebrating before God with all their might with songs and musical instruments.

Paul tells us in Colossians 3:16, "Let the Word of Christ dwell in you richly in all wisdom; teaching and admonishing one another in psalms and hymns and spiritual songs, singing with grace in your hearts to the Lord." Ephesians 5:19 tells us, "Speaking to yourselves in psalms and hymns and spiritual songs, singing and making melody in your heart to the Lord." We are to make melody in our hearts to the Lord. We are learning about God when we worship in music. Music has always been a powerful vehicle that aids learning. As for worship music in heaven, according to Revelation 5:8, the twenty-four elders and the four living creatures fell down before the Lamb, each holding a harp, and sang a new song worshipping the Lord Jesus, with a loud voice, saying, "Worthy is the Lamb," and ending with amen from the four living creatures and the elders falling down and worshipping. Does it sound like worship is important to God? Should we begin today and realize how important it is to the Lord and start practicing, getting ready for our blessed time with Him in heaven? Read some more in 14:2–3 and 15:3–4 to get more excited about what we can expect in the presence of our King!

Some references to Lucifer (later called satan) stated he was very instrumental in music and led all the created beings in heaven in worship to God. When he fell, it seems he used music, because it is so powerful, to draw humans away from the Lord with his satanic music.

We conclude this chapter asking you to evaluate your personal relationship with the Holy Spirit. Is it where you want it to be? In John 10:27, Jesus tells us, "My sheep hear my voice, and I know them, and they follow me, and I give them eternal life, and they shall never perish, and no one shall snatch them out of my hand." Do you hear His voice? Hopefully, the following chapters will make a difference in your walk with Him no matter at what stage your walk is. God wants us to have a relationship with Him, but more than that, He wants us to fellowship with Him daily.

Fellowship is greater than relationship. *Relationship* is defined as two or more people having a connection. *Fellowship* means friendly relationships with those who share one's interests. So you can see why the Lord wants us to fellowship, not merely have relationships with others. Jesus is truth, and truth never changes! This morning I awoke with the Lord explaining this truth, sort of like a parable Jesus used to explain situations to be better understood. Picture a big ball in the center of the table where we are seated, Bible studying or fellowshipping. When we are looking at the ball (I thought of the Sun), we each see a different spot on the ball. The truth is the whole ball, and each of us can see a tiny part of it, but when we share what each of us comprehends, the Lord can impart His wisdom to show us more of His Truth. The closer I draw to the truth, the more of truth can replace my limited amount. Expect the truth to grow as you allow more of the personality of Jesus to replace your will and your knowledge. We learn in part, but together more can be revealed as we come together. This reminds me of 1 Corinthians 13:12, "For now we see through a glass, darkly but then face to face, now I know in part, but then shall I know even as also I am known." This says to me, when Jesus comes, all truth will be revealed to us, but until then, we know in part, and each of us has a piece to fellowship with our brothers and sisters and learn together. We are essential to each other in our journey.

Perhaps you say, "I do not even know if there is a God or not." Well, God addressed that through Paul in Romans 1, starting in verse 16. Paul said he was not ashamed of the gospel. Then proceeded to tell them, "For what can be known about God is plain to them, because God has shown it to them. Ever since the creation of the world His invisible nature, namely, His eternal power and deity, has been clearly perceived in the things that have been made. So they are without excuse for although they knew God they did not honor Him as God or give thanks to Him but they became futile in their thinking and their senseless minds were darkened. Claiming to be wise, they became fools, and exchanged the glory of the immortal God for images resembling mortal man or birds or animals or reptiles. Therefore God gave them up to the lusts of their hearts to impurity...because they exchanged the truth about God for a lie and worshipped and served the creature rather than the Creator, who is blessed forever! Amen." I have always felt that God had allowed us to see the crucifixion in our spirits. I have not been able to prove that from the scripture, but Paul tells us God proves His existence all around us, so we know God exists because Paul said it in Romans.

Everywhere we look, God's Hand and is all around us. See the sky, the flowers, a new baby and study the human body. Do not try to explain how mankind hung the earth in space and it stays there, or that there are one hundred thousand miles of blood vessels in the average adult human if spread out in a single line; just look around and see the handiwork of our mighty God. Consider our breath. It is miraculous! It is available time and again, provided by our Creator. Not just the first time He breathed into us and made each of us a living creature but throughout our lives until we leave this earthly existence. Often I thank Him for that incredible gift. Bless you, God! You are real to me!

## Knowing God
## The Godhead, the Trinity

As the Lord was pouring out the table of contents to me, one chapter name when I began this book was "The Godhead, The Trinity." I said out loud, "Father, how could I attempt to talk about such a mystery as the Trinity?" I knew that we see in a glass darkly (1 Cor. 13:10). In my spirit, I felt the "Still Small Voice" impress on me that it was not my book, that it was His!

First, the word *Trinity* is not mentioned in the Bible even though we refer to the Godhead as the Trinity. I heard Dr. David Jeremiah talk about two examples that helped me better understand the triune God. He was explaining how important prayer really is and how all three manifestations of the Godhead (Trinity) are involved in prayer. He said, "We pray to Father God, in the Name of Jesus, through the Holy Spirit, who indwells us when we become believers." Another example Jeremiah mentioned was when John baptized Jesus in Matthew 3:13, "As soon as Jesus was baptized, He went up out of the water. At that moment heaven was opened, and He saw the Spirit of God descending like a dove and lighting on Him. And lo a voice from heaven, saying, 'This is my beloved Son, in whom I am well pleased.'" (The Father speaks, the Spirit descends, and the Son prays.) Also, in Luke 3:21, Heaven had been closed to man since the Fall, and now Jesus opened it! Let us hide in Jesus as believers for in Him, then God the Father can be pleased with us.

When I think of the Trinity, it reminds of how the Lord created each of us. For an example, I was born as a daughter, then married and became a wife; after that, I became a mother. Now, I am a grandmother and a great-grandmother. Am I one person or more? Of course I am one person functioning in three capacities. In Genesis 1:26, the scripture tells us God said, "Let us make man in our own image, in our likeness, and let them rule over...the earth." The three parts of the Trinity function in one capacity as I do as one person but when a daughter is needed I related to my parents as a daughter. I relate as a wife to a husband in that relationship, and as a mother to my children, and grandmother as well as great-grandmother. I deal with each situation according to the immediate need of the person I am relating to. That is one example that comes to my mind about the plurality of the Godhead. The problem here, however, is that I am not separate beings, operating as one. So this is not a very good example and has limitations.

Some people give the example of ice, water, and steam in three manifestations but all actually water. Perhaps that is a better way to discuss the functions of the Godhead. If we understand all the facets of God, then we will have the full mind of God, and of course, we do not! God cannot be put in a box as we see Him for our finite minds to explain! He is infinite! God is a spirit, and we contact Him through the Word of God, for that is His language. We look into the Spirit world through Faith; we can see things in faith before our eyes see them manifested. Faith comes by hearing and hearing the Word of God (Rom. 10:17).

Sometimes it seems God is three persons, and sometimes it seems like He is operating as a family. Perhaps because I am woman, I have always wondered, since mankind is created in the image of God, where is the female spirit and how is it designed to function? In Genesis, after God created anything, He said, "It is good." When He created Adam, He said, "It is not good for man to be alone." In Genesis 2:24, God made a creation from Adam, and they became one flesh. This is still a mystery for me, but I am asking the Lord to reveal His truth here. I never want to add or take away from His Holy Scriptures, and I encourage you always to question and prove everything from Scripture with the help of the Holy Spirit that is in you if you are a new creation. "Therefore if anyone is in Christ, he is a new creation; old things are passed away; behold, all things are become new" (2 Cor. 5:17).

We discussed the Godhead with our pastor Willie in our Bible class. It seems they all three operate in harmony. The Holy Spirit points to Jesus, and Jesus points to God the Father. Father God is shown to us in many examples in the Old and New Testament. We see His judgment, His jealously of His people, and His provision. There are instances in Scripture that show God the Father and Jesus at His right hand in heaven, showing two separate beings, and of course when Jesus was made flesh, He was separated from God the Father but fully functioning in perfect harmony with the Father's Will because He chose to do so, telling us that when we saw Him, we saw the Father (John 14:9). Jesus came not to abolish but to fulfill the law, God's law, and He was the only one who did and could. So He became the sacrifice for us to redeem our lives back to God. Jesus also told us it would be beneficial for Him to go be with the Father, for He would send the Holy Spirit, the Comforter, to be with us all the time and do greater things than He had done (John 14:12). The Holy Spirit is apparently the Power! The Holy Spirit enables us to go directly to the Father, through Jesus, and we can now fellowship directly without having to go through a Priest to commune with God, as was required in the Old Testament. Praise God! Often, the Holy Spirit operates much like a loving mother in a family, to create a harmonious situation in the family and to bring each member closer to the other members of the family. The Old Testament shows God as Judge, which seems to be Father God. Jesus brought a freedom mankind had not experienced before. He brought love, mercy, and truth. The Holy Spirit brought us intimacy and a personal relationship with God. However, we see in Revelation that Jesus is the Judge at the Great White Throne Judgment (Rev. 20:11–15). It seems they overlap in their manifestations at times.

As all these thoughts ran through my mind this morning, I believe the Lord gave me an example to clarify this thought. He had me visualize a coin. It has a head; turn it over and there is a tail. Then look at it on its side. There are three parts to a coin, but we still call it a coin, and it is also identified by its parts. The most important part of these three parts is that it takes all three parts to make up a single coin, reminding us that it takes all three parts of God, the Father, the Son, and the Holy Spirit, which manifest in different ways but work together as one, to make up the Godhead!

As we talk about the Godhead, let us be aware that when God created heaven and earth, and man, He had divine order and laws to govern everything. I am only now learning His laws and have been a believer for over fifty years! What is the matter with that picture! Just like gravity, when we operate in what He designed, we can live or die. The same is true with His spiritual laws of salvation and healing. As we take this journey together, allow me to share what I have learned about the subject and encourage you to start looking for His Wisdom on your journey.

In Genesis 1:26, God said, "Let us make man in our own image after Our likeness." (Also Genesis 5:1.) God had a plan and created everything perfect for mankind, put Adam and Eve in a lush garden, gave them everything they needed, but they were not robots without personal choices. God gave them the most incredible gift, a will of their own. He wanted them to obey Him and fellowship with Him in love! The scripture Genesis 3:8 tells us God walked in the Garden in the cool of the evening to fellowship with Adam and Eve. He wanted to spend time with His creations. Disobedience entered the Garden and destroyed that intimate fellowship between God and His creations. God still wants to spend time with us whenever we take the time to do so, and He made a way for us to.

All of God's creations were designed with a free will. Even Lucifer (satan), who was anointed and ordained as a guardian cherub, was created perfect with a free will, but iniquity was found in him. I believe this means that he perverted his freewill gift to make choices that he wanted to do that did not glorify God. One of his choices was to attempt to plant a question in the mind of Eve that God did not really mean what He said when He told them they could eat any of the trees of the Garden except the fruit of the Tree of Good and Evil.

Satan deceived Eve, but Adam then sinned deliberately, disobeyed God, and ate of that very fruit (Gen. 2:16–17). Through Adam and Eve the whole world has been deceived (Rev. 12:9). As punishment (Gen. 3:24), God drove them from the Garden and placed cherubim and a flaming sword that turned every way to guard the Tree of Life. God cursed the serpent that satan used to tempt the pair in Genesis 3:14, and Adam and Eve lost their paradise, and they now knew the difference in disobedience. God cursed the ground and punished mankind as a result. Their covering and protection was gone, and they had to leave the Garden. Not only life in a perfect setting was gone but the precious, intimate fellowship with God as well! But God always has a plan and a will for His creations. With the curses came a promise through woman (Gen. 3:13). "And I will put enmity between you and the woman, and between your offspring and hers, and He will crush your head and you will strike his heel." God killed an animal and made garments of skin to cover them, which was the first animal sacrifice for sin. Hebrews 9:22 tells us that the law requires that sin be cleaned with blood, and without the shedding of blood there is no remission of sins (forgiveness).

God is Spirit, and we contact Him through the Word of God, for that is His language. We look into the Spirit world through faith. We can see things in faith before our eyes see them, and before they are made manifest. Faith comes by hearing and the Word of God (Rom. 10:17). Hope is a golden cord that connects us to heaven.

We know that the Lord sees the earth tapestry from the finished (heavenly) side; thus, we only see the rough side in this life. The Lord reveals His mysteries to us a little at a time and gives each of His family pieces of the puzzle so we can come together and share His wisdom through His Body of Believers (Heb. 10:25). All three were present at Creation, and we see their mighty work through the Bible. The focus in the New Testament is on Jesus and the Holy Spirit. We know the character and workings of God by reading His Word, the Bible; making the Word in flesh, Jesus, our Savior; and experiencing His personality through spending time with the Holy Spirit on a daily basis.

This morning I awoke with impressions from the Lord about the Godhead. I saw in my mind an equilateral triangle with the Father at the top, Jesus on the left side, and the Holy Spirit on the right side.

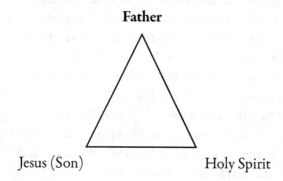

**Father**

Jesus (Son)                                    Holy Spirit

(I thought that was interesting, with the Father facing us, Jesus on the Father's right side, then after adding the Holy Spirit, the Trinity!) They operate as a Triune Being and manifest individually as well.

I may not be able to see God with my earthly eyes, but here are a few of the ways I know God is real:

- He has a purpose for my life, so He breathed His actual breath into me to give me physical life (Gen. 2:7). He created me with something inside that desires to come back to Him in love (Eph. 1:4) God has chosen us in Him before the Foundation of the Earth. The Holy Spirit wooed my spirit; I chose to come back to the Lord and have experienced the return.

- He told me He will never leave me, nor will He forsake me (Deut. 31:6; Heb. 13:5).

- Father God sent His Word, His Son, to save me out of this world so I can be with Him always (John 3:16), and He sent His Word, the Bible (written-down instructions), for me to read and internalize and live, day-to-day, and know how to fellowship with Him.

- Jesus sent the Holy Spirit to be with me all the time so I can fellowship with the Father and Son through the Holy Spirit. As a believer, God is always with me. He is ever present, available to commune with me at any time, day or night.

- He always answers my prayers, which is "Yes," "No," or "Wait." ("Wait" means with anticipation and expectancy. He will answer according to His Will, which is the best answer for my sake. That does not mean to just sit down and do nothing until He answers. He takes time to help me grow before the manifestation of the answer, so I can accept and work with His choice.) Allow me to state here that we can know the will of God by reading His Word; we can pray His Word and expect it to come to pass. We can pray what He says and stand on it and expect it to come to pass because He said His Will in Scripture. So when we pray, may we be mindful to say, "If it be His will," only when we are not sure He has stated His will in the scripture. Many times we say that because we have not studied and know He tells us His will in Scripture if we take time to study and learn. Everything points to the fact that He wants us well and reveals His will for healing as we search and ask for it. We need to constantly be learning His Word to know His Will, to know how to pray to get our prayers answered according to His Will. I am learning that a person's prayers are used to bring the Kingdom of God to the earth so His Will will be done on earth as it is in heaven.

Let me share one of the exciting things I have just learned. I have been asking the Lord if healing is in the atonement. I have felt so impressed that healing was in the atonement because I saw two scriptures, "By His Stripes we are healed" (Old Testament, Isa. 53:5) and "By His Stripes we were healed" (New Testament, 1 Pet. 2:24). I asked the Lord to show me if that meant healing was part of it when Jesus said, "It is finished," meaning He did it all for us. Just this week I was listening to Andrew Wommack, and he said the Greek word for salvation, sozo, meant salvation and healing. I always like to research and not believe everything I hear or read. When I did research it, I found out the meanings are "save or saved, whole, healed, preserve, and well." It is used in three different ways in Greek, to save from certain death, to be healed, or for salvation or getting born again. Praise God! When Jesus was crucified and said, "It is finished," I do know with His death and resurrection Jesus sent the Comforter to be with us. After the Comforter came, each believer became a priest after the order of Melchizedek (Heb. 7:17) and able to go directly to God through Jesus by way of the Holy Spirit. I know that part of the curse is over so men and women can go directly to God through the Holy Spirit now. Also, I am encouraged that Jesus is the best thing that ever happened to women because of His Word and treatment of women. He entrusted Mary to go "tell" his disciples, and if you study how the early church grew and worshipped, you'll see women were very instrumental in the growth of the new church as needed.

- He communicates with me. I hear His Still Small Voice (within) daily. I am aware of His presence in my day-to-day activities. I talk to Him and praise and worship God. He talks back, not audibly, but in the stillness. This means it is imperative I shut out the world to hear Him. I have had some amazing dreams that I wrote down that have strengthened my faith and helped me to help others. On two occasions, I heard a booming voice speak to me, once in prayer and once upon awaking, like the scripture account that His Voice is like thunder or mighty running water (Rev. 14:2). I have had a few visions that speak to me about plans the Lord has for me. Two different times, a man of God spoke prophetic words in church about my life that encouraged me and enabled me to draw closer to God.

- I have been blessed with fellow believers, both laymen and preachers/evangelists, who shared and encourage me in my walk with the Lord and strengthen my faith.

Some of the Names for Each Part of The Godhead
(There is overlap sometimes in the names and the function of the Godhead.)

Who Is God the Father?
Apparently, God did not have a name in the Old Testament until Moses said to Him, "Who shall I say sent me?" (To the Israelites after receiving the Ten Commandments.) God told Moses to tell them, "I AM That I AM!" (This tells me that He has always existed and exists in the present and will always exist.) He is known as Elohim, Adonai, and El Shaddai, referring to Him as a powerful ruler. Wikipedia says that Yahweh is the principal name in the Old Testament by which God reveals Himself and is the most sacred, distinctive, and incommunicable name of God. We know God as the Ancient of Days, Father/Abba (like Daddy).

Here are seven names of God in Christianity (Psalms 23:9, 10, 11).

- Jehovah-Jireh. "The Lord will provide" (Gen. 22:13–14).
- Jehovah-Rapha. "The Lord that healeth" (Exod. 15:26).
- Jehovah-Nissi. "The Lord our Banner" (Exod. 17:8–15) (my victory).

49

- Jehovah-Shalom. "The Lord our Peace" (Judg. 6:24).
- Jehovah-Raah. "The Lord is the Way, my Shepherd" (Ps. 23:1).
- Jehovah-Tsidkenu. "The Lord our Righteousness" (Jer. 23:6).
- Jehovah-Shammah. "The Lord is the Light, ever present" (Ezek. 48:35).

The scripture tells us about things God loves and things He hates. "Whoever sows sparingly reaps sparingly, whoever sews bountifully, reaps bountifully. God loves a cheerful giver" (2 Cor. 9:6–7).

Here are six things the Lord hates—yea, seven are an abomination to Him—from Proverbs 6:16–19: a proud look, a lying tongue, hands that shed innocent blood, a heart that devises wicked imaginations, feet that be swift in running to mischief, a false witness that speaks lies, and he who sows discord among brethren. (These is strange wording, but a commentary says "Six things, yea seven" is a figure of speech arresting attention and signifying that the list is not exhaustive.) We learn much about a person when we see what he or she likes or dislikes.

Who Is Jesus?
Here are some of the Names of Jesus: The Word of God (Rev. 19:12–13). The Word became flesh, Logos (John 1:1). He was the Light of the world (John 8:12). Word of life (1 John 1:1). Our Great High Priest (Heb. 3:1). The Great Shepherd (Heb. 13:20–21). The Good Shepherd (John 10:11–14). King of Kings and Lord of Lords (Rev. 19:16 and 1 Tim. 6:15). Emmanuel, God with us (Isa. 9:6 and Matt. 1:23). Lord of All (Acts 10:36). Jesus was slain from the foundation of the earth. The Way, the Truth, and the Life. "No man cometh unto the Father but by me." (John 14:6). He, by the grace of God, might taste death for everyone (Heb. 2:9 and Phil. 2:5–8). The Deliverer (Rom. 11:26). The only way to deliver us from death and bring many sons to glory (Heb. 2:10). He is the Resurrection and the Life (John 11:25–26). Firstborn of all creation (Col. 1:15). The Judge of all men

(Acts 10:42 and 2 Tim. 4:8). Prince of Peace (Isa. 9:6). Author and Perfecter of our faith (Heb. 12:2). The True God (1 John 5:20). He is known as Christ, Lord of All (Acts 10:36). Master, Savior (Matt. 1:21 and Luke 2:11). Rabbi (Great Teacher), Son of God (Luke 1:3). Son of Man (John 5:27). Son of David, Lamb of God, the Alpha and the Omega (Rev. 1:8 and 22:13). The Chief Cornerstone and the Sure Foundation, the Living Bread (John 6:35 and 6:48). The Door, the Great Physician, the Rose of Sharon, and the Lily of the Valley, the Rock of Ages, the Lamb of God (John 1:29). The Redeemer, Author, and Finisher of our faith, the True Vine (John 15:1). He is the Pearl of Great Price, the Counselor, the Lawgiver, and the Advocate, the Good Tidings of Great Joy, the Living Stone. He also was called I Am in John 8:58 and Exodus 3:14. The Rock (1 Cor. 10:4). And more! Jesus was slain from the foundation of the earth (Rev. 13:8).

Who Is The Holy Spirit?
The Holy Spirit is a person (He is not an *it*), so He desires to have a personal relationship with you.

Here are some to the things the Holy Spirit does. He is our Helper who Jesus sent when He ascended into heaven so we can have God with us at all times as a believer (Rom. 8:26). Jesus was limited to an earthly ministry on earth. He came in the flesh to redeem mankind from the curse of sin and death. He told us it was for our good that He should leave and send the Comforter (Acts 9:31) to live in us (Cor. 3:16) You were sealed with the promised Holy Spirit, which is the guarantee of our inheritance until we acquire possession of it, to the praise of His (Jesus's) glory (Eph. 1:13). The Holy Spirit gives us access to the Father through Jesus (Eph. 2:18), for through the Spirit, by faith, He helps us wait for the hope of righteousness (Gal. 5:5). "The renewing of the Holy Spirit" proclaims who carries out the work of the regeneration in the heart and life of a believer by His faith in Christ (Titus 3:5). He produces the Fruit of the Spirit, love, joy, peace, long-suffering, gentleness, goodness, faith meekness, temperance, as we allow ourselves to be led of the Spirit (Gal. 5:22). The Holy Spirit gives us gifts by carrying out the instructions of Christ, relative to who gets what: the Word of Wisdom, Knowledge, Faith, Gifts of Healing, working of Miracles, Prophecy, discerning of spirits, diverse kinds of Tongues, and the interpretation of Tongues (1 Cor. 12:13). He guides us (John 16:13), teaches and instructs us (John 14:26). He calls us for the work He has for us to do (Acts 13:2).

The Lord reveals His mysteries to us a little at a time. Truth, from His Word, is the center. We see portions, and God gives each of His family pieces of the puzzle so we can come together and share His wisdom through His Body of Believers (Heb. 10:25) A way to get to know God is through His Word and His Personality. He has always existed, from everlasting to everlasting. "I AM God!" Believing His Word, trusting Him, and spending time in His Presence are the best ways to learn His ways and learn about Him and know Him. He is infinitely wise. If you want to draw near to Him, all you have to do is lovingly whisper His Name. He is as close as a breath, Immanuel (God with us). He will never leave us nor forsake us. You are never alone! Today I heard Joyce Meyers say that someone asked a well-known preacher how he was able to accomplish all he did during his lifetime. He said, "I am never alone. There are two of us!" How much easier to carry a burden when two people carry it! Especially when your help is the Lord (Eccles. 4:9).

The Holy Spirit (The Spiritual Umbilical Cord)
Jesus called the Holy Spirit the Comforter. In John 14:16, Jesus said, "I will pray the Father and He shall give you another Comforter, that He may abide with you forever. Even the Spirit of Truth; whom the world cannot receive, because it seeks Him not, neither knows Him, but you know Him; for He dwells with you, and shall be in you. But the Comforter, which is the Holy Spirit, whom the Father will send

in my name, He shall teach you all things, and bring all things to your remembrance, and whatsoever I have said unto you." John 15:26 tells us, "When the Comforter is come, whom I will send unto you from the Father, even the Spirit of Truth, which proceed from the Father, He shall testify of me." Jesus said in 16:7, "Nevertheless I tell you the truth; it is for your good I am going away. Unless I go, the Counselor will not come to you; but if I go, I will send Him to you. When He comes He will convict the world of guilt in regard to sin and righteousness and judgment; in regard to sin, because men do not believe in me; in regard to righteousness, because I am going to the Father, where you can see me no longer, and in regard to judgment, because the prince of this world now stand condemned. I have much more to say to you, more than you can now bear. But when He, the Spirit of Truth, come He will guide you into all truth. He will not speak on His own; He will speak only what He hears, and He will tell you what is yet to come [prophesy]. He will bring glory to me by taking from what is mine and making it known to you. All that belongs to the Father is mine. That is why I said the Spirit will take from what is mine and make it know to you." If you are a believer in the Lord Jesus as your personal Savior and desire Him to be the Lord of your life, the Holy Spirit seals you (Eph. 1:13), lives in you (1 Cor. 3:16). He frees us (Rom. 8:2), prophesies through us (2 Pet. 1:21), and helps us obey (1 Pet. 1:22).

Some more of the things the Holy Spirit does is to testify of Jesus (John 15:26). He fills us (Acts 4:31), He bears witness to the Truth (Rom. 9:1), He helps us (Rom. 8:26), and He guides us (John 16:13).

This book has been such an incredible vehicle that the Lord has used to "grow me up" in the Way of the Lord. A function of the Holy Spirit is to reveal the truth of the Word (1 Cor. 2:10). He calls us (Acts 13:2), and then He instructs us (Acts 8:29). Here is an example of His speaking to me (Rev. 2:7). I awake in the mornings with words flowing through my mind that I attempt to get on paper as quickly as

I can so as not to forget any of the nuggets from Him. One morning, I felt His joy rushing out to greet me and heard Him say in my spirit something about "The Spiritual Umbilical Cord." I said, "And what?" I never heard that before! I knew He meant for me to research the umbilical cord in the physical, for so many lessons to be learned in the spiritual are easier to understand when we can relate to something in the physical. So of course, I researched the umbilical cord.

After I checked the dictionary for the meaning of the human umbilical cord, it made sense. Wikipedia calls the umbilical cord or birth cord a conduit between the embryo or fetus and the placenta as the mother is connected to the child and what she sends through the cord nourishes and develops the baby. During prenatal development, it is physiologically and genetically part of the fetus and contains two arteries and one vein buried within Wharton's jelly. The umbilical vein supplies the fetus with oxygenated, nutrient-rich blood from the placenta. Conversely, the fetal heart pumps deoxygenated, nutrient-depleted blood through the umbilical arteries back to the placenta. (*Wharton's jelly* is a gelatinous substance within the cord present in the vitreous humor of the eyeball. Cells in Wharton's jelly express several stem cell genes. They can be extracted, cultured, and induced to differentiate into mature cell types such as neurons. Wharton's jelly is therefore a potential source of adult stem cells.) The interchange from nourishment through the cord *from* the mother to the baby, and eliminating the wastes from the baby by pouring out the dross to return to the mother for filtering, is a strong visual of why the Lord would use this as an example. Wow! What an incredible example of our intimate fellowship with the Holy Spirit! His umbilical cord to us is vital for life as well!

There is a spiritual channel between the Lord and the worshipper that needs to be open and available for an interchange and for fellowship to flow between the two. As we allow the channel to be open and free for the necessary exchange, the arteries bring lifesaving properties from the host to the recipient. The vein returns the depleted properties to the host for cleansing. As I am a very visual person, it is now clearer to me about the exchange. We find so many human examples to explain the working of the spirit world. It is essential for our spiritual life for us to be connected to our Creator continually to be nourished and exchange the dross for something refined straight from our Creator. With sight being an integral part of the Wharton's jelly, perhaps our "spiritual insight" emanates from our Spiritual Umbilical Cord.

Clearing the Channel: Developing the Fruit
Well, then, how can we keep the channel clear for the proper exchange? Galatians 5:22 tells us about the fruit of the Spirit. He produces fruit! Developing the Fruit of the Spirit is similar to developing our physical muscles. We are given muscles, but for them to grow and be strong, there must be a developing process. First, how does fruit develop on a tree? Do we plant a seed for a tree and rush back the next day to see the fruit appear? Of course not! It takes some knowledge of how and what a tree needs to grow. It needs good soil, sunlight, water, and the environment needs to be considered. Then how can we develop this spiritual umbilical cord between the Lord and us? Perhaps it is the silver thread we hear spoken about; perhaps when we are born the silver thread connects us to our Maker and never leaves us, letting us have that opportunity for connection to Him. Paul tells us in Romans that the Lord put in all of us a desire to know Him and to seek Him. Some call it a vacuum, like a beacon that guides us to find our Source. If we desire a stronger communication, what do we do?

In order to be nourished from our Source, there must be an exchange in the Cord of a fresh cleansing allowed to flow from Him to us. If the Cord is jammed with fear, unforgiveness, hate, doubt, stress, impatience, etc., the blessings from the Lord cannot flow. They are impeded. Well, then, how do we get them going? We develop the fruit of the Spirit, which is a process, one moment at a time, one day at a time. The Holy Spirit is our Teacher (John 14:26) and comforts us (Acts 9:31). He prays for us (Rom. 8:26). When we learn to substitute the Word of God a little at a time, it is like nourishment to our whole being, Spirit, Soul, and Body. If we want to know the Will of God, we read His Word, the Bible, and if we want to be led of the Spirit, we do the Will of God. When we spend time with Him (fellowship), we learn His ways and take on more of His character. He strengthens us (Eph. 3:16). We learn to praise Him, glorify Him, and thank Him for all He is and does for us. As we take on more of His character in us, the Fruit of the Spirit is manifested. When we allow ourselves to be grafted into the tree, we become more mature, and the branches develop fruit. The Fruit of the Spirit will be addressed in a later section of the book. He brings freedom (2 Cor. 3:17) and joy (1 Thess. 1:6), and the Holy Spirit transforms us (2 Cor. 3:18).

Verses 4 to 16 say, "My message and my preaching [Paul is writing to the church at Corinth] were not with wise and persuasive words, but with a demonstration of the Spirit's power, so that your faith might not rest on men's wisdom, but on God's power. We do, however, speak a message of wisdom among the mature, but not the wisdom of this age or of the rulers of this age, who are coming to nothing. No, we speak of God's secret Wisdom, a Wisdom that has been hidden and that God destined for our glory before time began. None of the rulers of this age understood it, for if they had, they would not have crucified the Lord of glory. However, as it is written: 'No eye has seen no ear has heard, no mind has conceived what God has prepared for those who love Him, but God has revealed it to us by His Spirit.' The Spirit searched all things, even the deep things of God. For who among men knows the thoughts of a man except the man's spirit within him? In the same way no one knows the thoughts of God except the Spirit of God. We have not received the spirit of the world but the Spirit who is from God, that we may understand what God has freely given us. This is what we speak, not in words taught us by human wisdom but in words taught by the Spirit, expressing spiritual truths in spiritual words. The man without the Spirit does not accept the things that come from the Spirit of God, for they are foolishness to him, and he cannot understand them, because they are spiritually discerned. The spiritual man makes judgment about all things, but he himself is not subject to any man's judgment: 'For who has known the mind of the Lord that He may instruct him?' But we have the mind of Christ." This scripture has always been so fascinating to me. Now I understand it better as I study about the Holy Spirit. As more of the Lord's Spirit is invited into my spirit, I know the Lord's mysteries and understand better.

As we know the ways of the Lord, Paul says in 2 Corinthians 2:14, "But thanks be to God, who always leads us in triumphal procession in Christ and through us spreads everywhere the fragrance of the knowledge of him. For we are to God the aroma of Christ among those who are being saved and those who are perishing. To the one we are the smell of death, to the other, the fragrance of life."

## What Voices Are You Listening To?

Agree with God

What voices do we hear? The inside voice is the Holy Spirit, that "Still Small Voice" guiding our minds and consciences in the ways of the Lord, and the outside voices are ourselves and satan with his demons.

1. *Man* (self, human nature, influenced from this fallen world we live in).

2. Satan (who became the god of this world after his deception in the garden and usurped mankind's authority given to him by God). Sometimes it is difficult to determine which voice, man's or satan's, a person is listening to, so there is an overlap between number 1 and number 2. Satan points us away from God and His Word. Watch what comes out of your mouth if you want to keep satan at bay and not invite him into your lives. He is a defeated foe and only has the power in our lives that we give him with our words, actions, and choices. Jesus defeated him on the cross, and the same power that raised Jesus from the dead lives in you, if you are a believer. "If you confess with your mouth, Jesus is Lord, and believe in your heart that God raised Him from the dead, you will be saved. For it is with you heart that you believe and are justified, and it is with your mouth that you confess and are saved" (Rom. 10:9). The way this takes place is, when you truly believe and do what Scripture says, Jesus becomes Savior of your life and you become a new creation. "Therefore, if anyone is in Christ, he is a new creation; the old has passed away, behold, the new has come" (2 Cor. 5:17). Then you seek to do things God's way instead of your own. That is making God the Lord of your life. Anybody can say anything, but the proof is in what you seek after. Self is a very strong influence. God gives us His

Word to guide us into His way. Your actions and words prove if you have truly believed in Jesus as your Savior.

3. *God* (through the Holy Spirit, that Still Small Voice, and on rare occasions God sends His Word through an angel messenger, but the loudest voice He sends us is His Word, now written in the Bible for all to read). How do we know it is God talking to us? He never speaks against His Word, so you can read His will in the Bible. He never tells you to do anything against Scriptures. God always emphasizes life versus a religion of death. John 10:10 tells us, "The thief comes only to steal and kill and destroy; I come that they may have life, and have it abundantly. I am the good shepherd." If the voice you are listening to goes against the Word of God and lies, steals, and destroys, you must choose to turn away and stop listening to it. God's way is peace, love, and harmony.

Paul tells us in Romans 1:2–23 there is no excuse for men to not believe in God, the Great I Am. "For what can be known about God is plain to them, because God has shown it to them. Ever since the creation of the world His invisible nature, namely, His eternal power and deity has been clearly perceived in the things that have been made. So they are without excuse for although they knew God they did not honor Him as God or give thanks to Him, but they became futile in their thinking, and their senseless minds were darkened. Claiming to be wise, they became fools, and exchanged the glory of the immortal God for images resembling mortal men or birds or animals or reptiles." The remainder of the chapter tells what happens when God gives them up to their own lusts and the dishonoring of themselves.

Human conscience (that was put in mankind in the beginning from our Creator God; some call it a gut-level feeling)—everyone has it. Whether you are a believer or not, our mind and spirit are connected at birth, and this remains with a person unless he or her make decisions to sear the conscience with deliberate actions to the contrary. "Now the Spirit expressly says that in later times some will depart from the faith by giving heed to deceitful spirits and doctrines of demons, through the pretensions of liars whose consciences are seared" (1 Tim. 4:1). Verse 7 says, "Have nothing to do with godless and silly myths. Train yourself in Godliness; for while bodily training is of some value, Godliness is of value in every way, as it hold promise for the present life and also for the life to come."

God would not leave us in this fallen world without a viable weapon inside us to protect us against the enemy. We are told by many preachers there is a kind of a homing device that is our North Star to guide us safely home. Perhaps it is this conscience that our loving God provided for us to use daily, moment by moment. John 8:19, Acts 24:16, and Romans 13:5 all speak about the conscience. This is an inner feeling or voice acting as a guide to righteousness or wrongness of a person's behavior. (Take a moment and read what Paul has to say in Ephesians 3:1–6 and discover the mystery he talks about that can share together in the promise to Christ Jesus.) In Hebrews 13:18, Paul speaks about a clear conscience and desire to live honorably in every way. Hebrews 10:22 tells us to "draw near to God with a sincere heart in full assurance of faith, having our hearts sprinkled to cleanse us from a guilty conscience and having our bodies washed with pure water."

There is a voice we need to listen to each day, and that is the Voice of Jesus. His words will change your life! David Jeremiah produced an informative pamphlet about hearing the Voice of Jesus and suggested three ways, Prayer, Instruction, and Scripture. Read the chapter "Ways to Develop Intimacy with the Holy Spirit," and some of the ways to hear the Voice of Jesus will be explained.

When the question "What voices are you listening to?" is discussed, the subject of addiction comes up. What an insidious development to submission this is! Beth Moore, in her book *Praying God's Word,* is an excellent place to go for help to overcome addictions. That homing device our Heavenly Father planted in us to gently guide us back to Him was perverted by the adversary into addiction, taking away the free will the Lord gave each of us at creation. Remember, your free will gives you the right to choose whom you listen to, and if it does not agree with Scripture and a loving God, make your choice now to turn away as fast as you can.

Beth Moore says, "Addiction is one of the cruelest of all yokes. It comes to us like a friend, promising to bring comfort. It kisses us on the cheek like Judas, stealing from our treasury, then rents us for a cheap fee to the opposition. Addiction is a yoke that convinces us we must wear it to survive. Nothing makes us more powerless. No ungodly master is a more unyielding dictator. Countless people, even those in the family of our faith, have concluded that they are hopeless to overcome this relentless beast. After more failures than they can bear to count, many believers accept earthly defeat as compulsory and await a freedom that will only come in heaven. The accuser of the brethren chides them constantly with his tally of failures and convinces them that they are unable to derail the miserable cycle of self-loathing." This is the best definition and explanation of addiction available that I have seen. Please get her book if you want to read the whole chapter dedicated to addiction. Some very valuable points are that God can set you free, with your help. He requires time, trust, and cooperation. As with many of the facets of our walk with the Lord, He seldom delivers us immediately, for if we get the manifestation before we have learned the lessons of the journey, it is so easy to fall back into the old patterns we established for ourselves. The Lord is a God of new beginning; with repentance and choosing to follow His way, He is always available to us. David was an example of making bad choices at times, but he knew where to go when he sinned and asked the Lord for forgiveness, then truly repented. God said David was a man after His own heart, for he asked God for forgiveness and repented when he realized his choices were not God inspired. If you are battling addiction, realizing you have a problem is the first step. Praise the Lord for His mercy, and He is always available to you, day or night, never leaves you or forsakes you (Heb. 13:5). With each problem, He will give you the means to escape (1 Cor. 10:13).

Remember that your mind is a filter to sort through the good thoughts from the Holy Spirit and the destructive thoughts you receive from the adversary or your own carnal nature. You have the choice again. I heard that Kenneth Hagin said, "You are not responsible for the birds flying around your head, but you are responsible for allowing them to build a nest in your hair" (or something like that). Your behavior will attract people to you, knowing that the better person you become, the better person you will attract. Each of us has the responsibility and opportunity to grow as quickly as we can toward the Lord to be the servant He intended us to be. So have your thoughts pointed the way to freedom and wisdom in God's Word, or are you wallowing in stagnation where you are and doing the same old things over and over and expecting different results?

Dawna DeSilva says there is an unseen world working silently to control you and the atmosphere around you, but you can live in the atmosphere of heaven instead. She says you can exercise your authority over the unseen world operating around you. She also added that we are a walking transmitter, so be careful what you partner with in this lifetime. If the adversary tempts you with his negativity, say to him, "I see you, and I am not going to partner with you, and I send you back." The enemy is trying to get you to take the bait. When Jesus was tempted in the wilderness by satan, He quoted scriptures to the devil. "It is written" prefaced whatever issue was addressed with words coming from the Word. An example Dawna said if she has difficulty sleeping, she says, "Satan, I will not partner with you, I belong to the Lord, and He gives His beloved rest." Ignorance is not bliss! "My people perish from lack of knowledge" (Hosea 4:1). Remember to reject and replace the evil broadcasts with the wisdom of the Holy Spirit. She also said, "Satan, not on my watch, you don't control!"

Ideas and suggestions are being broadcast all around us. We need to know that we have a choice which frequency and entity we listen to. Dawna stated, "I have authority over the radio station I am listening to. I can choose to change the channel!" "Take your thoughts captive" (2 Cor. 10:5). Do not listen to everything; reject and send away what you do not need to be listening to. Shift the atmosphere by replacing lust with love, because love gives and lust takes. "God did not give you a spirit of fear but of love and a sound mind" (2 Tim. 1:7). When you are a walking transmitter for the Lord Jesus Christ, you are a broadcaster of peace!

*God can speak to us through other people* (prophesy and interpretation, through circumstances, and in rare cases, to hear His voice either while we are awake or asleep, in dreams, or in visions). Never forget to test all these ways with the Word of God (the Bible) and with discernment through the Holy Spirit. When we respond to the Word of God, we discover, "For the Word of God is living and active, sharper than any two-edged sword, piercing to the division of soul and body, of joints and marrow, and discerning the thoughts and intentions of the heart. And before Him no creature is hidden, but all are open and laid bare to the eyes of Him with whom we have to do" (Heb. 4:12–13). (We cannot hide from the Lord!) Diligently work on your discernment by meditating on the Word and allowing the Holy Spirit to teach, discipline (from which the word disciple comes), and fellowship to allow us to pattern out ways after His Ways. The more you can die to self (stop your selfish nature from controlling your thoughts and actions), the more the Holy Spirit can come to dwell in you, helping to shape your old nature into the new creation the Lord promised you are becoming. The second book of Corinthians 5:17 explains the process of becoming a new creation.

As you read this, continue on through chapter 6, as all this is part of working out your salvation and your part in becoming this new creation. It is a process. It reminds me of a marriage. First one says, "I do," then both work very day to make a successful marriage. So many times we are reminded of being the Body and Bride of Christ, and I believe the reason for the comparison is to learn how to be married to the Lord.

This is a good time to mention the books by Sarah Young, *Jesus Calling and Jesus Always*. She shares what the Lord says to her and the scriptures to back it up. They have helped me seek what the Lord is telling us, for it sends me to the Bible for conformation. When I look up the scriptures and study them, she is able to explain it in layman's terms for me to understand.

I urge you to make the time every day for the Lord to speak to you so you can learn His Ways and be in His Perfect Will. That does not happen by chance. Make decisions to be in the Lord's Presence; it will never disappoint you. He has much to teach all of us!

## Watch Your Words

Before we discuss the words that you speak out of your mouth, let's read again what Kenneth Copeland said about Ephesians 4 on becoming spiritually mature.

1. Meditate on God's Word.
2. Be a doer of the Word.
3. Put the Word first place in your life.
4. Obey the voice of your Spirit.
5. Do exactly as God tells you to do, now!

(Take these steps and you will grow spiritually.)

Reading, meditating, being a doer of the Word and obeying and learning to speak as the Lord would have you do brings life, not death. Shouldn't we learn the correct way to speak before we allow our mouths to send out words that can be used like satan does, to steal, kill, and destroy? One needs the desire, like a passion to know God, and the more we mature in Him, the closer we can grow to Him, learning His nature and learning about ourselves. We need to learn to speak truth straight from the Word to release blessings in the world and not to produce curses on anyone or anything. Kenneth reminds us that Mark 11:23–24 declares that we have whatever we believe and say. He also states that your words can bring life or death to your family line, your descendants. So speak healing words, not only for yourself, but also for your family and those around you.

Words Are Powerful!

Watch those words diligently that come out of your mouth, for they are powerful. Proverbs 18:21 states the tongue has the power of life and death, and those who love it will eat its fruit. Matthew 12:34–35 says, "For out of the abundance of the heart the mouth speaks." Words have the power to bless or curse. Remember, God spoke the world into being with words. In the first chapter of Genesis, read how many times "God said" was listed. Each time God spoke things into being with the power of words. "He said, He said!" (Gen. 1:3, 1:6, 1:9, 1:11, 1:14, 1:20, 1:24, 1:16, 1:28, and 1:29). Do you think speaking words are important? Words are powerful! Scripture tells us to stand on the Word with those who need our prayers, to speak healing, not negative words, to believe to receive because Scripture tells us we can trust the Lord at His Word. By the stripes of Jesus, we are healed (1 Pet. 2:21) and were healed (Isa. 53:5). His mighty blood in the atonement means He came for salvation and healing for us. (We are to speak those words that be not as though they are [Rom. 4:17].) Words are powerful, so speak them according to what Scripture says and stand on them to believe with others. May we watch what we say, and all of us can benefit from standing together and claiming the mighty Word of God.

You have often heard that we are what we eat. The body certainly responds to food, but we are what we think, what we inhale, what we see, what we hear, etc. With all our senses, we "drink" in this world. Never forget we are what we speak and say we are and what others speak and say we are. In Deuteronomy 30:14, the Bible states, "The Word is very near you, it is in your mouth and in your heart so that you can do it." The Word must be in two places, in your heart and in your mouth. Correct yourself when you hear yourself speaking negative or discouraging words.

While I was working at IBM, we learned GIGO—garbage in, garbage out. Be mindful of the atmosphere that is created when you are in the company of someone who spits out poison you do not want to internalize. You may find yourself needing to be more selective on whom you are around and what you bring into your daily life, such as television, books, movies, etc. You are filling your heart and mind all the time with something; let it be God's Word. Let the Word abide inside you, then you will always have an abundance that pleases God.

A tree is recognized by its fruit (Matt. 12:34–35). What kind of fruit are you displaying? The moment something comes out of your mouth, perhaps something you have heard and said all your life, you will soon start actually hearing what you are saying and will desire to change some phrases you have lived with for years. In verse 36, it is said, "But I say to you, that every idle word that men shall speak, they shall give account thereof in the day of judgment." It is certainly a sobering revelation that verse 37 says, "For by your words you shall be justified and by your words, you will be condemned!"

Words Are Used in Therapy
Some doctors are using "talk therapy" to treat patients suffering with depression. Instead of medicating the problem, the doctors instruct the patients to start making positive declarations over their lives, saying such things as "I have a bright future," "People like to be around me," or "Good things are in store." Some of the patients are depressed because they are facing life-threatening diseases and feel there is no hope. The doctor asks them, "Has anyone ever survived this disease?" The answers are always yes. So he tells them, "Then I want you to start saying, 'I will make it. I will be one of the people who beats the odds.'" Those patients obey the doctor's orders, and amazingly, many of them not only come out of their depression but also make full recoveries. It's time to use our words to declare good things. Speak blessings over your life and your family. Throughout the day, say things such as "I have the favor of God," "I am strong and healthy," "I'm well and able to do what I need to do." Do you know that what you say about yourself has greater impact on you than anything anybody else says about you? Many people are overly critical of themselves, saying, "I'm so clumsy. I can't do anything right." "I'm so overweight. I'll never get back into shape." "I never get any good breaks." They may not realize it, but they are cursing their future. Those words sink into their minds. Before long, they

develop a defeated mentality, low self-esteem, and diminished confidence. Worse yet, those negative mindsets can interfere with God's plan for their lives.

I was guilty of stating, "I can't remember names. I am awful with that!" One day I came upon the scripture that told me we have the mind of Christ (when we belong to Him, we are part of Him and have access to His Mind). That was a revelation to me to stop those works immediately. One of the best ways to break free from such strongholds is simply by speaking what the Bible says, words of victory. Every day, look in the mirror and declare, "God's Word says I am strong. God is fighting my battles for me. I'm excited about my future." Maybe you are lonely because you don't have a lot of friends. Instead of complaining, start declaring, "God is bringing great people into my life. I know He loves me so I can risk loving others." Speak blessings over your life, and as you do, you'll go out with more confidence, you'll be more congenial, and in turn, you will attract new friends. When discouragement comes (instead of sitting back and accepting it), say, "No, I'm a victor and not a victim. I may have been defeated before, but the past is the past. I can only learn from the past and look to the future. We only live now and have this moment, so start to speak what you want to come about. This is a new day." It's not enough just to think it you need to hear it, because what we constantly hear ourselves saying, we will eventually believe. Some people live in a perpetual state of financial crisis. They can't seem to pay their bills, "always living under their circumstances" and constantly speaking defeat. If you are struggling financially, remind yourself repeatedly, "The Lord has made me the head and not the tail," as the Word says in Deuteronomy 28:13 that I will lend and I will not borrow. "Everything I touch will prosper and succeed" (Deut. 15:6). You may be thinking, "None of that is true in my life." Yes, it is true! That is what faith is all about. The Bible promises are for you. Put your name in the sentence. Speak your faith! Kenneth

Copeland tells us to take the promises of God personally and read the Bible, putting your name in it as if it He were talking to you, for He is. "God is no respecter of persons" is in Acts 10:34. The spiritual forces of faith reach into the realm of the Spirit and transfer things to manifest in the material realm. The world says you need to see it to believe it, but God says you must believe and then you'll see it.

Worship comes in speaking to the Lord as if He were beside or in front of you, for His Spirit is there with you as you worship and praise Him. Worship is like drawing from a well of "living water." Draw from your well that you store within. It really is not a praise until you speak it. There is power in the Word, for words are containers and carry to you the mighty strength of our Lord. Read His Word, seek to think God's thoughts, rest in Him, and trust His Words, speaking His Words. No murmuring, like the children of Israel in the wilderness; murmuring only delays God's plan for us. You are putting stumbling blocks in your own way with murmuring. That only delays seeing the manifestation of the future that the Lord has planned for you. John Hagee used to say about the murmuring, "One more time around Mount Sinai." When we pray according to Scripture, which is the Will of God for us, He tells us to "delight ourselves in the Lord, and He gives us the desires of our heart" (Ps. 36:4) for He put the desires there!

Watch Your Words!
Watch what comes out of your mouth! I mentioned earlier while working for IBM, we learned GIGO—garbage in, garbage out. Watch what goes in. Remember, you are filling your heart with something, so let it be God's Word. Let the Word abide inside you, then you will always have an abundance that pleases God. A tree is recognized by its fruit (Matt. 12:34–35). What kind of fruit are you displaying? The moment something comes out of your mouth, perhaps something you have heard and said all your life, you will soon

start actually hearing what you are saying and will desire to change some phrases you have lived with for years.

Make a list of your goals, your dreams, and the areas where you want to see change. Confirm your desires by Scripture, and then every day before you leave the house, speak those blessings aloud. Maybe you struggle with condemnation because of past mistakes. Each day declare, "I am the righteousness of God in Christ Jesus [2 Cor. 5:21] because of what Jesus has done, not what I have done. God is pleased with me. He is on my side." If you say something like that consistently, guilt and condemnation won't hang around. Understand it's not enough to avoid saying anything negative; you must go on the offensive and start making positive declarations over your life. Remember, your own words will have more impact on your future than anything anybody else says about you. Our own words spoken out loud by us program our subconscious mind better than the voice of others. Do your part and speak words of victory. God will pour out His favor in exciting, fresh ways in your life, and you will live the abundant life He has in store for you.

Words Have the Power to Bless or to Wound
Be quick to listen, slow to speak, and slow to become angry. As you ask the Holy Spirit, "Help me, please, Lord," allow the Holy Spirit time to help you communicate properly. Allow your speaking to come under the control of the Holy Spirit, and you will respond properly. So often our habits of speaking result in a negative response or pattern of negativity in our environment and relationships. Discipline yourself to fix your thoughts on the Lord and expect Him to always be with you to guide and direct you. Words can never been taken back. Remember the scripture that tells us we will be accountable for every word that comes out of our mouths (Matt. 12:36).

Read about what James 3:9 says about the tongue with praises and curses from the same place. "With the tongue we praise our

Lord and Father. Out of the same mouth come praise and cursing. My brothers, this should not be."

Our belief grows as we speak the words we read from Scripture and pray God's Word. We build our spiritual muscles so our faith grows as well, for "faith comes from what is heard, and what is heard comes by the preaching of Christ," who is the Word and brings the Word to us (Rom. 10:17 RSV). We are given a measure of faith to each of us when we accept Jesus as our Savior (Rom. 12:3–8). Faith is like a muscle; it grows as we use it. As we speak the words of faith, we build that faith similar to how exercise builds our physical muscles. The more we work our physical muscles, the larger they grow, just like our spiritual muscles. Faith comes by hearing, and hearing the Word of God (Rom. 10:17). And then speak the Word! Change your words and your culture changes, then your journey changes, and then your world changes. You can make a difference in this world for the better.

An Excerpt from Our Church Newsletter
By Steve House
Here is the gist of an article from Christ Centered Church that blessed me from a fellow member, Steve House, who wrote for our newsletter. He was writing on thoughts to begin a new year, expecting the goodness of God and the excitement that can only come from the Lord for the New Year. He stated that the power to see change in your life can be found in the words you speak. You have the power to set the destiny for your life, by what comes out of your mouth. Proverbs 18:21 states that life and death are found in the words we speak and that no one gets to decide the words that come out of your mouth except you. Words have the power to set things in motion, good or bad. They are like little seeds that you plant in life.

He went on to encourage us to enjoy the fruit of faith, hope, and promise, then if your thoughts and words are positive, you will see your circumstances and situations changing for the better. Start by planting good seed through your words. Make your confessions personal and real and stated in a positive way. Say, "I am healed, blessed, and gifted. I am everything God has called me to be." Remember to bless others, and God has promised to bless you. Proverbs 25:11 says, "The right word at the right time is like precious gold set in silver."

To summarize, Steve said to be careful what you say; there is power of life and death in the tongue. An encouraging word to someone who is down can lift them up and help them make it through the day. A destructive word to someone who is down can be what it takes to kill them. Be careful what you say. Speak life to those who cross your path. Special is the individual who will take time to encourage another. "Let us continue to encourage each other, my Christ Centered family," Steve House wrote.

(Steve has gone to be with the Lord, but his words of encouragement live on here. He blessed us often with his articles.)

What Were the Last Words Jesus Told His Disciples?
If you knew you were going to die, would every word you told those around you be of utmost importance? Here are some of the words He left for us. He told us the hour had come for the Son of Man to be glorified (John 12:23). Verse 28 states that it was for this reason Jesus came to this hour to glorify the Father, Jesus and the Father as one. Verse 47 adds that He came to save the world, not judge it. The Father commanded Him what to say. Jesus came in love and brought a new commandment (13:34): "Love one another as I have loved you, so you must love one another. By this all men will know that you are my disciples if you love one another."

"Let not your heart be troubled; trust in God" (John 14:1). Jesus told what He was going to do for those who believed in Him. He was going to prepare a place for them.

Verse 6 says, "I am the Way, the Truth, and the Life. No one comes to the Father except through me." Verse 9 says, "Anyone who has seen me has seen the Father." Verse 12 adds, "Anyone who has faith in me will do greater things than this because I am going to the Father." Verse 23 finishes, "If anyone loves me, he will obey my teaching. My Father will love him and we will come to him and make our home with him."

John 14:16 to 16:14 tells us it is expedient for Jesus to leave so the Comforter (Holy Spirit) can come to us and abide in us forever. He is the Spirit of Truth to teach us all things and guide us. The Holy Spirit points the way to Jesus because the only way to get to the Father is through Jesus.

Verse 27 says, "Peace I leave you. Do not let your hearts be troubled and do not be afraid. John 15:1 tells us, "I am the true vine and my Father is the gardener. Remain in me and I will remain in you." Verse 5 adds, "I am the vine, you are the branches." Verse 8 continues, "This is to my Father's glory, bear much fruit, showing yourself to be my disciples." Verse 1 says, "I told you all these things so that my joy shall be in you and your joy may be complete." Verse 12 adds, "My commandment is to love one another as I have loved you." Then verse 16 finishes with, "Then the Father will give you whatever you ask in my Name."

After the Resurrection, He said, "Feed my sheep" (John 21:17).

In Matthew 28:18, the very last thing Jesus said before ascending into heaven was, "All authority in heaven and earth has been given to me." Verse 19 continues with, "Therefore, go and make disciples of all nations, baptizing them in the name of the Father, the Son, and the Holy Spirit, teaching them to obey everything I have commanded you. And surely I am with you always, to the end of the age." The is the good news that each of us as believers is told to share with the world everywhere we go and with everyone we come in contact with. It is the obedience of a believer disciple.

My son wrote the piece below for a group he founded to mentor on November 13, 2007. He allowed me to reprint it here because I felt it was so appropriate, and I could not say it any better than this!

## About the Word
## by Greg Millspaugh

Have you had your daily nutrition today? Have you fed on the Word of God? Babies need food to stay healthy. If you've been born of the Spirit of God, you'll have a healthy appetite as well. The Bible says in 1 Peter 2:2, "As new born babes, desire the sincere milk of the Word, that ye may grow thereby." Just like you feed your children, you must feed yourself every day without fail. Job 23:12 states, "Neither have I gone back from the commandment of His lips; I have esteemed the words of His mouth more than my necessary food." Many scientific hypotheses have proved that the more you eat, the quicker you will grow. You can speed up the process by simply vowing to read God's Word every day, without fail. Be like Job and put your Bible before your belly.

Do you remember the promise in the first book of Psalms? "Blessed is the man that walketh not in the counsel of the ungodly, nor standeth in the way of sinners, nor sitteth in the seat of the scornful, but his delight is the law of the Lord; and in His law doth he meditate day and night. And he shall be like a tree planted by the rivers of water, that bringeth forth his fruit in his season; his lead also shall not wither; and whatsoever he doeth shall prosper. The ungodly are not so; but are like the chaff which the wind driveth away. Therefore the ungodly shall not stand in the judgment, or sinners in the congregation of the righteous. For the Lord knoweth the way of the righteous; but the way of the ungodly shall perish" (Ps. 1:1–6). Those six verses represent the entire book of Psalm 1. You would do well to memorize those verses and keep them in your heart. This represents life's two roads— the life of the faithful servant contrasted with the life of the faithless person. Which path do you choose? If you choose wisely, God promised that you will be like a fruitful, strong, and healthy tree. Each morning, find somewhere quiet and thoroughly soak your soul in the Word of God!

There may be times when you read through its pages with great enthusiasm, and there may be other times when it seems dry and even boring. Doesn't food profit your body, whether you enjoy it or not? As a child, you probably ate desserts with greater enthusiasm than vegetables. If you were a normal child, you had to be encouraged to eat them before any sweets. Then, as you matured in life, you were taught to discipline yourself to eat vegetables. This is because they would physically benefit you, even though they may not have at the time brought pleasure to your taste buds.

Remember this saying and purpose in your heart to follow it: "No Bible, no breakfast. No read, no feed." Make God the first priority in your life, and He will provide you with the very treasures of your heart!

"A new commandment I give unto you, that ye love one another; as I have loved you, that ye also love one another. By this shall all men know that ye are not disciples, if ye have loved one to another" (John 13:34–35).

"Go ye therefore, and teach all nations, baptizing them in the name of the Father, and of the Son, and of the Holy Spirit: Teaching them to observe all things whatsoever I have commanded you: and, lo, I am with you always, even unto the end of the world. Amen" (Matt. 28:19–20).

Change your words; change your culture.

Change your culture; change your world!

## Taking Care of the Temple That Houses the Holy Spirit

We are three basic parts as a human being, a soul (mind, will, and emotions), which makes us an individual who has the very breath of God (His Spirit) breathed in us by Creator God, who lives in a body adaptable to our earth environment. So we must address all three parts of our being. Here, we will focus on the body, but it is difficult to isolate the body without involving the other two parts, so naturally there will be an overlap, but repetition helps learning.

How would you compare the way you take care of your body? Would you say you take better care of your car and your home from destructive forces than your own body? How about preventive maintenance? Do you take care of your children's bodies better than your own? Answer honestly, for it is time to consider a very vital fact—you can replace your car and your home, *but* you only have one body. Should you do less for your body than your possessions? The first book of Corinthians 6:19 states, "Do you know that your body is a temple of the Holy Spirit within you, which you have from God? You are not your own, you were bought with a price. So glorify God in your body." Are we cognizant of that fact? You are in this body 24-7, so it needs to work for you as well as it can for the number of years you need it. When you are ill or unhealthy, you must take time, money, and effort to get better and concentrate on the problem. When your body is healthy, you have choices for your time and can choose to pursue your spiritual growth and focus on intimacy with the Holy Spirit. Quality of life is vital and demands you feed your body healthy food and gain knowledge to prevent illness whenever possible. It is extremely difficult to rise above illness and pain to concentrate and draw on the peace the Lord promises us when we seek His Presence. Paul says in 2 Corinthians 4:1–15 that we have this treasure in earthen vessels to show that the transcendent power belongs to God and not to us; we are always carrying in the body the death of Jesus so that the life of Jesus may also be manifested in our bodies. Did you realize how important our body is? After Jesus ascended, He sent the Holy Spirit to come live in us so we can have a direct line to God.

David Jeremiah quoted E. Stanley Jones, who said, "When I met Christ, I felt that I had swallowed sunshine." David Jeremiah said about this treasure within in one of his devotionals, "[The Holy Spirit in us] leads to a life of thanksgiving as our hearts overflow. Gratitude isn't a momentary feeling; it's a constant attitude produced by the indwelling Holy Spirit as He reminds us of our blessings in Christ. Be thankful today, as though you had swallowed sunshine." Would you say our body is a valuable part of our being? Then let's determine today to take better care of this temple and glorify the Lord in it.

Most of us think of ourselves as a body (the part you can see with your eyes), which is the physical part that people look at and recognize us, calling us by our given names. The Bible tells us that we were created in God's image. This is the part that allows us to fellowship with God, the spiritual part of our being. Even though we may think of ourselves as a body, the other two parts are of major importance. The soul is our personality and will be the lasting part to define us and is made up of mind, will, and emotions. Those three parts seem to overlap at times but need to work together for optimum health, not struggle against one another. We do not see the soul or spirit with physical eyes, but we feel the effects like wind affects everything in its path. We also need to address the fact that while Jesus was on earth, He prayed and handled needs of the people with different methods and Words.

Healing

*Healing* is defined as the process of making or becoming sound or healthy again. Do you think God wants you healed, or do you think He can heal you? Healing is not a formula; it is a personal journey with the Lord in most cases, unless He chooses to heal you miraculously—and He can! Kenneth Copeland says, "God is not the author of sickness and pain. All sickness and pain came when the devil began running things on the earth but Jesus came and changed that!" Jehovah-Rapha, our healer, is alive and well!

I do believe that God wants His people healed of whatever comes between His people and Him, whether it is sickness or an obstacle. Isn't it interesting that the definition of *healing* is the process of being sound or being made whole again? It is a process or experience of, so those are action words. It paints a picture of expectation for action from more than one person. In 2 Corinthians 5:17, the Bible tells us we are a new creation in Christ when we accept Him as our Savior, so if He died for our salvation and healing, why would He not want us healed? Jesus came to restore us to Him as we were when we walked in the Garden with Him in the cool of the evening. The walk is a little different than it was then, but the Holy Spirit allows us to intimately delight in His Presence now. Philippians 2:12 says to work out our own salvation with fear and trembling. *Salvation* in the dictionary is defined as preservation or deliverance from harm, ruin, or loss. Surely, that means He wants us healed if He came for both salvation and healing. He does, however, have a pathway of healing for each of us. Sometimes doctors are involved, and sometimes He heals immediately, and we call that a miracle. Sometimes it is a process that involves us standing and quoting scripture, believing, expecting, and receiving. I heard somewhere that if you pray when you take your meds, it is a double whammy. At any rate, we have a definite part in our healing to receive it and keep it!

Let me share one of the exciting things I have just learned. I have been asking the Lord if healing is in the atonement because I have felt so impressed. It was because I saw two scriptures, "By His stripes we are healed" (Old Testament, Isa. 53:5) and "By His stripes we were healed" (New Testament, 1 Pet. 2:24). I asked the Lord to show me if that meant healing was part of it when Jesus said, "It is finished!" meaning He did it all for us. Just this week, I was listening to Andrew Wommack, and he said the Greek word for *salvation*, *sozo*, meant salvation and healing. I always like to research and not believe everything I hear or read. When I did research it, I found out the meanings are "save or saved, whole, healed, preserve, and well." It is used in three different ways in Greek, to save from certain death, to be healed, and for salvation or getting born again. Praise God! Whether or not the curse in Genesis 3:14–19 was released at the time Jesus was crucified and said, "It is finished," I don't know. I do know that with His death and resurrection, Jesus sent the Comforter to be with us. After the Comforter came, each believer became a priest after the order of Melchizedek (Hebrews 7:17) and able to go directly to God through Jesus by way of the Holy Spirit. I know that part of the curse is over and women can go directly to God through the Holy Spirit now. Also, I am encouraged that Jesus is the best thing that ever happened to women because of His Words and treatment of women. He entrusted Mary to go tell his disciples, and if you study how the early church grew and worshipped, you'll see women were very instrumental in the growth of the new church. I believe the Lord will get His message to His people with whoever is willing to be a servant and worker for the Lord's calling. He will use us as we are willing.

Getting Prayers Answered: God's Laws and Harmonious Creation

God had a miraculous plan that developed in love, peace, harmony, and fulfilment with His laws, running the universe smoothly. Sin destroyed the rhythm, but His laws remained the same. The Greek word *sozo* (the atonement) included salvation *and* healing, which have laws that produce the manifestation of both. For salvation and healing, we need to find out the Will of God. Do we say, "If it be the Will of God to save me, I want to be saved"? No, because Romans 10:9 tells us His Will to save us, along with others as well. In 2 Peter

3:9, it says, "He is not willing that any should perish, but that all should come to repentance." There are so many scriptures on healing that can show us without a doubt it is God's Will to heal us. Here are some: What about God's laws concerning healing? God's power flows through laws (Mark 5:28 and 30).

1. One must hear the Word (through the scripture, saying it to oneself, through others, and through preaching).
2. Giving praise, thanksgiving with worship, will keep the channel open for the power to flow to you from our God. Fear and worry keep you earthbound. Peace and joy lift you up heavenward. The Lord can do His best work when the chain of darkness of fear and worry (which is the adversary who tries to keep you earthbound) are broken. Do not cloud the channel between you and the Lord. As you look up to the Lord, you allow Him to break the chains of fear and worry, letting them fall back to earth, where they belong. As a believer, you are allowed to experience the Lord as the balm of Gilead. Jesus is our balm of Gilead. In Jeremiah 8:22 and other Old Testament references, we learn about it, and Jesus is the spiritual medicine that is able to heal Israel and all sinners.
3. Act on the Word (James 2:20). Faith apart from works is dead.
4. Speak the Word (Mark 5:28). Speak, say the words. Genesis 1:1 says God's power was voice activated. He created everything with "He said!" (Heb. 11:3). By faith we understand that the world was created by the Word of God so that what is seen was made out of things that do not appear (Prov. 18:21). Death and life are in the power of the tongue. Speak to the problem as Jesus did with the fig tree. He cursed it, and it withered and died (Mark 11:22). Jesus said, "Have faith in God. Truly, I say to you, whoever says to

this mountain, be taken up and cast into the sea, and does not doubt in his heart but believes that what he says will come to pass, it will be done for him. Therefore, I tell you, whatever you ask in prayer, believe that you receive it, and you will. And whenever you stand praying, forgive, if you have anything against any one; so that your Father also who is in heaven may forgive you your trespasses." Speak to the specific thing like Jesus did to the wind (Mark 4:39). "Peace! Be still!" And the wind ceased, and there was great calm. Speak to the disease or anything else that needs to be healed. When you got born again, you received the same incredible power that raised Jesus from the dead two thousand years ago. Jesus restored the power of the believer that satan stole in the Garden.

5. Stand on the Word. When others speak incorrectly about your healing, counter with the Word of God. "The Bible says I am healed. By the stripes or wounds of Jesus, I am healed. I was healed" (Isa. 53:5; 1 Pet. 2:21). Stand on the Word, not what you have heard over and over. "If it be your will!" When we read the Bible all through, we learn the Will of God, and it is His Will to save us and heal us (Ps. 107:20). Watch out for the *if* word that mankind puts in there, for it leads to death and destruction. The remainder of the verse says, "He sent His Word and heals them, and delivers them from their graves... delivered them from their destruction...out of their trouble... out of their distresses....He sent His Word and healed them." Words release power or release fear and death. Do not deny the problem but say what you want (Rom. 4:17). Call those things that be not as though they are.

Continue believing the Word of God and speaking what you were promised in the Scripture and what Jesus came to give you and restore your authority, which was lost when sin entered the Garden. Unfortunately, well-meaning people who are ignorant of God's word, who have been taught contrary to God's Word, or whose level of faith does not match yours will be used by the adversary to lie to you about what God did. Did he not do the same to Eve in the Garden by questioning God's Word? This is the oldest trick of his in the Bible—do not fall prey to it! Jesus is very personal through the Holy Spirit. Believe Him, for you are staking your life on Him. You can trust Him, for He is trustworthy.

Some Suggestions to Get Prayers Answered as a Believer
We know God answers all prayers we lift up to Him, but sometimes He say "Yes," sometimes He says "No," and sometimes He says "Wait." It is the "No" and the "Wait" that we have trouble accepting. What we need to realize is, the wait means God is working on situations to achieve your prayers. God never goes against a person's will, for He gave us free will from our creation. When other people's wills are involved, God takes longer to work out the situation because He deals with us so individually, as if we were His only child. My son Greg posted a scripture on Facebook (Isaiah 40:31). In this scripture is the word *wait*, and in the Hebrew it is qavah and means "to bring together by twisting." The sense is that if we delay waiting upon the Lord, we will be constantly seeking His face and being bound together with Him. We will be desirous of carrying out His Will. Ultimately, the Lord's will for us is the very best He can do for us, but sometimes we need to be ready to accept it or others need to be ready, and that can delay our receiving His answer of yes to us.

1.  Learn the Word of God and His laws to be able to know God's Will. Meditate on His Word day and night and internalize those words. Build your bank of scriptures to be able to speak them when needed for yourself and others.

2. Know who created you and whom you belong to. God created you, then after the fall of mankind, you were bought back with a price, the mighty blood of Jesus at Calvary. Learn about the importance of the Blood of Jesus and what it can do in your life. (Please keep in mind; it is impossible to really talk about healing until addressing the issue that we are a triune being, spirit, soul, and body.)

3. Develop a relationship with the Lord. This is vital if you want Him to do anything for you. You need to know your Heavenly Father personally. Get in His Presence. Ask the Holy Spirit to lead you into the Presence of the Lord. Praise, worship, and thanksgiving, in fellowship, draw us near to "listen to His still small Voice!" The Lord is able to do His best work in you to transform you by the renewing of your mind during this quiet time, so do not rush (Rom. 12:2). This sounds simple, and as you practice spending time with the Lord, it becomes easier. "His sheep hear His voice" (John 10:27). He is able to lead you as you listen to His instructions. Relax and feel the true joy of being in His Presence! This is a delightful privilege (Ps . 16:11) (This is aimed at physical healing but can be used to help a Christian develop into the new creation the Lord wants us to work toward, where the emotional, the physical, and our will, with the spiritual, work hand in hand to help us be the person the Lord desires us to be. As stated before, Scripture says, "Work out your own salvation with fear and trembling" (Phil. 2:12). We have an important part as well as what we expect Him to do. (Even though He knows our problem before we tell Him, if you want to state it, remember to pray the solution and do not dwell on the problem.) See the answer in your imagination (which Andrew Wommack says is the "womb," to manifest the answer).

4. Cooperate with the Will of God. God's Will does not just happen. We need to stretch and believe His Word and Him. Get over fears, of failure, of success, of people and what they think, of persecution, etc. God gave mankind the ability to imagine. When you pray, see yourself healed. Look in the mirror and talk to your subconscious and reprogram it according to the Word and Will of God. Use the scriptures you hear from the Lord and those you seek out to speak out loud. This method works and has been used by many for years to strengthen the inner man to be able to overcome present conditions. See yourself well! Put a picture of you that shows you well and happy where you dress each morning and visualize yourself healed. *Yetser* is the word in the Bible for *imagination*, and it means conception, to conceive something. The imagination is the spiritual womb for the Holy Spirit to operate. Give Him something to work with, your new thoughts, your new words, and your new actions, your new beliefs. Realize that your old way of talking, acting, and receiving adds to the present condition, so stop and regroup! Watch your words and only let them glorify the Lord. Negative words of any kind at any time are detrimental not only to healing but to your personality and to everyone you speak to as well. We were created to create, so watch what you want to result from your words. As you practice this in your everyday activities, you develop a sort of check in your spirit any words you have chosen to say from the past or present that damage you and others. Let your words offer life and not death. Watch what you create for you and others will live with it (Rom. 12:2). Do not be conformed to the pattern of this world but be transformed by the renewing of your mind. Then you will be able to test and approve what God's will is—His good, pleasing, and perfect will!

5.  Forgive those who hurt you and forgive yourself. This has to be a vital part of healing, because on the Cross the Lord asked Father God to forgive those who were killing Him because they knew not what they were doing. When we do not forgive, it seems like a negative mass develops and continues to be fed and grows with more hurt, anger, etc. Our fallen world certainly adds to the scenario, but we must do what we are able to do to free us of destructive habits, words, and actions that interfere with our healing of any kind. So break the chains that hold you captive with unforgiveness and be free! Here is a personal example. I went through a divorce that left me leveled because I had loved with all my heart, and in the healing process afterward, I really thought I had forgiven my ex-husband. In the middle of the night, I was awakened by a "booming voice" that said to me, "You have not forgiven Larry," my ex-husband. I burst out crying and said, "Oh, dear God, forgive me. I thought I had!" Well, I did not take that lightly, for He was teaching me about how important forgiveness is in our growth with Him. I had more work to do, and the Lord patiently worked with me until I felt in my spirit I had forgiven my ex-husband. It took a while, but finally, the peace was there when I spoke of him or encountered him personally. God is so faithful when you ask for His healing touch; He works with you so gently and lovingly for your healing to be complete.

6.  Stand with the scriptures and instructions you receive. Speak out loud the scriptures you were given and listen daily as you dress to the scriptures you record that are personal to you about healing or any other issue you are believing for the Lord to do. Speak to your mountain (which is the problem) as Jesus did to the fig tree. God told you to speak to it, not Him, about your problem. He gave us His life and left His

Word to let you know He gave you the authority as a believer to stand against what is coming against you. In Mark 11:23, Jesus said, "That whosoever shall say unto this mountain, be thou removed, and cast into the sea; and shall not doubt in his heart; but shall believe that those things which he saith shall come to pass; he shall have whatsoever he saith."

7. Then thank the Lord, praising Him for healing you and restoring you, as you see yourself healed!

Read Luke 11:1–28 and Matthew 6:5–15 as they are somewhat similar. The disciples asked Jesus how to pray, and both passages have the Lord's Prayer as we have been taught, except Luke's is shorter. Everything Jesus had to say to us was essential to our spiritual growth. There are many suggestions of attitudes by Jesus for us to read and obey in praying, so please take a few minutes and follow His instructions to really learn the way He told us to pray.

The Prayer of Relinquishment

There is also the Prayer of Relinquishment. In one of Catherine Marshall's book, she told a story about her own healing. She had tried all she knew and still was ill, in bed. She prayed the prayer she called the Prayer of Relinquishment, where she completely turned over the problem to the Lord, took her hands off, and trusted whatever the Lord had for her, then she experienced her healing. So she learned to let go and let God, thus trusting Him. We know trust grows as we are able to get ourselves out of the way and let the Lord have His way. His Will is far better than anything we can come up with or dream.

Another thought about healing that should never be forgotten is that sometimes the Lord allows us to enter into His suffering. There are various ways He can do this. (I have had one very dramatic experience with entering into His suffering. In my early days, as I was focusing on learning the Bible and obeying His instructions of studying an hour each day in the Word, I was praying with a prayer partner and the Lord allowed both of us to experience a unique event. There are no words to express the feelings. They were short-lived but intense, and afterward both of us knew what the Lord was teaching us through this time.) Another way it seems is He can use our sickness, distress, pain, etc. to allow us to enter into His suffering for us to catch a glimpse of His suffering for us. When people experience events together, intimacy grows. There is a scripture, 1 Thessalonians 5:18, that tells us to give thanks in everything, for this is the Will of God in Christ Jesus concerning you. Quench not the spirit. I could handle Romans 8:28, "We know that all things work together for the good of those who are called according to His purpose." God can use anything to work together for our good, but all of us have something totally unbelievable in this fallen world happen to us or those we care about, like cancer, murder, rape, etc., that it is extremely difficult to truly give thanks to the Lord after it happens. We know He can use it to further something to help us grow spiritually in Him and for His Kingdom, but it is so difficult to accept. Unfortunately, we see only our patch in the tapestry of eternity that only the Lord can see. "For my thoughts are not your thoughts, neither are your ways my ways," declares the Lord in Isaiah 55:8–9. We cannot see into the future as He does. God's eternal purpose for us extends way past the present existence here.

In the article from Jerry Evans about healing, he says healing is a partnership and we are expected to do things. Do you want to be well? Do you speak healing, or is most of your time spent talking about sickness, aches, pains, and operations? If the true answer is yes, then change is underway if you really want to be healed. You did not get there overnight, so unless the Lord heals in a miracle, which He can do, normally He uses the healing to teach you how to be an overcomer so the healing will last. Healing is a journey; recovery is a road. Your body sometimes needs time to undo what has happened to it and give it time to come back to healing. I believe the Lord has a pathway of healing for you. Your first avenue to pursue is to start speaking healing and get quiet with the Lord to learn what He wants you to do. Be willing to do something different from what you have been doing because you know you have heard that you cannot keep doing the same thing and expecting different results, which is very true. Healing is not just an event; it becomes a lifestyle. Are you willing to do what the Lord asks you to do? Be honest with the Lord, bring Him your hurts, and listen. Take this opportunity to forgive others and yourself for weaknesses and sin. Part of Scripture, Matthew 5:25, tells us that if you have anything against your brother, go ask his forgiveness, because unforgiveness can come between you and your relationship with the Lord. It can also manifest into other negative results in your life. Forgiveness does not make the action right but breaks the chain to free one from the bondage and to overcome, with the Lord's help. Sin will destroy a person. Another thing Jerry Evans, in his article, states is this: "Tell me what you eat, and I will tell you your illness." Many things can cause illnesses. In this imperfect, fallen world, a person collects toxins of all kind that work against our bodies and minds. You have heard "We are what we eat," but we are many things—what we breathe, see, hear, ingest, think, speak, dwell on, and on and on. Sometimes our healing comes from working through emotional traumas from our childhood; sometimes the problem comes from a lack of forgiveness that festers and manifests into various places to be worked through, and Scripture tells us to go make things right with a brother. Sometimes diseases come from improper nutrition and toxins we ingest. These things need a change of diet, change of actions, etc. Spending time with the Lord will allow one to focus in the area He wants you to work on first.

If it is emotional, the Lord may take you back to the time of the trauma, allow you to see the hurt, and as you give it to Him and receive His loving touch, you can experience His peace, which surpasses all understanding, and you can be free of that negative emotion. Drs.

Dennis and Jen Clark have a book, workbook, and CD that have really helped me. The title is *A Practical Guide to Self-Deliverance: Simple Keys to Receiving Freedom.* The information teaches you to "drop down" into your belly and find the hurtful experience and allow the Holy Spirit to heal it and free you of the bondage. The peace is a blessed result of dealing with the experience. This is something I continue to do as I am led to with my walk, learning that nothing should come between me and my Jesus, and if anything does, it needs to be dealt with this way. They have had others use this healing method, and even the veterans returning from war and others who have experienced terrifying events can be helped with posttraumatic shock through these things the Lord has taught them to share.

Because worship, praise, and thanksgiving are so important to the Lord, getting in His Presence with the Living Word He gave us seems an important place to start. Make it personal, as the God we serve wants a personal relationship with us. Find scriptures to express why you believe He is your God and above everything on earth. Everything has to bow down to God Almighty. Some things I say are, "You are the King of Kings and Lord of Lords" (1 Tim. 6:15; Rev. 19:16), "Jesus, you are the Holy One" (Acts 3:14; Ps. 16:10), "You are the Word made manifest" (John 1:1), "You are the great I Am" (John 8:58; Exod. 3:14), "You are Lord of all" (Acts 10:16). Find your own words to speak to Him. I do not quote scriptures only, and here are some more words: "God, you are an awesome God!" "Lord, You are my Jehovah-Jireh, my provider!" "You are our Savior and our Lord!" This is not a formula. God is very personal. I start with recognizing who He is and what He means to me, seeking His face first, then His Hand. Worship and fellowship are the two main reasons that I believe He created us. Then, since He did it all on the cross, let us draw near to the King of Kings for His glory to envelop us with His mighty power. Worship and praise draw us closer to Him, make us aware of His Presence, and are the part we give back to Him. After a time of worship and praise, talk to Him as you would a loving father and tell Him what you want Him to do. This builds your intimacy with Him. Relax and allow His Presence to envelop you. The peace that comes in His Presence shows a person how vital it is to never let anything come between you and your Jesus. "Peace which surpasses all understanding will guard your hearts and your minds in Christ Jesus" (Phil. 4:7) and comes as a gift when you are able to give it all to the Lord and trust Him. Be certain to allow the Holy Spirit to guide you into prayer, and pray as He leads. Pray for His anointing and allow Him to let it flow through you. The language today is, "Just hang out with Jesus and spend time with Him, learning His way and enjoying His Presence, listening and learning and experiencing." The joy you experience is priceless!

Here is a prayer for Terry, my cousin Shelby's son, who is going through treatment at the time I was writing this. It is exactly how I sent it to her to pray for him, and then I will answer her questions and explain anything if she may want more information.

Dear Lord, we praise you and thank you for what you did at the Cross, bringing us salvation and healing. When you said "It is finished," you restored the authority we had lost in the Garden. Thank you for being the Holy One and the King of Kings, who is above all things. We stand today with Terry and speak to this disease of cancer and the spirit of infirmity to leave Terry's body, now, in the name of Jesus of Nazareth, for you told us in Mark 11:23 to speak to the mountain and say, "Be thou removed and be thou cast into the sea—and we shall not doubt in our heart but shall believe those things which you said shall come to pass, whatsoever we say." Terry is disease-free; all signs of the cancer are gone, and the body is healthy from the top of his head to the bottom of his feet. He will rejoice and praise your holy name for the mighty work you are doing in him. (See him completely healed as he was before this cancer bout, share with him what you are praying, and ask him and Sharon [his wife] to speak all words of healing, not sickness, because negative words reach toward death, and they can find their own scriptures to stand on, such as, "By the stripes of Jesus, I am healed," in Isaiah, and then Paul says, "By His stripes we were healed!" Speak out loud, since there is power in speaking words. "I am healed by the stripes of Jesus." Searching out and saying scripture out loud, along with believing you will receive, build your faith muscles. Using those powerful words of scripture will give the Lord something to work with. Seeds you are planting for Him to harvest! Encourage each other and keep that healed vision in your head at all times, no matter what a report looks like or what someone says (that is tough, but you can do it.) God bless you all, and may the Lord be glorified throughout this journey, and may we remember who we are in Him!

This is the hardest part of being a prayer warrior, if prayer seems unanswered. Jesus does answer all prayers. Some are answered "Yes," some are answered "No," and some are answered "Wait!" Terry just died, and I was tempted to delete the paragraph altogether. Sometimes our prayers are not answered the way we want them to be. God has a bigger plan that we cannot see. We all must face death unless Jesus returns before we die. So when a body wears out for whatever reason, that body is unable to house the Holy Spirit, so our spirit must leave. The most difficult part for me was that I was really standing with my cousin Shelby, expecting the Lord to perform a miracle and heal Terry. I know He can, and I have seen it happen, so I wanted Him to do so this time. I know the Lord has really become more real to Shelby during this time, and she has grown tremendously spiritually, but what a difficult acceptance she had because she really thought the Lord would give her a miracle, for that was what we both were praying. Now, my part will be to help her through the grieving process and be there for her however the Lord leads. I know the Lord will sustain her, but losing one's child when she is a widow has to be such a tremendously painful time in her life. As King David stated when his infant son died, "He cannot come back to me, but I shall go to him." The best comforting thought now is that Terry was permanently healed and is out of pain and suffering, has gone to be with the Lord, and Shelby shall go to him someday. Unfortunately, grief and pain entered our world with sin, and even though God had a plan to reunite us with Him, we must all die some time. Preparing for our wonderful home with the Lord is what is expected of us here on earth, and trusting Him for our future is what we all must do. Let us all encourage each other in this endeavor, knowing we can build our treasures in heaven as we live out our lives here.

As I pondered over my desire not to address the death of Terry, it reminded me of the three Hebrew men in the Old Testament who were thrown into the fiery furnace and what they said. "Our God whom we serve can deliver us from the fiery furnace (and save our lives)....but we will not serve your gods or worship the golden image which you have set up" (Dan. 3:17). This could mean, "I know our God can perform a miracle for whatever our needs are, but if He chooses not to answer the prayer the way I have prayed for Him to do, I will worship and serve Him anyway." Sometimes we do not understand the Lord's way, but we must stand with Him and not be shaken in our faith because the Lord sees the tapestry of life from the top side, and we are limited with our vision, only seeing the underside. Remember what Jesus did in the garden of Gethsemane when He asked for the cup to be removed from Him (about the Cross). "Not my will, but yours, Father!" As difficult as it is to accept, I do believe the Lord expects us to accept His Will, no matter how difficult it is to do, for He does have a better plan for us that we must trust Him for, promising that "He will never leave us nor forsake us" (Deut. 31:6). I know the Lord can use our challenges, struggles, losses, etc. to help others and bring them into the Kingdom. I do not understand everything, but I do know my God personally and know He works out things for my good when I can keep my focus on Him. We learn to grieve with others and lift them up when they have difficulty doing so for themselves. As a believer, overcoming death by living eternally with the Lord is far better than anything I can think of; we just have to deal here with loss and sorrow that live with us in this world. We do not understand all the Lord's plan. The first book of Corinthians 13:12 tells us, "We see in a mirror dimly, but then face to face: now I know in part; but then shall I know even as also I am known." When Jesus comes, the whole truth will be revealed.

In Streams in the Desert, a devotional I had years ago from a missionary named Cowman, there was a story about the wood that the carver chose to use for a strong ax handle that came from not the prettiest tree in the forest but the one that had been beaten by the storms, gnarled and sometimes bent over by the wind. It was the strongest because it had endured the cruelty of the elements and still was standing. The Lord allows us to experience many things in life to strengthen us and so we can help others through the difficulties of the journey. It is almost impossible to give what you have not experienced; you can try, but when you have been through similar situations, your compassion and depth show the qualities the Lord wants you to use to lift others up and minister to them out of loving concern.

Some Ways That Jesus Healed
Jesus healed many ways. Do not forget that the laying on of hands is Biblical when appropriate or possible. In Luke 4:40, all those who were sick with various diseases were brought to Him (Jesus), and laying His Hands on each one of them, He was healing them. Also,

anointing with oil and having the spiritual leaders pray for a healing. James 5:14 says, "Is any of you sick? Let them call the elders of the church to pray over them and anoint them with oil in the name of the Lord." What about the time in John 9:6 "when He [Jesus] had thus spoken, He spat on the ground, and made clay of the spittle and He anointed the eyes of the blind man with the clay. And He said unto him, Go wash in the pool of Siloam." He went his way therefore and washed and came seeing. Also, when people touched Him or the hem of His garment, they were healed (Matt. 14:36, Mark 3:10, Mark 6:56). Then there was the prayer of faith (Mark 5:34 and James 5:15). Prayers for one another were important (James 5:6 and James 5:13). The prayer of faith was mentioned in James 5:15 and Mark 5:34. Singing psalms was also mentioned in James 5:13. These are some ways, and you can surely find more ways as you peruse the Holy Scriptures yourselves.

All this tells me a personal relationship with the Holy Spirit will guide you to the Lord's pathway of healing for you. Sometimes He heals through doctors or a combination of different things, teaching you and others along the journey the ways of the Lord. Scripture states, "My people are destroyed from lack of knowledge" (Hosea 4:6). Sometimes a person needs to be mindful of all the perversion that has entered our food chain and begin to read labels, seeking the most wholesome foods available. The body is designed for food that nourishes and balances for a healthy body. If the body breaks down, it totally affects spiritual growth. Being forced to focus on ill health with pain and whatnot gives little time to spend seeking after the Lord. Who does that glorify? It certainly is not the Lord but the adversary. Everyone knows what the drug world has done to our health. Something that was designed to help heal has often escalated into addiction and destruction of the body, soul, and mind. I believe with all my heart that the Lord wants us healed because that is a freedom He gave us on the cross along with salvation. Take the time and get quiet. Jesus wants us to abide in Him. He is the Vine, and we are the branches (John 15:5). "If you remain in me and I in you, you will bear much fruit; apart from me you can do nothing."

Do not ever forget to "Plead the blood of Jesus," for Jesus did it all with His Blood.

## Pleading the Blood of Jesus

What does *pleading* mean? We have heard the word in the legal context and have some idea what it means. The definition for plead is to make an emotional appeal. Beg is defined as asking earnestly or humbly for something. As I researched the meanings of the word, I noticed some sources use each as a synonym for the other, but other sources do not. Some say begging and pleading both together, so they most probably do not mean exactly the same. You must decide for yourself here. The connotation of begging to me is almost forcing one's will to achieve something. It reminds me of a child or someone immature trying to get its own way. *Pleading*, I think, means an earnest desire. I do not mean to make an issue, but anything I write, I want to be in alignment with Scripture, and I want to be certain I listen to the truth from the Holy Spirit, who is teaching me along with others. I would never want to mislead or add anything to Scripture but be as accurate as I can be. I do not think God wants us to be a beggar but learn what authority He gave us in this world in the beginning, which we gave away to satan in the Garden at the fall of mankind. Since Jesus came as the ultimate sacrifice, the authority has been restored, but do we act as if it has been? Jack Hayford said in his article "Pleading the Blood" that through the blood of sacrifice there is deliverance, protection, and a God-provided future. This mighty forecasting was fulfilled in the Person of Jesus. Understanding the sacrificial laws that were required in the Old Testament that God gave to the Israelites is so important and helps us understand the question "Why was it necessary for Jesus to have to come to earth, anyway?" Please never forget how vital the blood is to our redemption and that it fulfills the plan that God has to bring us back into fellowship with Him through Jesus's work at the Cross and the work of the Holy Spirit in us now. Jesus put His Blood between us and God because God cannot look upon sin, and that blood covering restores the fellowship God has in mind to be able to have an intimate relationship with Him. Hebrews 9:22 says, "Under the law almost everything is purified with blood, and without the shedding of blood, there is no forgiveness of sin." Since Jesus came to fulfill the law, His blood was essential for our sins to be forgiven, and it was the Lord's way to restore us to intimate communion with Him. So you can see how powerful the Blood of Jesus is to His created beings.

Washing in the Blood of Jesus

This is a new concept for me. I was listening to Sid Roth's program, and a lady named Sandra Kennedy was his guest. If you want to hear this in-depth, go to sidroth.org and listen to the whole interview. It will explain in detail. I am only highlighting some of her conversation. Sandra said, "I think a new season has broken loose. I think back in August, when we had that eclipse that took place, I think there's a shift in the heavenly dimensions that happened on that day. Something broke loose and we are just on a road to see the Glory of God."

Sid asked her, "What is the devil's greatest strategy to cause believers to be so defeated?"

Sandra responded with, "He doesn't want you to know the power of the Blood, and he doesn't want you to know that you really are cleansed. He just doesn't want you to understand who you really are in Christ Jesus is the best way I would put it. He just doesn't want you to understand what Jesus has really done for you. This is the part that really just blows my mind, the forgiveness of Almighty God. You know, not only when He comes in and you're born again, we forget what the blood does. We remember that it cleanses us of our sins, but we forget that the blood can take care of every area of our heart."

Sandra used to work in mental health as a therapist and got a six-year degree in religious psychology. And then when she became a pastor, she realized everybody in the church had the same problem that everybody in the world had, which made no sense to her. She said, "We remember that the Blood cleanses us of our sins, but we forget that the Blood can take care of every area of our heart."

She knew something was terribly wrong here, so that was when she began to really delve in the power of the Blood of Jesus and gained understanding that there is something that looks like a stain, called defilement. She went on to tell the audience that when a person backslides, they rededicate their lives so many times they break the rededicator. Then she said, "But you and I cannot grab hold of the fact of how wonderful Jesus is. And so we walk around knowing that we're saved, but not holding our head down, shameful, thinking somebody is going to find it out, somebody is going to bring that up. I'm embarrassed because of who I was or what I did. Listen, I'm talking about myself now. I've walked these roads."

Sid asked her about a term she used, *thoroughly cleansed*. Her response was, "You're so clean and you accept it by faith. You're just so clean that you almost can't believe it, to tell you the truth. And so if somebody were to bring it up, this is what the Blood does. If somebody were to bring it up, 'I knew you when,' you automatically would begin to say, 'Uh-uh, that person is dead. I don't even know who you're talking about.' There's a place that we can get there. We can get there. The Lord is waiting for the church to lead the way. All the powerhouse of God is inside of us, and the Lord is waiting on us to be shining lights and lead people to the Lord Jesus Christ. This is harvest time."

Sid mentioned she said that the priests in the Old Covenant cleansed themselves twice a day, and he said, "I know you do this. I want to find out exactly how you do it for yourself, and I want to find out the twin of atonement of sin and forgiveness of sin. I want to find out that same Blood, how that operates in healing."

Sandra went on to tell Sid she wasn't getting her healing the way she wanted to get it, and the devil began to talk and say, "Well, you don't deserve this," like he does everybody. "You don't deserve this." When she began to say this to the Lord, He said back to her, "But my blood took care of that." And so with everything she mentioned to the Lord, He said, "But my Blood took care of that." No matter what she said, she received the same answer from Jesus. When she began to name all the people in the church who had told her why they couldn't get healed or why things weren't happening, He said, "But my blood took care of that. But my blood took care of that." There wasn't a thing. What a powerful statement, which means that no one could ever come to you with anything that He would have said to them that cannot be cured. So no matter what anyone is going through, family problems, any kind of sickness, someone on death's bed, remember "But my Blood took care of it." Every sickness, every disease. We remember to thank God that the blood took care of all the sins. She said, "Praise the name of the Lord, Hallelujah, but also His Blood at the whipping post. His Blood came out of the wounds."

Sid asked her, "So you're saying to me that every believer that is convinced because of the death and resurrection and the shedding of the Blood of Jesus they are forgiven of all sins should be just as convinced that by his blood you are healed."

Sandra said to Sid that it took place at the same time. Sid asked her to show the audience very briefly what she prayed and how she prayed the Blood every morning and every evening, in her home, for herself when no one was looking but she and God.

Here is Sandra's reply: "Okay. As if I have taken a shower, I take the Blood. I wash my eyes in the Blood, I wash my ears in the Blood, I wash my mouth in the Blood so that my ears will hear only what God says, my eyes will see only what God wants me to see, my mouth will speak only what God wants me to say by the power of the tongue. I wash my hands so that my hands can be used for God

Almighty, because hands can get you in trouble. They can do all kinds of bad things and get very defiled. I wash my hands. I wash my feet, and if there's, say, I have a tumor or something, I wash that tumor in the Name of Jesus, in the Blood of Jesus, and command it to go in Jesus's name with the Blood of Jesus. Just like you're taking a bath. Believe it or not, when you get through, you feel like you've had another bath. Hallelujah."

Sandra also mentioned to wash their mind and wash their dream life, to wash it in the Blood of the Lamb. "It's amazing what it will do," she said. "God just, you know, He just goes into every area of our life."

Sid asked her to pray the Blood over everyone watching right then to have the shame removed and be physically healed.

Here is Sandra's prayer:

Yes. In the name of Jesus, I'm telling you right now, I come against that which has come against you, all shame, all guilt, all dirtiness, all filthy feelings, all those things that you feel that you can't even hold your head up. I wash you in the Blood of Jesus. If you've invited Jesus into your heart, you already belong to Him. Now take His Blood and just cleanse yourself in it from the top of your head to the soles of your feet, any kind of sickness. We hold up the Blood and wash ourselves from any kind of defilement, wounds, any kind of defilements, in the name of Jesus. And I expect you to absolutely, just as you have been dirty going into a shower, and you come out feeling refreshed, you ought to feel totally refreshed once you have bathed yourselves in the supernatural power of the Blood of Jesus. And I call it done in Jesus's name.

Sid's final remarks were, "Outstanding!" He reminded us that Jesus said, "I shall never leave you." That means in this life and all eternity. Who would want to live this life without knowing God, without having experiential knowledge of God? You want to have your own experiential knowledge, open the door, tell Jesus you're sorry for your mistakes, which are called sins, and believe that Blood washes them away and He doesn't remember them anymore. Then when you're clean, ask Jesus to live inside of you and be your Lord. "Do that and you and I will be together for eternity," he said.

A Personal Testimony of Healing

Allow me to give you a personal testimony about the healing of allergies I had since childhood. In my small town, and when I was a child, they were diagnosed as colds. Later, when medicine became more sophisticated, I found out what the problem really was. I had suffered terribly for years. My symptoms were severe, and for about three days, my eyes streamed with water, which seriously hampered my day-to-day activities. So as I grew in the Lord, I saw healing was mentioned in the Bible, and I wanted healing. So I began to seek spiritually, physically, mentally, and emotionally. The Lord used doctors to give me allergy shots, which relieved my symptoms and allowed me to function more normally. This was wonderful, but I wanted more. In the worst times, I had two shots (one in each arm) weekly or twice a week, depending on the severity of the allergies. I cried out to God, "I want to be healed!" My spiritual growth was coming along, and the hunger to know Scripture was foremost. I began learning about nutrition, what I was eating, how I prepared food, and what is in the food. I read labels; I ate wholesome, fresh as much as possible, etc., so the physical was being ministered to. The mind is such an important and integral part of our being that I read books I was led to improve my mind. How the mind functions was always fascinating to me, so as I asked the Lord to teach me, I grew by leaps and bounds. My will has always been very strong, but wanting balance in my being, I sought to adjust my will to what the Lord was teaching and showing me of Himself. My pathway of healing and the journey I was on led me straight to the Lord, and I praise Him and thank Him for His mercy. Inside, I believe the Holy Spirit was impressing me that He had healed me and that I did not need my medicine anymore and to throw it away. Well, I was excited but still unsure of whether it was the Holy Spirit or myself just wanting the healing so much that I asked God if He would give me a scripture, and then I would throw it away. I wanted my faith to do it, but unfortunately, I was hesitant. He gave me a scripture in May of 1974, and I have not had another shot for allergies since then. Of course, my part afterward was to stand against the adversary who tried to make the symptoms show up again. I quoted my life-giving, healing scriptures constantly and *stood*, speaking out loud the words of faith, and praised my Lord for healing me and seeing myself free of symptoms. This was a time that I was the speaker at seminars all over Dallas and during the worst season for outdoor allergies (my major problem).

So I believed. I stood, quoted, listened to my healing scriptures daily as I dressed, allowed the Word of God to rise big inside me, and when I felt weaker and needed more assurance of the fact I was healed, I continued my part and experienced the Presence of the Lord more and more, drawing closer to Him, feeling His healing touch. Praise God! And now, as the seasonal allergies hit, I continue to praise God for His miraculous healing for something I suffered so many years with before I discovered He was willing and able to heal me.

While writing this book, I have experienced an incredible gift from the Lord that needs to be shared before the chapter is closed. It is difficult to understand sometimes why and how God works in the healing department, but I have another healing that is so exciting to share with you. For a few years the eye doctor diagnosed me with glaucoma, and that was a difficult blow, as important as our eyes are. I read up on it and realized it could cause blindness. Apparently, it was on the low end of pressure, because my doctor was encouraging and said, "You probably will not have to do anything but put one drop of solution in each eye once a day for the rest of your life." The eye drops were faithfully administered daily, never missing a day. I had experience healing from the Lord years before from horrible allergies, so I knew He could heal, so I started standing with my scriptures, taking the scripture for the truth it states, believing, visualizing, praising, and thanking the Lord for His mighty touch of healing for my eyes.

On July 29 (the day after my birthday), when I was at the lake where I did live with my mother and her husband, as I started to awake, I heard in my spirit like I do in my intimate times of fellowship with the Lord His Still Small Voice (not aloud with my ears) say, "I am giving you a late birthday present. Your eyes are healed of glaucoma!" I woke up rejoicing and shared it with my husband. From that day on, I did not use the eye drops, for I believed what I heard, that it was from the Lord, and acted on it. When I went back to the eye doctor, I told him my testimony and what I had done. He checked me and said I had not done any damage to my optic nerve. The eyes were not any worse, but I am not sure if they were any lower. I should have asked, but still I was believing for complete healing. He said I needed cataract surgery on both eyes and that often that cataract surgery would lessen the pressure. When I went for the surgery on the first eye, they checked my pressure; it was 18 in one and 22 in the other, which is the normal range. After surgery, it was 18 in one eye, and when I went for a follow-up on the second eye, it was 28, but the assistant offered this explanation: because of the eye drops that were being used, it could account for the slightly higher reading. In November, just before I saw the eye doctor, my left eye had begun watering, and I mentioned it to him. He said it was probably dry eye, which did not make sense, but after I learned more about how the eyes lubricate themselves, it was understandable. So glaucoma was healed, and along came the dry-eye situation. I just went to a specialist for the dry eye, and both eyes were 18 for pressure, praise God, and healed. But now the dry eye that waters is left to deal with. One might wonder, as I did, "Lord, you healed the glaucoma miraculously, so why not the dry eye?" I do not have the answer for that. The eye doctor recommended to me a top specialist in his field who trains other doctors, so he knows his field. The summary to this situation, I believe, is that God can heal as He determines; our part is to trust Him, believe His Word, and expect His best. My journey is not over with the dry eye, but when it is, another could come, so we just keep on standing on the Word and believing the Lord at His Word.

Before I could close out this chapter, another major crisis developed that I need to share with you. Check note below.*

My 2019 Journey to Healing: Gentle Healing
As I sat on the patio and began drinking in the gentle, warm sunlight, my mind took me back to my childhood when I visualized the Lord sending His warm shafts of light to let me feel a hug from Him. But I had actually forgotten that experience as I grew into adulthood, until now. (Anytime I needed to feel the Lord reaching out to me,

---

* After the stroke, the watering dry eye seemed back to normal. Thank you, Lord. Another touch of your mighty Hand! You are awesome, God! God provided the way for this book to be published, but after I signed the contract and before I sent in my final manuscript, another physical hurdle hit me. I tripped and fell in front of my house, breaking my hip. Therefore, another delay in getting my book published. While I was recuperating, the Lord was still teaching me a great deal. We can only live moment to moment, obeying that Still Small Voice. Thank you, Lord, for your promise to never leave me or forsake me. Please realize that one of the most difficult things I have encountered is to speak healing and keep visualizing that healing when you are in pain and everything feels overwhelming to your senses. But you must speak healing and not allow the words of others to lessen that power from the Lord, for it can. Speak to the mountain and speak words of healing only. God is faithful, and His words are true. You can trust him!

I went outside and paused until the warm sunlight caressed me and that special feeling returned. I certainly needed that healing light now. Thank you, Lord, for reminding me of that very special time with you. I told no one! I am sure it was God's way of making me feel special to Him.) Then here I am now, recovering from a life-threatening experience called a subarachnoid hemorrhage, actually two aneurysms, one of which broke and bled on my brain. A few years ago, that meant sudden death, but because the Lord gave the medical profession more insight and wisdom, there is indeed more hope today. Along with that wisdom, my healing journey progressed because of intense power from so many praying for me with their faith and speaking healing on me, encouraging me with their words. I am so blessed. Praise God!

In the morning hours of July 31, 2019, I collapsed on the floor and my legs would not hold me to get up. I called out to my husband, Jim, and told him that my legs would not hold me to stand up! He came quickly, and when he was unable to get me to stand, he brought a pillow to put under my head and then called 911. They arrived within fifteen minutes to take me to the hospital, and they asked me where we wanted them to take me. We told them Saint Joseph on Broadway. The last I remember was their putting me on a gurney in the hall, until four weeks later. Later I was told that we first went to Saint Joe; they did a few tests and sent me to UK, where I remained for three weeks, had a procedure to pack the aneurysms with coils to keep them quiet so they would not break open and bleed on the brain. I was diagnosed with two aneurysms in the brain. Three weeks later, I woke up in the Cardinal Hill Rehab Center with no memory of the past three weeks. My stepfather, Jim, and our friend Evelyn came for the surgery along with our pastor, Willie, to support my husband, Jim. My son Greg and my daughter, Julie, and son-in-law, Chris, drove in from Texas the next day. My son James called, checking on me, and Julie came back to Lexington when I came home from rehab to help me settle in. As we went over what I had endured, Julie told me my pain was tremendous in the beginning. I asked her how she knew. She told me she could see it all over my face as I kept telling them to give me something for pain for it hurt so badly. God's mercy spared me from remembering the pain. Thank you, Lord! I do not remember their even being there at all!

The third week, I woke up at Cardinal Hill with my hair shaved on top and sides and thinning hair on either side of my ears. That was a shock! It seems a small price to pay for the doctors saving my life. I found out I was on prayer chains and had a myriad of people and groups praying for my recovery all over the country. I had lived in so many different places over the years and had so many wonderful friends it really came in handy for prayers.

It had to be difficult for my family and friends to hear the doctors tell them it was hour to hour about my recovery. So I thank the Lord for sustaining my life and helping me to return almost to normal. After the initial collapse and stroke, I heard the Holy Spirit in my spirit tell me He did not cause this to happen but He wanted me to give Him the glory from the experience. So from the time it happened, I praised Him and thanked Him for being with me and my loved ones to comfort, heal, and help me during this extremely difficult challenge. There are several places in Scripture where we are told that the Lord will never leave us or forsake us. So I held on to that and expected His best!

Jim did everything timely and got me to the hospital quickly, with 911 arriving at my home within a few minutes after he called. Last year, so many people died with strokes, even much younger people than I. I told Jim how thankful I was to be alive and that he did everything so well toward my recovery. He has been an incredible caregiver! I am so thankful for all those people who prayed for me, cared about my well-being, and encouraged me. I truly could feel all the prayers from all over the country. Also, I thank the Lord and send praises to Him for imparting all the medical knowledge to the doctors and medical staff that saved my life and extended my days on this earth. That and all the prayers certainly made the difference in my life. The Lord still has much for me to do before I leave this earth, and I thank Him for allowing a second lease on life for me. The beginning of December, they did another procedure on the aneurysm that burst and bled and put a stent in and another coil to keep the aneurysm quiet to prevent another bleed. Everything went well. I bounced back quickly. When I returned to my normal routine, at church, at the YMCA, and with friends, they called me a walking miracle. At first, it made me a little uncomfortable, but I soon realized that was affirming, giving the glory to God! I felt it glorified God to agree with everyone. So I rejoiced in hearing others saying that.

There is so much to praise God for. I am not on a walker or cane or in a wheelchair, which often happens after a stroke, and am close to being back to normal. There is no paralysis or permanent damage that I am aware of. I discovered another very helpful technique, tapping. This works like acupuncture without the needles. It helps with stress and sleep. If you are interested in more information, go to www.thetappingsolution.com and check out the simple and free techniques. I bought the book *The Tapping Solution: A Revolutionary System for Stress-Free Living*. It has really helped me calm down and ease my stress level and lessen the cortisol production. It also helps work through trauma in one's earlier life and to correct detrimental habits. It is well worth checking out for well-being. It has really helped me in many ways.

My part now is to use my imagination, which is our spiritual womb, to see myself healed, to speak healing from the scriptures on healing, and to take extra good care of my physical, spiritual, and emotional, knowing a lot of my permanent healing is up to me. Jim and I have worked out at the YMCA for twelve years, so I know that has helped me bounce back, for the doctor said he had not seen anyone in my situation overcome as quickly as I did. Praise God! The Loudon Family YMCA has helped me stay in good physical condition since I have worked out three to four times a week in classes and on the equipment. Also, the comradery and emotional support at the YMCA is marvelous. We encourage one another and have developed many close relationships there. This is vital for recovery. I am so blessed! My church, friends, family, and children have checked on me often and are so caring and loving. Now it is up to me to quote my healing scriptures from the Bible, keep myself healthy, exercise, and focus on the Great Physician and encourage others with what I have experienced. God has proved Himself again and again.

Additional Thoughts

As this chapter comes to a close, another subject must be dealt with. We know the Lord answers prayers. He may say yes, no, or wait. The wait answer is sometimes more difficult than no. Why would the Lord delay our healing when He clearly says, "By His stripes we are and were healed"? Here are some thoughts on the matter. In one of my intimate times with the Lord, I cried out to Him because I did not understand why complete healing had not taken place for two people I had been praying for. He had healed others I had prayed for. There was much improvement, and I had seen them grow closer to the Lord in their journey, seeking their healing, but they were not completely healed. Here is what I felt the Lord revealed to me. (This is for you as well.)

"Child, I feel your pain. I know your disappointment. Be patient. I am teaching you as you can learn about my healing. My Words are true. Never doubt them. They are there for a purpose to give you wisdom and power. Understanding my Will is another thing. I see the end from the beginning, and you are unable now to view everything as I do, so you must be willing to trust me as my wisdom unfolds to you." Then, I received something personal I do not wish to share at this time. "You are being taught one thing at a time what I have in store for you. Do not chafe at my method. My way is the right way for you to learn. Keep looking up. I am always here with you, teaching you and loving you, my child, for I loved you so much I died for you! I left heaven for you so you can always be with me through the Holy Spirit. My ways are not your ways, but soon you will operate in my ways as I have planned for you. My peace I give you, my child! Abide in me."

I realize that God's timing is not our timing, and one of the hardest things I have to do is wait and trust and allow the Lord to work His timing. We sometimes forget that God gives us free will and He does not go against that free will, so when the wills of others sometimes stand in the way of our receiving even what the Lord desires us to have, we must allow Him to do things in His timing. This is very difficult sometimes, but necessary. Our part is to stand, to keep fortifying ourselves by speaking the Word and believing the Lord will make that Word manifest in our lives.

In Mark 29:23–25, Jesus said all things are possible to him who believes. Then in verse 24, the father says to Jesus, "Lord, I believe! Please help my unbelief!"

I heard Henry Gruver on Sid Roth's TV program say that when he had stage 5 cancer, he said out loud to the devil, "Devil, I refuse to give my life to cancer when Jesus gave his life for me at the Cross." Henry kept saying, "I am standing against cancer. By Jesus's stripes I am healed and was healed!" (He is cancer-free today as far as I know!)

Ask (speak out loud), seek, believe, and receive. Healing is for today! Healing most often is a journey, and it is a partnership. We are expected to do our part as believers and overcomers because of the sacrificial Blood of Jesus. Healing becomes a lifestyle. A prayer I use, as a believer in Jesus Christ, by putting together several scriptures is, "Lord, I submit myself to you, and satan must flee in the name of Jesus of Nazareth, for greater is He that is within me than he that is in the world, and no weapon formed against me shall prosper." Make up your own collection of scriptures that relate to you and speak them, expecting results, for the Lord is faithful and very personal.

Remember, our body is a temple that houses the Holy Spirit. Do you think God would want your temple healed so we could be freer to worship Him and help ourselves and others? I surely do! I see nowhere in the Bible that God says sickness glorifies Him—quite the opposite! Jesus came to save us and heal us!

Summary: Steps to Healing

There are many factors involved in a healing. It can be miraculous—God can certainly do that, but most of the time it seems like He is teaching us through a journey of working with us for our healing. We learn so much about Him and His Ways during that time.

Try using your imagination to birth your new provision (or healing) today (Rom. 1:21).

1. *Glorify God.* Spend time getting to know our mighty God. We will spend eternity praising and worshipping Him, so develop that precious time with Him here.
2. *Be thankful.* Psalm 69:30 states to Praise the name of God with a song and magnify Him with thanksgiving. List the myriad of blessings you are thankful for and show Him your appreciation.
3. *Use your imagination,* for it is the ability to see with the heart what you are unable to see with your eyes now. As you visualize, you'll compel yourself to inspired action. It is your spiritual womb where your mind can create what it visualizes and believe to receive from our Creator. Walking by faith is the opposite of worry, but you use the same imagination that worries and feels lacking to "call those things that be not as though they were" (Rom. 4:17). This is referring to speaking, but those words are visualized before they are spoken. Close

your eyes. (It helps you see in your mind's eye what you want manifested in your life before you see it in the natural.) And see in your imagination what God has in store for you this day. Declare out loud God's position. "God, you are bigger than any of my problems. Healing, lack, job, money, etc., the same power that raised Jesus from the dead, is in me. I can do all things through Christ, who strengthens me" (Phil. 4:13). (Put your own words and scriptures here). Plan your day by putting Jesus first and asking Him to do His part and show you what is your part. Praise and glory and magnify the Lord together with imagining the results. Make the plan unfold before you. Remember what is His part and what is yours and thank and praise Him, and see your provision.

See yourself healed or the final product of what you are believing for. "He will keep him in perfect peace whose mind is stayed on Him [God] because he trusts God" (Isa. 26:3). Verse 4 says, "Trust in the Lord forever; for in the Lord is everlasting strength."

Keep thanking and praising God for your healing and keep seeing yourself healed. And watch your words! In my studies a few days ago, I felt this in my spirit as I was writing and wanted to share it here. Believing and speaking the truth of God's Word is like receiving blessed CPR from the Holy Spirit. How great is God!

Scriptures and Information Helping Secure Answered Prayers: Holding on to Your Healing
To help you stand, enabling the Lord to totally heal you with His pathway of healing, your part is to worship and magnify Him and enter into His presence with thanksgiving.

1. Accept His healing.
2. Speak His words while Standing on His promises.
3. Build your faith in Him.

4. Trust Him to completely heal you.
5. Believe His Word.
6. Praise Him for caring for you so especially.
7. Give thanks for your healing.
8. Share God's mercy and work with others.

Do not listen to the world or the adversity to cause doubts in what the Lord has done in your life!

After having prayer and receiving words of knowledge about a specific need, the recipient's part is to be prepared to stand against the world and the adversary, equipped by putting on the armor of God for war. After I believed the Lord for my healing in 1974 from allergies suffered since childhood, I recorded scriptures on my tape recorder that strengthened me, in my own voice, and listened to them each morning while I dressed. I combined scriptures and made them very personal to me. Find some that have special meaning to you to help you stand, but you can use some that have blessed me while you search for your own.

- Dear Lord, I submit myself to you, and satan must flee, in the name of Jesus, for greater is He that is within me than he that is in the world, and no weapon formed against me shall prosper. (James 4:7; 1 John 4:4)
- "With His stripes I am healed!" "By His wounds I have been healed." (Isa. 53:5; 1 Peter 2:24).
- "Calleth those things which be not as though they were." (Speak your healing in your own words and this special gift you have accepted from the Lord for specific things.) (Rom. 4:17)
- "My Maker is my husband, the Lord of hosts is His name." (Isa. 54:5)
- "Put on the whole armor of God, that you may be able to stand against the wiles of the devil. For we are not contending

against flesh and blood, but against the principalities, against the powers, against the world rulers of this present darkness, against the spiritual hosts of wickedness in the heavenly places. Therefore take the whole armor of God, that you may be able to withstand in the evil day, and having done all, to stand. Stand therefore, having girded your loins with truth, and having put on the breastplate of righteousness and having shod your feet with the equipment of the gospel of peace, above all things taking the shield of faith, with which you can quench all the flaming darts of the evil one. And take the helmet of salvation, and the sword of the Spirit, which is the Word of God. Pray at all times in the Spirit, with all prayer and supplication. To that end keep alert with all perseverance, making supplication for all the saints." (Ephesians 6:10–13)

Add those scriptures you are led to include because the Lord is a personal God and will tell you what you need to say. He tells us in 1 Corinthians 2:16, "But we have the mind of Christ" (when He is our Savior). So let Him be the personal God He desires to be for you alone. This is meant to point the way to your own pathway of healing that He has chosen for you and desires you to have. Blessings to you as you stand!

# The Facts of Life

- Life is short.
- Death is certain.
- Everyone is a sinner.
- Everyone has a judgment to face.
- There is a literal hell to avoid.
- There is a heaven to gain.
- Freedom is now!

1. Life is a mist that appears for a short while. (James 4:13)
2. There is appointed unto man once to die, then the judgment. (Heb. 9:27)
3. Death is no respecter of persons. (Rom. 2:11)
4. The wages of sin is death, but the gift of God is eternal life in Christ Jesus our Lord. (Rom. 6:23)
5. The promise depends on faith. (Rom. 4:10)
6. Revelation 20:11 tells about the Great White Throne Judgment; there is a hell to avoid. (Cast out from the Presence of the Lord.)
7. Revelation 21:1 describes the New Jerusalem (being in the Presence of the Lord).
8. Luke 4:16 tells us that Jesus goes to prepare a place for us, so we have a reservation if we know how to make one. Do you know how to make a reservation? Have you made a reservation for yourself?
9. Romans 10:9 states, "If you confess with your lips that Jesus is Lord and believe in your heart that God raised Him from the dead, you will be saved."
10. Galatians 2:16 says, "By grace are you saved through faith and not of works, least any man should boast."
11. Jesus says, "I am the resurrection and the life. He who believes in me will live, even though he dies and whoever lives and

believes in me will never die." (John 11:25)

12. Salvation is found in no one else; there is no other name under heaven given to men by which we must be saved. (Acts 4:12)

13. At the name of Jesus, every knee shall bow in heaven and earth and under the earth, and every tongue shall confess that Jesus Christ is Lord, to the glory of God the Father. (Phil. 2:10)

14. "I [Jesus] am the Way and the Truth and the Life. No one comes to the Father except through me." (John 14:6)

Remember, everyone has a god, something you spend most of your time with or are pursuing. Ask yourself, "Who or what is my god?" If it is not the God who created you and is desirous to fellowship with you in an intimate, personal relationship, or you want to know Him better, now is the time to reach out. You are assured only of this moment, this one second of life, no more. He wants you to know Him better.

What if you say, "I do not believe in God." You can be assured He will never force His Will on you. He gives you the freedom of a freewill choice. So may I ask you, "Where does the breath you take for granted come from?" You can only live less than ten minutes without breathing. How do you explain the breath? Where does it come from? Start searching and asking questions. You have a short time to get the questions answered, and you are assured only of this moment. It could be your last breath. What then? Do you want to live as Adam and Eve lived before sin entered the world? I believe the Lord wants us to return to that marvelous existence before sin and to fellowship with Him one-on-one in a perfect world, and He gives you the choice to determine where you spend eternity. Do you want a choice? Choose now while you have the breath to make that choice!

Have you accepted Jesus Christ as Savior? You must make the most important decision of your life to accept the Lord as your

Savior, or you will have already made a decision by default. Stop and read Romans 10:9 out loud. The scripture says, "If you confess with your mouth, Jesus is Lord, and believe in your heart that God raised Him from the dead, you will be saved. For it is with your heart you believe, and are justified, and it is with your mouth that you confess and are saved." Continuing on in verse 13, we are told, "Everyone who calls on the name of the Lord will be saved." There is your hope made manifest!

The good news is, that everyone's debt has been paid! (In Romans 5:8, Christ died for us, and Romans 10:9 tells us how to be saved.) Everyone can be saved! Just receive the gift the Lord has given us in His Son. John 3:16 states, "For God so loved the world that He gave His only begotten Son that whoever believes in Him shall not perish but have everlasting life!"

1. Admit you are a sinner.
2. Tell Him you believe in your heart Christ died for your sins.
3. Ask for forgiveness.
4. Believe He promised to save you.
5. We are assured everyone who asks receives.

Making Jesus Lord of your life is a journey. (We will discuss later.)

The Lord wants us to be a family (His arms and legs) to bless one another and draw closer to Him. May God richly bless all who ready this, and it is my sincere prayer that Father God, in the name of Jesus, will send His Holy Spirit to bless you and bring a closer fellowship with Him. "Behold, I stand at the door and knock, if anyone hears my voice and opens the door, I will come to him and eat with him and he with me" (Rev. 3:20). Why not just ask Him in and change your life for the better? Jesus said, "If you love, obey my commandments."

(Much of this is from a sermon that Pastor Mark Wyatt of Timbercreek Church gave to bless everyone who has ears to hear.) If you are blessed, pass on this information.

What About Heaven and Hell?

Is there a literal hell? Of course, we want to believe there is a heaven, but hell? Surely, a loving God would not sentence us to hell! Can't we throw out all the talk about hell and skip that part? Questions, questions. What is the truth? In the Bible, Jesus talked about hell more than about heaven! Surprise you?

Let's explore the subject. If a loving parent takes the time to inform its own child to avoid certain dangers that that child could face in life that could destroy its quality or final destination, wouldn't that be a good thing?

Facts

God did not create hell for you; He never intended for you to go there, but the choice is up to you. There is a literal hell that had to be created for the spiritual being Lucifer and his followers when he rebelled against the Lord and took a third of the angels with him. This place created for Lucifer gave God's created beings a choice of who to follow. Hell was never meant for God's children, but if a created being chose to follow after Lucifer, then the die is cast; that person would be there with Lucifer. Hell is a place without the Presence of God. You definitely do not want to go there!

The Salvation Experience

What is this, anyway? God is so personal. First, He gave us free will at the creation of mankind, and then He gives each person a unique experience after making the decision to come back to Him. God knew we would take the gift of free will and disobey, so He loved us so much and wanted a personal relationship with each of us. He had already prepared a way for us to return to His presence. The Word (which is Jesus) was made flesh and dwelled among us to give us a hope and a payment for the sin of disobedience. Just as we are born into this world, one at a time, we come back to Him one at a time in our own experience with Him. His progressive revelation starts here, and truth is unveiled over a period of time throughout the Bible in our life as we seek Him and are willing to die to self to allow Him more of our life.

Everyone does not have a "Damascus Road experience" as Paul did when he encountered Jesus and was knocked to the ground as he was riding. The change in each life is dramatic because Jesus came to give us the ultimate sacrifice for the penalty of sin that mankind incurred with disobedience in the Garden. He makes us a New Creation in Him (2 Cor. 5:17). "The old has gone, the new has come" when we repent and seek His forgiveness. The Spirit woos us like He did in the beginning, in Genesis 1:1, "The Spirit hovered over the waters," to create a new creation out of chaos. Read the rest of that chapter and discover that "God made Him [Jesus] who had no sin to be sin for us, so that in Him we might become the righteousness of God." We have a progressive revelation from the Lord as we learn His Word and experience the journey of refining (getting the dross out of us) and making us the new creation in Him. It would appear that some individual salvation experiences are more dramatic than others. This is the point we all begin our journey back to Him. You have the choice how quickly you get to know Him intimately. The more time you spend with Him, the quicker you learn His Perfect Will for your life. The adventurous journey becomes richer and fuller then to mine the precious metals He has planned for you.

So how do we make this encounter? The Word tells us to repent and ask Jesus to take away our sins and invite Him to come into our lives so we can make Him the Lord and start returning to the Garden to be with Him and experience that day-to-day fellowship He enjoyed and mankind enjoyed in the Garden.

Have you made your reservations for heaven yet? Do you want your name in the Lamb's Book of Life? Well, you might say, "How do I do that?" Here is an interesting story for you.

Dr. David Jeremiah, pastor and teacher, told a story about the importance of RSVP to the calling of the Lord and to make your reservation to heaven, now, without delay. You must RSVP! Here is the gist of the story Dr. Jeremiah tells that appeared in *Guidepost* about Dr. Ruthanna Metzgar, who was a world-famous professional singer, instructor, lecturer, and director of choirs/orchestras all across the globe. She was invited to sing at a millionaire's wedding in the tallest skyscraper in Seattle to an elegant affair with an atmosphere of grace and sophistication. After the ceremony, the bride and groom ascended the beautiful glass-and-brass staircase, ascending to the top floor leading to the reception. There at the top was a tuxedoed gentleman with an ornately bound book containing the names of all invited to the reception. Dr. Metzgar approached and gave him her name. The gentleman said, "I am sorry, but your name is not here." She explained who she was and her part in the wedding, to which he replied, "It does not matter who you are or what you did. Without your name in the book, you cannot attend the banquet." She and her husband were escorted to her car, and on the way home, she told him she was too busy when the invitation arrived and did not bother to return the RSVP, feeling sure that because she was in the wedding, surely she could go to the reception.

Is your name in the Lamb's Book of Life? There is one place that is vital to one's eternal existence that must be responded to if one will be allowed into heaven, and that is in the Lamb's Book of Life. Dr. Jeremiah continues by saying, "You may say, I can't be left out of anything I do not know about, or a loving God will surely let me in, I try to be a good person and help others, or perhaps, I am active in the church, or my father was a pastor, and I went to church all the time, or some other excuse." The Bible tells us that Jesus stands at the door, knocking, asking to be invited into your life. Have you invited Him in? Jesus shows us that we must have a personal relationship with Him to be invited to His banquet after this life. Have you asked Him to come into your heart, and have you decided to make him your Savior and Lord? Do you know what the Lamb's Book of Life is? The Scripture tells us in Revelation 20:15 that at the Great White Throne Judgment, if anyone's name is not found written in the Book of Life, he or she would be thrown into the lake of fire. How do we get our name in the Lamb's Book of Life? Romans 10:10 states, "If you confess with your mouth, Jesus is Lord, and believe in your heart that God raised Him from the dead, you will be saved. For it is with your heart that you believe and are justified, and it is with your mouth that you confess and are saved. Everyone who calls on the name of the Lord will be saved." You are promised a place in the Book of Life if you respond to Jesus knocking at the door of your heart. Dr. Metzgar's response was like that of so many others who hear of God's plan but never take time to respond. God laid out in His plan in and through Jesus Christ, who tells us plainly, "I am the way, the truth, and the life. No one comes to the Father except through me" (John 14:6).

Dr. Jeremiah had a daily devotional where he wrote, "God is writing the pages of history, time is swiftly flying by, and the pages are blowing off the calendar like leaves in the wind. The last days will be full of surprises, and Christ will come like a thief in the night." The apostle Paul said, "The day of the Lord will come as a thief in the night, in which the heavens will pass away with a great noise, and the elements will melt with fervent heat" (2 Pet. 3:10).

Do you have your place reserved in God's city? Our reservations are held under the name of Jesus, and He alone is our ticket there. Make sure your name is written in the Lamb's Book of Life. Dr. Jeremiah continues with, "Make sure you travel light, for this world is not our home; we're just passing through. Today, pack your mind with God's Word and anticipate your eternal home." In John 14:2–3, Jesus tells us about going to prepare a place for us and about His Father's house, and where He is, we may be also. Just remember we are just passing through this world, and we have an incredible future to look for if you have made your reservations to be at the Lamb's Banquet. "Establish your hearts, for the coming of the Lord is at hand" (James 5:8).

Accepting Jesus as your Savior is the first step, then the next step in your life's journey is making him Lord of your life.

God's Word is seed; saturate yourself in it and keep saying and believing the Word. It produces freedom. It works, so keep working it. Our discipleship is a lifelong, total commitment and grows each day as we read the Word, speak the Word, internalize the Word, and live the Word. May I ask all of us the question, "How much time have I given the Word today?" Knowing the truth from the Word sets a person free. In John 8:32, Jesus said, "If you continue in my Word, you are truly my disciples, and you will know the truth, and the truth will make you free."

The last thing that Jesus said to His disciples after He was resurrected had to be vitally important since it was His last instructions to them. Jesus said, "Go therefore and make disciples of all nations, baptizing them in the name of the Father, and of the Son, and of the Holy Spirit, teaching them to observe all that I have commanded you; and lo, I am with you always, to the close of the age" (Matt. 28:19).

To be a disciple, one must be constantly renewing one's mind. Romans 12:2 says, "Do not be conformed to this world but be transformed by the renewing of your mind, that you may prove what is the will of God, what is good and acceptable and perfect." How does one renew one's mind? By the washing of the Word (Eph. 5:25). The Lord honors our efforts to "spend time with Him and sit at His Feet to learn His Wisdom and His ways." We then become the New Creation in Christ He intended us to become (2 Cor. 5:17).

This reminds me of the law of displacement. If I take a cup of coffee and run clean water in the cup, the clean water will displace the coffee and soon the coffee is replaced by the water. If you, as a believer, spend time in the Bible, which is the Word of God, seek His Presence, and learn His ways, the world's teachings and your own sinful nature will become displaced with the "washing of the Word" (who actually is Jesus) to the nature of the Lord through the Holy Spirit (the Comforter) that Jesus sent, and He promises to never leave us or forsake us, as He teaches us in Deuteronomy 31:6. Why not now make your goal to know Jesus intimately through the Holy Spirit, who is with you 24-7, available whenever you are?

The Books in Heaven

If you knew your name was written in a book in heaven, wouldn't you be interested in why and where it is written? The Bible mentions several books that are in heaven. The exact number does not seem to be as important as what we know about the ones mentioned. It would seem the Lord would expect us to be sure we knew what He was trying to communicate with the ones He mentioned in Scripture. Revelation 20:12 tell us, "I saw the dead, great and small, standing before the throne, and books were opened. Another book was opened, which is the Book of Life. The dead were judged according to what they had done as recorded in the books." So there were books, not one book; how many is not exactly mentioned, but here are some things we have been told.

Book of the Living: The Lamb's Book of Life

The Lamb's Book of Life (sometimes referred to as the Book of the Living), surely, must be the most important one, for John tells us it is opened by Jesus in Revelation to determine who attains eternal life with Jesus. He is the only one found worthy to open the scroll. Jesus told us to rejoice for our names are written in heaven. The dead are judged according to their works (Rev. 20:12; Dan. 7:10; Luke 10:20).

It would seem that when everyone is born, that name is recorded in the Book of Life, for the Lord intended everyone to have his or her name in the Lamb's Book of Life, so He would fellowship eternally with him or her. So He intended everyone to go to heaven and remain with Him. However, there are examples of blotting that name out of the book so it does not spell out the exact reasons for it. Exodus 32:33 states, "But the Lord said to Moses, whoever has sinned against me, him will I blot out of my book." So it would seem that everyone's name is placed in the Book of Life when the Lord gives life to a person. Only when that person literally turns away from God does his name get blotted out of the most important book in heaven.

Book of Deeds
(The Old Testament states that "a book of remembrance was written before Him of those who feared [reverenced] the Lord and thought on His name." Perhaps these two books are the same.) In this book is a record of everything a person has done while on this earth during his or her lifetime. It would seem that each person must have a book with his or her name on it, because we are told we will be held accountable for every deed we do and every word that comes out of our mouths. We know God records our words (Matt. 12:36–37). (Those are all the things done in our bodies, good or bad, and the words uttered from our mouths [2 Cor. 5:10].) The Bible tells us we are responsible and held accountable for every idle word that comes out of our mouths. Wow! That is a sobering thought. We are told the very hairs on our head are numbered and God knows that. Think how often that count changes every day (Luke 12:7). A tree is known by its fruit (Matt. 12:33). Nehemiah cried out to God to remember his deeds. God will render to every man according to his deeds (Rom. 2:6). The Lord documents the deeds of the believer, and no acts of kindness go unnoticed before the Lord, and the other that we do not want to think about is also recorded. Surely, one book could not hold all the people ever born and every moment of each person's life (unless the books were stored in a computer and filed as

Book of Deeds). Hmmmm. With our computer and tech age now, we certainly can see how that can be recorded and stored. The Book of Remembrance is mentioned in Malachi 3:16–18. It surely seems the Book of Deeds and Book of Remembrance could be the same book. The Kings had books about their subjects and had scribes write down what all the subjects did, so it was probably a similar activity. But the Lord knows everything each person does every minute of the day along with his or her thoughts and words, along with the heart's intent, which is vastly different. This makes me more aware of the importance of every unkind thought or action along with every kind thought and act of kindness. For in this we see how important it is to do unto others and realizing God created that person and how important we should deal kindly with God's creations (Mark 9:41). When we do any act of kindness, like a cup of water, God remembers it, so we are building our treasures in heaven. This is a sobering fact for me and makes me want to repent, ask for forgiveness, and allow the Lord to guide and lead me in relationships from His perspective and not mine. Job cried out to God for his words to be written, and they are. (They are remembered in the book of Job in Scripture.)

I looked for a Book of Tears because I had heard of tears in a bottle being saved and thought there might be a Book of Tears, but I was unable to find one. (The tears in a bottle proclaim an ancient custom of pain and suffering, and some people even saved the tears in a bottle.) In Psalm 56:8, David said, "You [God] have kept count of my tears in your bottle. Are they not in your book?" This is the only scripture I can find with *tears* and *book* together. So here it would seem like these situations can be included in each person's book because the challenges each person encounters on this earth will certainly be included in the book since the Lord cares and has compassion on what happens to us either by our actions, others' actions toward us, or the adversary's actions against us.

The Book of Scriptures: The Bible
This is God's book written through mankind (2 Tim. 3:16–17). All Scripture is inspired by God and is profitable for teaching, for reproof, for correction, and for training in righteousness, that the man of God may be complete, equipped for every good work. "For the Word of God is quick, and powerful, and sharper than any two-edged sword, piercing even to the dividing asunder of soul and spirit, and of the joints and marrow, and is a discerner of the thoughts and intents of the heart" (Heb. 4:12). The Bible is probably the only book that occupies library space both on earth and in heaven.

The Bible, of course, should be in heaven, for it is our history and God's account of His dealings with mankind. Matthew 24:35 says, "Heaven and earth will pass away, but my words will never pass away." The Bible is God's two covenants, with mankind before Jesus and His covenant with mankind after Jesus came to earth. Has the thought ever occurred to you, Why should you study all that Old Testament and even New Testament information? Because you can't take it to heaven. Now, with the Bible in heaven as one of the books, it must be important since it is already there. God's Word never changes, so there must be a record of it in heaven. Psalm 119:89 tells us, "Your Word, O Lord, is eternal: it stands firm in the heavens." Randy Alcorn says, "Presumably, we will read, study, contemplate, and discuss God's Word there." We have heard, "Oh, we can't take things with us." It appears all our studying and learning spiritual things will be eternal. So read and learn your Bible; that wisdom is something that goes on with you after this life.

We are told that the good news is that the Bible is more accessible in our generation than at any other point in history. The bad news is that fewer people are reading it today. The Gideons have done an amazing job with all the Bibles and New Testaments they have given away. The Bible is on the internet, available in the spoken languages in a way that it has never been before. You can find scriptures daily by using Google or Siri. What a blessing that is!

We are told a person reads less than one hundred books in his or her lifetime. Sadly, usually the Bible is not one of those books. This is one reason this book you are reading now is filled with scriptures, to perhaps introduce you to the words in the Bible to encourage you to search for treasure on your own and learn how to discover the wisdom to enjoy your life each day. It certainly has changed my life. Then, you can share your discovery with others to help them find out how they can shape their futures, now, with choices.

From the internet, I read that 92 percent of Americans own a Bible, and 72 percent say they would like to read the entire Bible sometime in their lives. But are they making any choices in their lives to achieve that statement? The Bible is an awesome book that contains 1,260 promises, 6,468 commands, more than 8,000 predictions, and 3,294 questions/answers. Aren't you just a little bit interested in reading what it says to you? Each promise can have your name in it, for the Lord tells us He is no respecter of persons (Acts 10:34). This means we all have the same opportunities. What a God!

His Will or Mine? Actor Vs. Reactor

Many times I have directed a person to be an actor, not a reactor, in my crime awareness and prevention seminars, to be prepared for unexpected, unpleasant conditions. It was wisdom for things of this world, because when you "practice your lines" in the play, you are prepared to express them, and that is good advice in this natural, human world, like saying "No to drugs" and practicing what to say if one is confronted. Today, however, as I was listening to my husband read to us a daily devotional from *Jesus Calling,* I realized a different advice about spiritual things was needed and what to focus on in response to God. When we act, we use our will to accomplish something and put self on the throne. However, when we are giving up our self and its direction, then allowing the Lord to guide our actions, He can direct our path into the journey He has planned for us and allows us to be part of the journey He has planned for us—His Will being made manifested in our lives!

Why would we want to allow anyone to take control of our lives, anyway? When the Lord created us and placed us in our mother's womb, He had a plan for us. Each of us must have a book in heaven with our name on it in the Library of God about our lives. In Revelation, the books are opened and we are to give an account of the life the Lord bestowed upon us for our earth's journey. Did you ever give that a thought?

Have you thought past what will occur after the life in this body you were given has ebbed and the breath you took for granted is no longer available to you in this clay shell? What then? We need to know there is an existence on beyond this lifetime, but the choices you make here on earth determine where and how you go and live beyond here on earth. What the Bible says is all I know to expect, and we are told by Jesus in Romans 14:11, for it has been written, "I live, says the Lord, that every knee will bow to Me, and every tongue confess to God so then every one of us shall give account of himself to God." So you are writing the book of yourself daily, moment to moment. What will you record?

The next subject addressed here is rewards. You surely will want to know about those and what you can expect when we stand before Christ and give an account of ourselves.

Rewards

Judgment Day will not occur without the Lord preparing us through His Word what He plans to do and what is expected of us (Amos 3:7). If we know in advance, then we are better prepared. This is what God did with us. Judgment will not be a surprise because God has given us the information ahead of time. Jesus said, "The word that I have spoken, the same shall judge him in the last day" (John 12:48). Paul said, "In the day when God shall judge the secrets of men by Jesus Christ according to my gospel" (Rom. 2:16). Since the entire New Testament is the last will and testament of Jesus Christ, it is all spoken by Him.

How important is it to know what your future holds? If your life depended on passing a test, would you read the material it covered before taking it? Your future place to dwell is riding on the choices you make in this lifetime. Do you want to spend eternity with God in heaven, or will you choose an agony beyond description with satan in hell? Matthew 25:46 states, "And they will go away into eternal punishment, but the righteous into eternal life." If you do not choose Jesus, you will choose satan by default. Where do you want your eternal soul to live?

"For we shall all stand before the judgment seat of God: for it is written, As I live, says the Lord, every knee shall bow to me, and every tongue shall give praise to God" (Rom. 14:10). So each of us shall give an account of himself to God. Did you ever know that every one of us, without exception, will have to stand before The Judgment Seat of God after we die, to give an account to Jesus for everything that we have ever done on this earth, then receive rewards for what we did for Him? The second book of Corinthians 5:10 states, "For we must all appear before the judgment seat of Christ, that each one may receive the things done in the body, according to what He has done, whether good or bad." Not everyone who says "Lord, Lord" will be entering into the Kingdom of heaven—but only those who are willing do the Will of God the Father (Matt. 7:21). (The rewards discussed here are lasting ones that the Lord issues, not the temporal ones here on earth.) The first book of Corinthians 3:8 tells us His rewards to us are according to our own labor for God. God did not say *successful* but *faithful* to what the Lord calls a person to do.

Rewards come only after you have accepted Jesus as your Savior and the Lord of your life. You cannot get into heaven by good works!

Ephesians 2:8 states, "You are saved by grace through faith; and it is not of yourself, it is the gift of God, not of works, lest any man should boast." The Lord tells us, "I am He who searches the minds and hearts. And I will give to each one of you according to your works" (Rev. 2:23).

The gift of eternal salvation is a free gift from God and is something that has to be accepted by faith. However, once you are saved, God expects you to do something with the time you still have left here on earth. Scripture (Philippians 2:12) tells us to work out our own salvation with fear and trembling. This probably means with great humility and respect for the journey the Lord has planned for us and the awesome nature of the plans of the Lord for us. He expects you to come to Him and work for Him. He has a Will for each of us when we come to earth, and the sooner we determine His Will in our lives, the closer our fellowship will be with Him, and we will start working toward the rewards He has for His children who do His Will. With the capacity the Lord has to reward us, what a wonderful time we will have in His Presence and the extras He has planned for us with rewards!

The Crowns

David Jeremiah lists five crowns in his book *Answers to Questions About Heaven*. He states there could be many more but the Lord Himself is our chief reward. "No crown could ever compare to the splendor of seeing our Lord and Savior face to face!" The exciting thing is that everyone can obtain this awesome reward by accepting Jesus as one's personal Savior and making Him Lord of one's life now, today!

1. Victor's crown (1 Cor. 9:25). Jeremiah calls it an award for self-discipline. Jimmy Swaggart's *The Expositor's Study Bible* says it means to fight the good fight of faith, anchored exclusively in the Cross.
2. Crown of rejoicing (1 Thess. 2:19). Jeremiah reminds us that

this crown is for those who lead others to Christ.

3. Crown of righteousness (2 Tim. 4:8). This crown is laid up for those who are being right and doing right with God, who yearn for and welcome His coming.

4. Crown of life (James 1:12; Rev. 2:10). If being tempted and tested for endurance and being faithful even unto death, secure this crown.

5. Crown of glory (1 Pet. 5:4). This crown comes from tending the sheep (those in leadership roles) with Godly wisdom and care, allowing the Great Shepherd to lead.

So what do we do with these crowns (rewards) after receiving them? We have the opportunity to choose to take the crowns and cast them at the feet of Jesus at His throne after He gives them to us as a gift of love and honor to our Lord while we worship and praise Him for who He is and what He means to each of us. We will only have ourselves and the crowns the Lord has given us in heaven with which to honor Him. David Jeremiah mentions that we will definitely not want to arrive empty-handed to the Savior. Our honor and joy will be that we are able to worship and praise our Savior face-to-face. We should be accustomed to worship and praise to God here on earth, so much so that it would be the first thing we should want to do when we see the Lord. *Worship* is defined as honor with extravagant love and extreme submission. The priority we give to God in our lives expresses itself in many ways from time spent with Him, how we treat others in love because He created them, what we are willing to do as the Lord leads, giving to others in money, time, and action, etc. Would we not want to give everything we had to Him at this moment?

This chapter closes with the scripture John 10:27, which says, "My sheep hear my voice, and I know them, and they follow me; and I will give them eternal life, and they shall never perish, and no one shall snatch them out of my hand. My Father, who has given them to me, is greater than all, and no one is able to snatch them out of the Father's hand. I and the Father are one." Then there will be one flock and one shepherd.

## Ways to Develop Intimacy with the Holy Spirit
### Remembering Your First Love

The freshness and promise of a lovely sunrise mimic the emotion of discovering the joy and intimacy of a first love. Almost everyone has either experienced falling in love or has observed others in this state. Your emotions are heightened, you see the world from a fresh approach, and you even feel physically changed. Perhaps we are allowed to experience this wonderful event as a "first fruit" to falling in love with our Lord, who is our Creator, our Savior, and the Mighty Counselor. In Isaiah 54:5, He tells us He is our Maker, our husband, and the Lord of Hosts is His name. He desires us to know Him intimately, and the same way we develop an earthly love relationship can apply here. We receive those love letters that mean so much to us and find out what the object of our affection is, thinking about and what that person desires for the relationship. Father God sends His Word through a written love letter, which is the Bible, and even went further by sending His only Son as the Word made flesh to dwell among us for a season. We spend time and think about our loved one constantly day and night and actually daydream about him or her.

To know God better, He tells us to meditate on Him day and night (Ps. 1:2). We spend as much time as we can, making time, not just an hour or two on Sunday. The relationship grows as we learn what our loved one desires for our happiness as we fellowship deeper. We do offer prayers to God and talk to Him about our needs, our wants for ourselves and others, but do we get quiet and listen to our mighty God as we do to the object of our earthly affections? The Lord desires for us to know Him intimately and to know what He wants for our lives and desires us to express to Him our thoughts and requests. Our love relationship with another human on earth is limited, but the limitations we put on our love relationship with Him come from us. The Lord is available day and night and is as close as a brother who will never leave us or forsake us (Heb. 13:5). He is as close as a breath. Allow Him to show you what real love is through what He gave us, Jesus, and allow that Savior to pour out the Holy Spirit more in your life and experience all the Lord wants you to hear, see, and experience. You were bought for a purpose with the precious Blood of the perfect Sacrifice for our sins. Draw close to Him and He will draw close to you (James 4:8). In 2 Chronicles 15:2, He tells us, if you seek Him, He will be found by you.

Rejoice and remember the Lord is the lover of your soul, the eternal part, forever and ever. The soul is the real you, transformed from Glory to Glory, and will continue long after the physical body has expired. He is transforming us into His image, seeing the best in us even though He knows the rest. The Lord wants to be intimate with us and have us trust Him completely, for you feel free to be yourself with someone you trust. The Lord says, "Trust me and be real with me, my refinement process draws out the dross...and brings out the gold in you so I may give you all the gifts I have planned for you. Rejoice, relax, and be blessed by our intimacy!"

We look forward (the Body of Believers, the real church) to the wedding supper of the Lamb and the banquet prepared for those who love the Lord and plan to be with the Bridegroom throughout eternity and desire to experience all the blessings our Mighty God has planned for us personally.

Perhaps you are thinking, "I do not know how to do that." Continue reading this chapter about ways to develop intimacy with the Holy Spirit and you will understand the purpose of sharing my thoughts on this subject. What if the Holy Spirit said, "Beloved, come away with me"?

First, one must choose to develop a love relationship.

In the first stage, everything is exciting, new, discovering, enjoying the ride, desiring each other's company and pleasing each other, and wanting to be together all the time. There is a searching for depth, relating to the other person, common interests, and similarities from the past perhaps, learning common ground and dislikes.

Second stage is to settle in, learning about the loved one in-depth, learning to give and take, getting more comfortable in the relationship and contentment. There is a realizing of the void when apart and finding quality time to be together. One realizes that the other person fulfills a portion of one's life. One never forgets the feelings of that fresh, new relationship and desires to balance one's life to keep that relationship fresh and new as it becomes comfortable.

The third stage is to always remember the excitement and passion that come with that first love, keeping love alive with all it takes to help grow that relationship. Learning in-depth what is important to the other person and having a desire and longing to please the one whose affections you are desirous to obtain.

Later in the relationship, to find out life is not nearly as enjoyable without that person when apart. Their importance and influence in day-to-day living is vitally important, whether together or apart. Of course, the above is referring to a human relationship, but much can be applied to your relationship with the Lord.

Desiring God above all is the best focus of a life. When that occurs, all other worthwhile relationships fit in one's life in harmony. Of course, developing a relationship with the Holy Spirit starts with a perfect being to love and communicate with, so we spend our time learning His Ways and the Word and we learn to adapt to His guidance and wisdom. God must be first in one's life. Is He really first in yours? God is perfect, and we are not, so we can trust Him explicitly. Each of us falls short, but we have options to restore and repent. So God promises to never leave us or forsake us, which gives us assurance of His love and care for us. He is always available as close as our breath because He gives us our breath. I think He allows us to feel that special, first-love feeling with another human being to catch a heavenly glimpse of our relationship as the bride of Christ at the

Marriage Supper of the Lamb. Interested? When we do not know how or what to pray, we can Pray in the Spirit. We speak directly to God in His language. This dispatches the angels on our behalf to achieve the Will of God. So when we do not know how to pray, that prayer language is what we know will bring the Kingdom of God to earth.

The Bible tells us about the end-time events and, when we see them come to pass, to look up, for our redemption draws nigh (Luke 21:28). Should we not learn all we can about our Bridegroom and all that Scripture tells us about Him coming so we can prepare for that mighty event and will be ready when He comes back for us?

Let's start learning to praise and worship the Lord, for when we are with Him after this lifetime, we will be praising and worshipping Him for eternity, so let's get ready now for that wonderful time.

This is a good time to review Psalm 100, written by King David, who knew God intimately even in the Old Testament and told us how to worship God.

> Make a joyful noise unto the Lord, all ye lands [that certainly means everyone]. Serve the Lord with gladness: come before His Presence with singing. Know ye that the Lord He is God: it is He that hath made us, and not we ourselves; we are His people, and the sheep of His pasture. Enter into His gates with thanksgiving, and into His courts with praise: be thankful unto Him, and bless His name. For the Lord is good, His mercy is everlasting; and His truth endureth to all generations! (Psalm 100:1–5)

Break that down verse by verse and meditate on each one to incorporate that in your daily life and see the relationship you have with the Lord just grow and grow. Worship needs to always be God centered, focusing on Him with all your might, abandoning what people think, and getting yourself out of the way. It is about entering into the Presence of Almighty God. Sometimes this is easier than other times. God honors our efforts, and we grow as we reach out to experience His Mighty Spirit.

Developing That Intimacy with the Holy Spirit
The first step in knowing God is to feel His love for you and experience Him as Savior. The chapter called the "Facts of Life" explained how to do that, and since you are reading this next chapter, we assume that is taken care of, because that step develops a hunger within you to know Him more in-depth and to discover what He wants for you in your life.

In order to increase your intimacy with the Lord, according to *Jesus Calling,* written by Sarah Young, who, by the way, inspired me to journal and seek the Lord in a more intimate way, you need these two traits, receptivity and attentiveness. *Receptivity* is opening up your innermost being to be filled with His abundant riches. *Attentiveness* is directing your gaze to the Lord, searching for Him in all your moments. It is possible to stay your mind on Him, as the Prophet Isaiah wrote; through such attentiveness you will receive a glorious gift: His perfect peace" (Isa. 26:3).

In *Jesus Always,* Sarah writes, "Knowing that you are perfectly and eternally loved helps you grow into the one I designed you to be. Grasping how wide and long and high and deep is My love for you, leads you into worship. This is where your intimacy with Me grows by leaps and bounds—as you joyously celebrate My magnificent Presence!" (Eph. 3:17)

When I began my serious study of the Word of God in 1973, the Lord was so long-suffering with me. I had a million questions and desired so especially to grow as fast as I could to learn more about the Lord and to experience His ways as I saw others doing. My eagerness often ended up in my running ahead of Him, which I did not want to do. He often answered my questions by directing me to scriptures in the Bible, through opening the Bible and guiding me to His truth.

How loving for the Father to do, but it lasted only for a time! He expected me to study and learn the scriptures so when I or anyone else needed a Word, I would know it or where to search for it. He expected His children to learn the meat of the Word and not have to be fed only milk, as a child is (Heb. 5:12).

One needs the desire, like a passion to know God, and the more we mature in Him, the closer we can grow to Him, learning His nature and learning about ourselves. Kenneth Copeland says, to spiritually mature as sons and daughters, as described in Ephesian 4, we need to take these steps:

1. Meditate on God's Word.
2. Be a doer of the Word.
3. Put the Word first place in your life.
4. Obey the voice of your Spirit.
5. Do exactly as God tells you to do now!

(Take these steps and you will grow spiritually.)

The Holy Spirit has led me to spent time studying the Living Word from the Bible in prayer times, learning to sit quietly and listen to that Still Small Voice as He desired to share the time with me and experience His love. Since God is a Spirit and the way to contact Him is through the Word of God, starting with reading the Word is an excellent way to begin. Soon, the habit was developed to sit in my prayer area, reading my daily devotional of *Jesus Calling* or David Jeremiah's devotional. From there I would go wherever I was led. Praying for the needs of others and my own needs along with the nation, our soldiers, etc. is normally next. Then praising God for all our blessings would follow. At this time I pray in the spirit (please do not get hung up on this phrase; it will be addressed later), then submit myself to His Perfect Will and listen for the Holy Spirit to join in the fellowship. He is as close as a brother and will surely communicate if you will listen. Then I pray for an interpretation from the Holy Spirit.

Years ago, the title was given, *Our Fellowship with His Holy Spirit,* which my friend Elaine and I used to call the Bible Studies we conducted. Knowing the Lord is no respecter of persons (Acts 10:34), I sat there listening to see if the Holy Spirit would speak to me in the same way He did to Sarah Young. The words began to flow. I felt the intimate fellowship of exchange and realized I could ask questions and even make statements, then wait and, in my spirit, would obtain a response. Glory be. What a joy! Phrases that blessed and encouraged me came, and as I hesitantly shared some passages with others, they seemed to be blessed as well, and they encouraged me to not keep them to myself. I had been journaling for some years, but only my thoughts of the moments. Feeling the closeness and the intimacy of my Maker, my Husband, the Lord of Hosts is His name (Isa. 54:5), then a total, new worship time came into being. The Lord led me to this scripture in Isaiah at an extremely difficult time in my life, and what a revelation that was! I went from a praying woman to an involved woman with my prayers of surrender, trust, praise, and thanksgiving. The richness in this new relationship gave my life new meaning as prayers were answered and mysteries of the Bible revealed as He had promised to share with me years before. From this step I went further into the refining process with learning more about repentance, forgiveness, and most of all, His love. As I was able to put away my own selfish wishes and desire and look to Him for His wisdom and guidance, and the more of Him I allowed to flow to my spirit and affect my life, the more excited I became to know Him even more intimately. Praise God for His many blessings and healings! He was patient and kind and loving! I began to discover Him more in-depth as described in Psalm 103. This is a short but mighty praise Psalm from David, who seemed to know the Lord intimately. Please take time to read the whole Psalm. Verse 3 tells us that He forgives all our iniquities and heals all our diseases, redeems our lives from the Pit, and crowns us with steadfast love and mercy, who satisfies you with good as long as you live and renews your youth like the eagle's (restores us). Verse 17 says the steadfast love of the Lord is from everlasting to everlasting. What a joy this Psalm is to read again and again! "Bless the Lord, oh my soul; and all that is within me, bless His holy name!"

Preparing for Intimate Worship
Discernment. (Watch your daily environment.) It really does not take long to "catch" the attitude of another person. Just observe and listen so you can determine whether you desire the "atmosphere" of another. Whom are you spending time with? Where are you spending time? How much default time do you spend in front of the TV? Remember, boundaries are important, and even though we need to minister to the needs of others, even that should be talked over with the Lord, for we often allow people and things to become idols in our lives and put the Lord on the back burner. Hurry away from a negative environment as quickly as you can, for it is like coffee spilled on a white shirt—the stain overwhelms the article! Then when you know you must encounter that negativity, prepare for it by standing strong and putting on your armor. Find the Scripture in Ephesians 6:10, "Be strong in the Lord and in His mighty power. Put on the full armor of God!" Read about the garments we put on and visualize the process for it to become part of you. Meditate on what each piece is designed to do for your warfare. This requires a commitment but is well worth the effort. Take some time with this and allow the Holy Spirit to sharpen your spiritual skills to avoid circumstances that can deter your walk with Him and lengthen your obedience to His walk with you. Quickly turn away from circumstances that do not glorify your walk. The Lord gives you freedom to choose, so choose wisely. If the Lord desires you to witness in a situation such as described, He will prepare you for it, but the preparation includes your choices to grow and be able to be used by the Lord to witness. He will prepare

you, but you need to be willing to allow Him to mature you in Him to be used effectively with that mission.

Practice the Presence of God. Wherever you are, the Holy Spirit is available to you. Jesus said He is closer than a brother (Prov. 18:24) and breathed into your nostrils the breath of life to make you a living being (Gen. 2:6–7). Take the time you drive, wash dishes, stand in line, or wherever you can to quietly call out to the Lord like a best friend, for He is better than a best friend. He listens, strengthens, and holds you up when you need something extra. Focus on Him, like Brother Lawrence did in a little book called Practice the Presence of God, which was written in the 1600s, when he washed dishes and did menial chores but spent his time in pure joy being in His Presence, no matter where he was. Brother Lawrence was joyful and spread that joy with everyone he met, for he had found the secret of "blooming where one is planted," in whatever capacity one finds oneself in, and knowing God intimately. Remember to operate in the present. We learn from the past and look forward to a future we can trust the Lord for. But God is in the moment and is all we have to live in, only this moment, now. The Scripture tells us, "He who truly seeks the Lord will find Him" (Jer. 29:13).

Thanksgiving, Worship, and Praise. Psalms 89:15 tells us about the festal shout. *Festal* is a word that has to do with festivals or festivities, one that connotes joy and celebration, and it grows out of a heartfelt desire to stand in the Presence of God. This defines God's character and relationship with Israel (and us who are adopted in Him). Jim Freeman said, "It is a glad offering of our very selves to the will of God. The psalmist knew that the festal shout of Israel indicated a relationship between the worshiper and God. We, too, may demonstrate that relationship when we allow ourselves to be guided in our worship, yes, but also in our living by the God of Israel whom we come to know in Jesus Christ." Psalms 106:1 says to praise the Lord and give thanks (read it all for yourself). Psalms 105:4 tells us to seek the Lord and His strength continually. Keep reading. Then Psalms 46:1 tells us He is our refuge and our strength. Keep reading. Isaiah 41:13 makes it clear to fear not, for He holds our right hand and will help us. Isaiah 61:10 gives us a blessing and tells us to rejoice in the Lord. "My soul shall exult in my God: for He has clothed me with the garments of salvation, He has covered me with the robe of righteousness, as a bridegroom decks himself with a garland, and as a bride adorns herself with her jewels, for as the earth brings forth its shoots, and as a garden causes what is sown in it to spring up, so the Lord God will cause righteousness and praise to spring forth before all the nations." The Psalms are full of rich praises, worship, and thanksgiving. Spend time like David did to get alone with the Lord and really get to know Him intimately.

Never forget confession, praise, worship, and thanksgiving in your time with the Lord. Worship invites the Presence of God in, quickly. Also, it seemed impressed on me that speaking "Hallelujah, hallelujah, hallelujah" with praise and worship (and even arms extended upward to heaven), speaking His Mighty Name, "Jesus, Jesus, Jesus," took me quicker into His Presence in the quietness. A blessed hymn such as "O the Glory of Your Presence" or "Jesus, Jesus, Jesus" takes me there when I finish the song. There is power in the name of Jesus! Demons have to flee, and satan knows he is a defeated foe and only has the power that we give him, through his lies, to steal, kill, and destroy. So we focus on Jesus, our Savior and Healer. Learn His Word and what the promises are for you to stand on and become an overcomer. The book *In God's Presence* by T. W. Hunt and Claude V. King has excellent suggestions on Confession, responding to God's Holiness; Praise, responding to God's Attributes; Worship, responding to God's Glory; Thanksgiving, responding to God's Riches; and never forget responding together. Worship is not about us; it is about God. Mainly to get our minds off the things of earth and into things of heaven (Col. 3:1–2), for we have died and our life is hidden in Christ. Worship is the corridor through which we exchange the things of this world for the reality of heaven. Never forget, we will be worshipping God in heaven, and the very core of our existence was created to worship God.

Forgiveness and repentance. Maybe you think this is strange to include in intimacy with the Holy Spirit; however, I have learned that anything you hold against your brother impairs a relationship with the Lord. He tells us before giving a gift at the altar that if we have anything against our brother, go make it right before coming to Him and offering this gift (Matt. 5:24). Forgiveness is for your freedom. It does not mean you think the person acted appropriately with you; it means you are giving up the right to the Lord to handle the situation and are trusting Him to free you from bad thoughts or actions that can result from unforgiveness. The chains are broken, and you are free by releasing someone with forgiveness. "Vengeance is mine, sayeth the Lord" (Rom. 12:9). With repentance, we must denounce our sin, repent, and turn away from the sin. Any sin without repentance becomes a barrier between you and the Lord and closes the channel of intimacy. Our relationship with the Lord is not static, but we must be ever changing and growing toward Him to develop and maintain that closeness He desires for us with Him. It is not our job to judge—that is the Lord's, because He knows all the facts and has earned the right to be the Judge. Your job is to keep the channel clear between you and God through the Holy Spirit.

(Remember that there is power in prayer, together. Even though this is not addressed when one is entering into His Presence during the quiet time, it is very important. We discover the Lord's truth and more information about a subject we are seeking an answer to and are kept accountable to the truth by "not forsaking the assembling ourselves together, as is the manner of some, but exhorting one another." The scripture Matthew 18:20 tells us, "When two are more gathered unto my name, there am I in their midst." Communion with other true believers brings answers and the vision that the Lord has for us. We are the Body of Christ, who become more powerful as we gather in His Name.)

David Jeremiah says in one of his devotionals that "when we talk to God, it's called prayer; when He speaks to us, it's called Bible study. When you meet with the Lord each day in personal Bible study, it's more than a routine, ritual, or resource—it is a relationship. You're listening to His voice in Scripture and enjoying the pleasure of His company." He goes on later to say, "After meeting with the Lord in our secret room each day, we open the door and leave; but we do not leave God behind. He walks with us into the day, into the night, and into all the situations we face. We continue to pray anytime, day or night, at any hour, for any reason and His Word can go with us too, for God has given us an amazing ability to remember things—to learn."

"Never forget that the main reason for prayer is to fellowship with the Lord and feel His intimate Presence." This is only necessary while we are on this earth and away from God; soon we will be able to meet Him face-to-face, and prayer will be unnecessary. It is necessary now, but not forever, for we will be able to walk with Him and commune with Him like Adam and Eve did in The Garden once again.

Thanksgiving is an attitude of the heart that produces joy, and it is a Biblical command. It is impossible to worship God with an ungrateful heart. You may go through the motions. Sarah Young writes in her book *Jesus Always* that no matter what is happening, you can be joyful in God, your Savior. Because of His finished work on the Cross, you have a glorious future that is guaranteed forever. Rejoice in this free gift of salvation—for you, for all who trust Jesus as Savior. Let your heart overflow with thankfulness, and He will fill you with His joy. Thank Him for the glorious gift of grace (Eph. 2:8–9). Your sins are forgiven, so let this gratitude for grace fill you with joy and increase your thankfulness for the many other blessings the

Lord has given you. (When you are joyful, you are in His presence and feel the intimacy of fellowship.)

If you are led to a scripture or your spirit is quickened to a specific subject during the day, write it down; that could just be what the Lord has planned for you to enjoy together today. You have your adventure with the Lord started for the day. Start yourself a special book on Scripture, or if He leads you to a scripture in the Bible, write in the Bible "To me" and the date, and every time you come across it for any reason, you can "hear" the Lord personally saying, "I gave that scripture to you." It is like a love letter from Him! Stand on that scripture throughout your walk with Him. Also, start a notebook on subjects like healing, peace, worship, salvation, etc. You will need it later. This brings intimacy as the Lord uses you to quote scriptures to others to meet their needs. When you are especially stressed or just need encouragement, you can read and re-read those gathered words, and it will lift your spirits and put you back on the high road the Lord wants you to travel with His help. Also, so important to me, I began to record my favorite scriptures needed for strengthening me on a cassette, listening to them daily as I dressed in the mornings, to feed my spirit and soul with His healing Words. I felt stronger and could face the fallen world each day when I feasted on the Word. One cannot give what one does not have! Think about how often we feed our physical body and how much our focus is on food. Then determine how much you feed your spirit with the Living Word and drawing close to the Lord. Our spirit needs feeding daily, and we must make the choice to do so.

The thrill of discovering each jewel in the Lord's mine is indescribable. The deeper the journey, the more valuable the jewels become—garnets, rubies, emeralds, diamonds. The Living Word produces pearls of unbelievable size! The joy in writing this book is to know that some people will respond and God will reveal that priceless time with Him in a new way. God bless you, reader, and may the words on these pages stir your heart to seek Him in a new, more personal way as Father, Teacher, Friend, and more, instead of Creator only!

"Great," you say, "but how do I start working toward that intimacy?" Are you serious, or is the question just lip service? For it will take time and commitment to follow through. There is a price to pay, but it's well worth it in every way. A relationship does not evolve overnight but is a journey of experiences to get to know another, very much like a marriage and learning about your spouse. Be patient with yourself but know that life has a way of trying to change your mind unless you take your commitment seriously (like a marriage), day to day. Ask two questions, "How well do I want to know the Lord?" and "What time am I willing to devote to this endeavor?"

One, you must make time and schedule time to spend with the Lord. This is like any activity you desire to engage in; it does not just happen without preparation. You must make it happen by setting a priority to it! I believe the Lord led me to study His Word, fellowship with others in His Word, and pray and praise Him an hour a day. Through this direction, my friend Elaine, who had also been called to do the same, studied in person or on the phone or any opportunity we could crowd in during the day. Even while we watched the children play at the playground, we learned by sharing the goodness of the Lord. If you truly desire to grow in Him, you can carve some time in your day. Do you not have time to do anything you really want to do? During this hour with this discipline, I learned scripture and the instructions for life from the Word. It is amazing what the Lord can teach you when you "sacrifice" time to Him. It really is not a sacrifice, but in the beginning, like starting an exercise program, it takes time to develop a habit that improves the body, mind, or spirit. So be patient. Do not beat yourself up if you miss a day. Do what you can and soon that special time with Him will be so rewarding you will want to schedule it ahead of many of the lesser-important things in your life. When you say "I do not have an hour a day," start seeing where your time is spent. Keep a journal for one week of your hourly activities. You will be very surprised where your time goes—TV is a wasteland to eat up your time for sure. Be honest with yourself and set your priorities the way you want them to be, not just letting things happen. Everyone has the same number of hours, and for the most part, a person can control a great portion of his or her time, so you are master of your time. Use it wisely for the good of yourself and others. Your spiritual muscles will start to develop and get stronger and stronger as you use them, just the way physical muscles respond to weight lifting and the like.

Trusting the Lord to guide my life, I found years later, because of that dedicated time, the Lord developed a "bank" within me that I can withdraw life-giving words for myself and others to encourage and share life lessons to those who need them and help myself. We know one cannot withdraw without first placing a deposit in the bank. So even if you have not done any research and study and are starting this as a new adventure, start where you are now and use some of the following suggestions to develop your own intimate relationship with the Trinity through the Holy Spirit. God honors any efforts and sees the desires of your heart. Each of His children is so special to Him. Just like loving parents who have multiple children, parents relate individually with each child and each child is special in talents and abilities that delight that parent. Relationships grow as time is spent individually with each child and fellowshipping with others. There are testimonies in the chapter entitled "Extra Goodies" to illustrate the way the Lord works with us individually, and you will surely benefit from their life experiences with the Lord.

Second, find a place, a prayer "closet" that is a comfortable place for you to develop intimacy with Him. In one of my houses, I literally had a large closet I prayed in and went over my past seven years at a time starting with the present. I went back as far as I could remember as a child, asking the Lord to show me what I needed to do to heal from past emotional experiences, losses, who I needed to forgive, how to forgive myself when I fell short or sinned, etc. You get the picture here. Moving forward, since I lived alone for years, and even after I remarried, I go to my living room couch and have my special time with the Lord. A designated place reminds you of your commitment, but you can keep your Bible, materials, prayer list, etc. available to you at a moment's notice. There will be more later on emotional healing and the Lord's work on getting the dross out of our lives.

Third, allow God to show up. God speaks to us in many ways. He speaks mainly through His Word, but there are other ways He talks to us. Start with counting your blessings, one by one. That develops into worship and praise as you lift your spirit up to reach out to our Mighty God. In turn, that draws Him ever closer to your presence as you experience His Presence. If one needs a place to start drawing nearer to the Lord, hearing that Still Small Voice, then start thanking the Lord for all the blessings you have at this moment. We all have an incredible amount. The Still Small Voice a person can hear within oneself, but the Scripture also tells us in Joel 2:28, and Jesus referred to it in Act 2:17, that it shall come to pass in the last days, that He will pour out His Spirit on all flesh. "Your sons and your daughters shall prophesy, your old men shall dream dreams and your young men shall see visions. Even upon the menservants and maidservants in those days, I will pour out my Spirit." I have been asking the Lord to specifically share with me how to write in the book about entering into His Presence and drawing near to Him. I have always felt like praise and thanksgiving were how we drew Him closer.

The Lord just gave me a special dream about how to come into His Presence. Here is a little of it, but I know there is more to learn from the dream. Part of the dream revealed to me is that I am living in one physical room but have access to a spiritual room whenever I desire to enter. Many objects showed me the supernatural was there, but what I need to share with you is, I believe the Lord confirmed what I felt was true worship to draw Him closer and manifest to us when we desire that closeness of His Fellowship. Even though I have not been in the habit of raising my hands to praise, my hand went up, and I started praising Him and worshipping Him with these words: "Hallelujah, hallelujah, hallelujah!" (three times). I was in heaven, then my husband woke me up as I was speaking these words out loud in the physical while feeling like I was in both dimensions. The Lord impressed on me that this is the way to enter into fellowship with the Lord, almost like calling to Him when you need to come into His Presence—the way to engage Him. Perhaps this is His address. He is always available to us and tells us so, but to really have that closeness He desires and we desire, we speak the words of praise to call Him.

Another time, I awoke at three o'clock that morning and felt the Lord had something to share with me. The thoughts started flooding into my mind. I heard the word amoeba and listened to hear what was next. I am a very visual person, and in a science class in high school, we studied this single-cell organism. We were told the way they eat is to wrap themselves around something and encompass it into their body. Then it occurred to me that we could internalize the Holy Spirit that came to visit us when we studied God's Word and wanted to have more of Him, by wrapping ourselves around Him and bringing more of Him into our body. This reminded me of dying to self and desiring more of the Holy Spirit to dwell in us. Then it also reminded me of taking communion in Matthew 26:26 when Jesus said, "Take this in remembrance of me," about drinking the wine and eating the bread, which is interpreted as internalizing what Jesus came to do that ultimately would refer to the Holy Spirit we welcome in after He leaves the earth. (The Holy Spirit points to Jesus and goes on to the Father.)

Very often, thanksgiving develops into worship and praise, but sometimes worship and praise can be individual or all three at once. I feel certain the Lord is pleased with all or focuses on one because one leads to the others. These actions draw the Holy Spirit closer so we are able to commune with Him.

Start singing songs of worship and praise or sing your own tune with Psalms and Scriptures you have memorized over the years. The Lord impressed to me that our voices are precious in praise and worship to Him as He judges from the heart, not whether we can carry a tune or not. Perhaps it is a blessing to Him to get ourselves out of the way by humbling ourselves to sing when we do not feel our voice is adequate to praise. Sometimes it is a lie we have believed that we cannot sing; sometimes it is a feeling of inadequacy we have or even that our singing voice has faded into something we do not want others to hear. But our Father created our voices to praise Him, so let go and let Him be blessed. I heard Perry Stone talking about Solomon wanting to get the glory into the temple. He tried Moses's way, which was through the law, then David's, which was worship, and still the Glory did not come, so there were singers outside the temple that had been singing there, and when they came into the temple, the glory came in. Singing/music was that important!

Your journey to intimacy begins with spending time with the Lord. Then say, "Lord, I submit myself to you and desire your perfect will for me" (1 James 4:7). Speak it out loud, mean it, sit, close your eyes, and allow the Still Small Voice (the Lord) to draw near (1 Kings 19:12). Each person's journey is unique with the Lord, who wants that intimate relationship to guide each very special child of His, at the helm. Talk to Him as if He were right in the room with you, for He is! There is a time for worship, praise, thanksgiving, etc., and there is a time to sit at His feet and listen, and there is a time to stand up with His strength and to go into all the world, proclaiming the good news (Matt. 28:19; Mark 16:15). As we develop this personal relationship, He can guide you throughout the day as He desires. This takes time, so remember that each day you become stronger than the day before, if you take time to listen and obey. This reminds me of a dream I had years ago. The gist of it is that I was driving home from work and felt led to stop at a parched lot with weeds growing and was instructed to get out and walk around the lot. It was getting late, almost dark, and I thought, "What am I doing here?" As I started to walk back to the car, I heard in my spirit, "Some of the things I ask you to do may not make much sense to you. I just want your obedience." Obedience is a key to spiritual growth. That statement has guided me to pray and seek Him, to not run ahead of Him, nor do I want to lag behind when He instructs me to do something. If either occurs, then I must stop and ask His forgiveness for my actions or lack thereof and accept the forgiveness, learn from it, and give it to Him. The freedom one gets from the repentance is that the chains are broken and we are given a clean slate with Him. Praise God! This, too, is a process. Jesus came to set us free, so accept that fact and live like a Child of the King. We are constantly being corrected for our own good and to free us so we can maintain that constant relationship with our Maker. Learn from it, accept His forgiveness, and endeavor to grown in grace. He chastens those whom He loves to be Sons of His. (Prov. 3:12; Hebrews 12:6). If you make the effort, the Lord will guide your personal time with Him. Sit quietly and listen to the Still Small Voice. He wants to, and He will show up.

Solomon's Dream

As you seek a more intimate relationship with the Lord, may I challenge you for a moment? While I was reading the story in 2 Chronicles verse 7, when God appeared to Solomon in a dream, asking him what He should give Solomon, it made me pause and think, If God asked me, what would I ask of Him? Solomon asked for wisdom and knowledge. Why not read from verse 7 to 14 and see what all the Lord told him? And then take a moment to reflect on what you would ask God if He asked you the same question. Now, what would you ask for? God is no respecter of persons, the Bible says, so you could be ready if He did ask you (and He could)! The time you spend pondering this question can give you some insight about your walk with the Lord.

Entering into My Presence

This is a page I received on January 15, 2018, as I was spending intimate time with the Holy Spirit. I believe the Lord gave me the title.

"Your blessed Redeemer calls to you and desires you to sit still and listen. Relax your body and sit back and await my Presence! Your whole being is awaiting my touch to direct your path following my glory, just as the children of Israel in the wilderness moved when they saw the cloud by day and the fire by night, moved when I moved. So shall my children on earth do the same. Do not run ahead of my plan or lag behind. I just want your obedience! That comes from abiding in me and allowing me to plot the course that you are to follow. When I speak, move. If not, stay where you are until you sense my change and move as quickly as you can. I know your heart, but you need to know your own heart and see your reaction to circumstances. The Holy Spirit is with you to teach, guide, and direct. You can trust the Holy Spirit. Learn your Bible well, and the Holy Spirit will help you carry out what is from me. Knowledge and wisdom come as you seek me, trusting me that I have your good ever most in mind as my will is carried out by my children. My Kingdom will come as you obey my calling."

So now, do you want to actually hear the Lord communicate in your worship time? Here is how I normally start. Please remember that this is only a guide. You are individually important to the Lord, and as with each of His children, He will deal with you in His own way. Just listen; He will guide. Truly seek and you will find. Remember, this is not a formula. Allow the Holy Spirit to lead and be willing to change whatever you planned. If He has another plan,

I promise you, His Will be better than what you planned. He has a Perfect Will for your life, so just allow Him to carry it out. It is better than anything you could have imagined. You can trust Him.

I sit in my quiet worship place and relax my body and mind. If I feel stressful, I may do deep breathing for a few times to help me focus. Try four, four, and four: breathe in through the nose for a count of four, hold the breath for a count of four, then slowly release the breath through the mouth for four counts. I usually do it four times so it is easy to remember. Most times I read either *Jesus Calling* or *Jesus Always* or another daily devotional. Sometimes I am interested in a particular subject and may focus on that or something I want to know more about. That gets me focused on spiritual things and away from the earthly pull. Praise and worship is always sprinkled throughout the time with the Lord. Often I am asked to pray for someone or something, then I offer that prayer up to the Lord. I meditate on the love God has for us, remembering scriptures where He mentions how much He loves us, like John 3:16, "For God so loved the world that He gave…" Read it for yourself and learn to quote it, for it is the essence of God's love for us.

Then I pray for a short time in my heavenly prayer language. (If you do not have one, no problem; I started seeking Him intimately before I had one. Just skip this step for now and read about it at the end of this chapter for later. Then I pray for an interpretation and listen. There is a journal at my special place of worship, so I write down what I hear in my spirit. I do not stop and edit, just listen and write. Sometimes it seems to come from Jesus, and sometimes the Father. As I re-read the writings I receive, I feel His Presence and continue worship by thanking and praising the Lord for His time with me.)

My focus has totally changed since my intimate times with the Lord began. I can feel Him and enter into His Presence by just getting quiet when I need or want to. Like any relationship, the more time is spent together, the closer the relationship becomes. Your mind makes you feel guilty for taking this time to be quiet, still, and alone. I promise you, this is the most productive, freeing experience you can have. In the past, I had allowed myself to be driven by a perfection-type makeup so that I would strive in the beginning with sitting still and listening, but the Lord promises that taking this valuable time with Him not only lifts you closer to Him by putting Him first, but also, He redeems the time you have for the rest of the day. I cannot explain that, but it does occur. It seems like if I schedule our time in the morning as soon as I am able, the rest of the day flows with better choices and is smoother. Jim and I work out at the YMCA three to four times a week. Sometimes I stay home after breakfast while he works out, then my quiet time with the Lord, and the joy I feel during and after this time, sets the mood for the day. The Holy Spirit teaches me, brings things to mind what I need to address. If my actions have not glorified Him, He gently disciplines and guides me as I ask for forgiveness and respond out loud to Him about the solution. Sometimes I can feel the dross melting away as I feel His Hand. When I find myself grumpy or irritable during the day, I can slip away into my quiet place to work on myself with worship and praise time, or even when that much time is not possible, I can start praising and speaking my uplifting scriptures out loud. Sometimes Jim will come into a room where I am and hear me speaking and, thinking I am talking to him, ask me, "What did you say, dear?" I will say, "Oh, honey, I am just talking to the Lord." He has gotten used to me after all this time and understands. He actually benefits from my time with the Lord and does not seem to mind. It helps my stress and keeps my mood on a level plane.

You might ask me how long you should plan to spend with the Lord. Sometimes you only have a little window, which is better than nothing. Use the time you can carve out of your day, but plan that activity or it will not happen. The world has a way of gobbling up your time. The time you choose to spend getting to know our God benefits you in all areas and gives you more of everything to give others. I wish I had known this amazing fact when I became a single parent, raising three children and entering the work world while I was grieving and adjusting to the necessary healing that had to take place in me. You cannot give what you do not have, but in spending time with the Lord, He is able to meet your needs as you allow Him to do. Taking time to feel His Love for us and making time to spend with Him feels like discovering a great treasure. Thank the Lord now, for I know what I need, and I realize it helps the relationships I have with others as the Lord gently teaches me His ways. As I die to self, I can draw on more of His personality to replace mine and be more like Him. If you desire to grow in Him, He is there, waiting to help you at any time, and is as close as your breath. Remember, He was the one who gave you that breath, so we can start by praising Him for that. This may seem like a lot to digest, but these are only suggestions. You will develop your own relationship with the Lord, and that Fellowship will be so beautiful that you will be excited to seek His face and experience His Presence as much as possible, for how it will bless your life and the lives of those you encounter along the way.

Footnote
(This is some additional information on the prayer language discussed above.)

My personal observation of Praying in the Spirit from all I have learned is that everyone can have a prayer language if he or she desires, but they do not have to. It is a choice. You can stop and start anytime you want to. Just like a foreign language. No one makes you speak. It took me a while to accept this prayer language, but the more intimate I grew with our Heavenly Father, the more I realized I want everything He has to give me. I have never been led to speak in front of others because I am not aware that I have the Gift of Tongues. If the Lord asked me to, I would obey. My feeling is, we should not get hung up on any gift of the Holy Spirit; just focus on Him. We definitely do not want to cause our brother to stumble in anything we do (Rom. 14:13). Nowhere have I read that speaking in tongues is needed for salvation, but it certainly does draw you closer to the Lord, because you get yourself out of the way and allow room for the Holy Spirit to enable you to impress what God has for you. This is a freeing experience and allows one to get oneself out of the way and allows the Lord to lead. My understanding is that there are two types of Speaking in Tongues. One is for a personal relationship with the Holy Spirit, and the other is one of the Gifts of the Holy Spirit to edify the Church, and an interpretation is required so the whole congregation can understand the Words the Lord has for them. Paul speaks about Tongues in 1 Corinthians chapters 13 and 14. In a church service, there are rules of order which are required. In everything, let us never forget that love is the most important element in our universe, placed there by God, and John 3:16 tells us that God so loved the world that He gave His own Son, that whosoever believes in Him shall not perish but have everlasting life.

Sid Roth's program *It's Supernatural* had a guest, Kevin Zadai, who said he had an after-death experience and went to heaven, met Jesus face-to-face, and saw many things there. Kevin said, "Jesus told me that beyond anything else you could do on this earth, it would be the only thing that He would want you to do is yield to the Spirit of God, and that that would bring forth that utterance which they call speaking in tongues. If you will Pray in the Spirit and bring out the depths and the mysteries of God out into this realm, that the spiritual realm would become so close to me that I'd begin to operate in the spiritual realm here on earth." He stated that each of us has a book that is written about us before we are born (which sounds like the Lord's Perfect Will for us). The books that are written about every individual person are available to the angels that are assigned to each person. Those angels look at those books. They're briefed. Decisions are made on who would influence a group of people, and those angels go to work in bringing the truth to those people and helping them to get other people involved and walking in the spirit with God. Kevin said that when we pray in our heavenly prayer language, the angels are sent to carry out the Lord's will in our lives. They read the book and know what God has in store for us and do what they can to help us (not force us, for we have free will) enter into the Perfect Will of the Lord. (This would certainly be an extremely important reason for desiring the prayer language if a person is truly desirous to allow the Lord to lead his or her life.)

Kevin went on to say, "I found that the most serious asset or liability that we have is our own will. I know that God loves us, but He has to get that across to us. We have to have revelation from the Spirit of God, and many people don't have the revelation of God's love and His concern for us or His plan for us, but these books are full of pages that Jesus said some of them will never be opened, because people don't yield to the Spirit and they don't give their will over. There is a walking in the Spirit that requires you to hand your life over and carry your own cross, and Jesus wanted everyone to know this, that there is power available, but it's going to be by you losing and Him gaining you." Kevin also said Jesus said, "You've got to teach people to receive from me. I want to bless them." Kevin said we receive by turning over our will to the Almighty God.

Dawna DeSilva says, "Speaking in tongues disengaged my mind and engaged the Spirit world and the Lord. It chases fear, dispels a thick atmosphere, and releases peace. I believe it prepares our mind to hear the Holy Spirit talking to us."

Here is what *Charisma News* reports about scientific tests on the brain when a subject is speaking in tongues (which was very interesting to me) that I found on Google.

In 2006, researchers at the University of Pennsylvania took brain images of five people while they spoke in tongues. Their research was published in *The New York Times*. The leader of the study team was Dr. Andrew Newberg, who arrived at this conclusion:

> We noticed a number of changes that occurred functionally in the brain. Our finding of decreased activity in the frontal lobes during the practice of speaking in tongues is fascinating because these subjects truly believe that the spirit of God is moving through them and controlling them to speak. Our brain-imaging research shows us that these subjects are not in control of the usual language centers during this activity, which is consistent with their description of a lack of intentional control while speaking in tongues.

When they prayed in tongues, their frontal lobes, the willful part of the brain we use to think and control what we do, were quiet. The language center of their brains—the part we use to speak in our native language—were quiet as well. The people were not in a trance; they were fully aware of what was happening. The researchers were unable to pinpoint which part of the brain was controlling this behavior of speaking in tongues. Dr. Newberg went on to say, "The amazing thing was how the images supported people's interpretation of what was happening. The way they describe it, and what they believe, is that God is talking through them."

Speaking in Tongues is clearly not a fabricated language, as these scientists have confirmed. It is a spiritual language given to us by God to communicate with Him.

There has been much written and debated about the prayer language. I will not elaborate on this very special gift from the Lord, just enough to say that it is a gift from God for today, and if you are desirous to have it, ask the Lord to show you His way for obtaining it. As mentioned before, nowhere in Scripture does it state speaking in tongues or a prayer language is necessary for salvation. The Holy Spirit brings it to you as He did in the time of Pentecost. In Verse

5, Jesus said, "For John truly baptized with water; but ye shall be baptized with the Holy Spirit." Jesus told His disciples to tarry and wait (Acts 1:4). In verse 8, the Lord said, "Ye shall receive POWER after the Holy Spirit is come upon you, and you shall be witnesses unto me both in Jerusalem, and in all Judea, and in Samaria and unto the uttermost part of the earth." Jesus is giving them power to be witnesses and telling them to desire to be baptized in the Holy Spirit as part of the Discipleship process of making Jesus Lord of their lives. Acts 2:2–3 (at Pentecost) states, "Suddenly there came a sound from heaven as of a rushing mighty wind, and it [He] filled all the house where they were sitting. And there appeared unto them cloven tongues like as of fire, and it sat upon each of them. And they were filled with the Holy Spirit and began to speak with other tongues as the Spirit gave them utterance." In verse 16, there is reference to what was spoken by the prophet Joel in the last days. Read about the end-time signs so you will know what to expect (verses 17 through 20). In verse 21, it finishes the thought with, "And it shall come to pass that whosoever shall call on the name of the Lord shall be saved!" This shows the importance of becoming an empowered disciple to go into the world and spread the good news (Mark 16:15; Matt. 28:19). Read what vital instruction the Lord told His disciples just before He left the earth and ascended to His Father.

Please note that Paul encouraged Christians to follow the practice of speaking in tongues in their private prayer lives, as it is the doorway to the supernatural (1 Cor. 12:1) and it magnifies God. It also builds up oneself when one needs strengthening in the Lord through the supernatural. We all need spiritual encouragement when journeying through this fallen world. My personal thought is that I want all the Lord has for me that can draw me closer to where He wants me to be. We sometimes desire to tell God how we want Him to deal with us, but our prayer needs to have thine own will, Lord.

## Weapons Provided for a Believer
## Spiritual Warfare

These weapons are meant to be used by believers. These subjects discussed here are weapons to be used by the believer of the Lord Jesus Christ after He has become Savior and Lord of the believer's life. Only then can one use the Blood of Jesus for a sin covering and protection. If you have not made that commitment, please stop here and read Romans 10:9, which says, "Because, if you confess with your lips that Jesus is Lord and believe in your heart that God raised Him from the dead, you will be saved. For man believes with his heart and so is justified, and he confesses with his lips and so is saved." Then verse 13 says, "For everyone who calls upon the name of the Lord will be saved." Admit to God you are a sinner, ask the Lord Jesus into your heart to take away your sins and cleanse you, then commit to making Him Lord of your life with each day, looking to Him for your answers. Find a Bible-preaching church with warm fellowship, read your Bible often, and learn to love your fellow men and treat them as Christ treated us while He was here on earth. Start walking the path the Lord intended you to have. As you read and search the Bible, you will feel excited, like you are on a treasure hunt for the golden nuggets the Lord has in store for you. Be patient with yourself but never stop learning and growing in Him. (It is like being on a diet. You did not get all that weight overnight. It takes time and patience to overcome.) This first step is essential. Then as you share your new life in fellowship, you grow, and others grow in turn. God honors even little steps and gently lifts you up when you fall down. I think of the process as this: I accept the Lord as my Savior, then each day I prove I made that decision by putting the Lord first and His Will for me, which makes Him Lord of my life. It is like putting my actions where my mouth is. There is a scripture that tells us to work out our own salvation with fear (reverence) and trembling (Phil. 2:12).

Love

Remember how we began our walk in this book? God is love. Everything He did for us in the beginning was love. When Adam and Eve disobeyed in the garden, He had a plan of love to bring mankind back to Him, in love. John 1:1 tells us, "In the beginning was the Word, and the Word was with God, and the Word was God." Verse 12 states, "But to all who received Him, who believed in His name, He gave power to become children of God; who were born, not of blood nor of the will of the flesh nor of the will of man, but of God!" Verse 14 says, "And the Word became flesh [Jesus] and dwelt among us, full of grace and truth; we have beheld His Glory, glory as of the only Son from the Father." John 3:16 says, "For God so loved the world that He gave His only begotten Son that whoever believed in Him shall not perish but have everlasting life!" What a gift to mankind was that! Believing and acting upon the first and Great Commandment that Jesus said. "Love the Lord your God with all your heart and soul and mind and your neighbor as yourself" (Matt. 22:3; Luke 10:27). This gives you a strength and power straight from the Lord. Obeying the wisdom of the Ten Commandments condensed as a guide to live by creates an atmosphere of love and caring the Lord desires us to operate in daily. How our world could change if we kept these instructions from the Lord operating in our relationship with others! Jesus came to earth to show us the Father's love and to make the ultimate sacrifice so His creation could return to Him in a perfect world that He had intended for us. This power of love lifts us above the chaos of this world into the heavenly realm if we allow it to do so, and we can truly live on both planes simultaneously if we allow the Lord to help us soar on the wings of love straight to His Heart. Drawing on His love during our intimacy with Him allows His Love to manifest in our lives and in all we do and then produces power to stand against with adversary when he tries to influence or overwhelm us!

The Mighty Name of Jesus and the Blood of Jesus
When God created the world, He gave mankind dominion to rule over all His creations, but sin entered the perfect environment He created, and mankind sold out that dominion to satan, who now is the god of this world. When Jesus came the first time to restore what mankind had lost, His precious Blood on the Cross was the ultimate sacrifice for sin. He cried out, "It is finished!" He came to restore mankind to an intimate relationship with God. Mankind could now fellowship directly to the Father through the Holy Spirit because Jesus Christ had paid the price for mankind's sin. We can plead the Blood to cover us and protect us. We can use the Name of Jesus because we belong to Him, and He has made us overcomers to be able to speak His Name with authority. We speak that with our voice out loud because the Blood of the Lord Jesus fulfilled the scripture in Genesis 3:15 when God cursed the serpent. "I will put enmity between you and the woman, and between your seed and her seed: He shall bruise your head and you shall bruise His heel." God said to satan, who had used the serpent to bring down the human race, the woman shall be used an instrument to bring the Redeemer into the world to save the human race from the clutches of satan. "He will overcome you and restore mankind to the place I planned for mankind before the sin entered the garden." (Satan was a defeated foe at the cross by the precious blood of Jesus!)

Bloodline Prayers
These are prayers to issue a restraining order to reverse generational curses (redeeming your bloodline from curses). Jesus set us free to live a full life of peace, joy, and strength. In the spiritual realm, the adversary (accuser) is bringing claims against us in the Spiritual Court and praying the bloodline prayers can dissolve ancient spiritual covenants and claims that affect our everyday lives. There are several good books on this principle and prayers to overcome the adversary!

Hrvoje Sirovina and Robert Henderson have a book, *Redeeming Your Bloodline*. I Googled the subject and found a very illuminating article by Michael Bradley in Bible-Knowledge.com that is certainly worth reading. When you pray bloodline prayers, you actively apply the power of Jesus's Blood to your life. Always end your request and prayers with "In the name of Jesus." There is power in His Name!

Discernment, Awareness of the Enemy: Take Control of Your Own Mind

Choose what enters and stays in your mind. Be aware and alert. Your adversary, the devil, walks around like a roaring lion to deceive you (1 Pet. 5:8). I saw a cartoon of an angel sitting on the right shoulder and the devil sitting on the left shoulder. Both were whispering into the ear of the person. This probably is not just a cartoon. We can fine-tune our discernment to distinguish where the voices come from. If it agrees with Scripture, it is of the Lord; if it does not, stand against it, for you do not want to be lured into the wrong path and decision. The Lord gave us free will, and He will never take that away from us. We were made in His Image and are the only part of creation that was given a free will. Your wisdom to seek the Lord is found in James 3:13–18. Do you realize there are three voices speaking to your subconscious mind? There is the Lord, the adversary, and your own self (which actually is influenced by the adversary). After reading many books about the mind and how it controls our being, I realized the most effective way to control ourselves and reprogram any detrimental or nonproductive habit is our own spoken word, which goes directly into our subconscious. Whom do you listen to? Have you believed a lie straight from the pit of hell? So many people I have talked to certainly have. I am sorry to say I did. It seemed like my Dad did not love me, because he did not discipline me or show me affection—I did not feel his love. The truth was, he was concerned he would hurt me if he spanked me, and it was difficult for him to show me "daughter" affection. He was very affectionate with Mother, so as I watched that, I felt rejection, which carried through much of my adulthood. It was a lie! Later as the healing process began with my seeking the Lord and learning more about myself and how the mind works, I felt freedom. I had locked on to a lie and believed it from the adversary. Free yourself from the lies you have believed during your lifetime because freedom from the adversary and his tricks unchain you to be freer to worship the Lord and grow in His wisdom and direction more quickly. Spend time allowing the Holy Spirit to free your past with forgiveness and love so you will not be drawn back at the mention of it by the enemy.

God offers freedom, so choose to seek Him now while He may be found (Isa. 55:6–7).

(The chapter "What Voices Are You Listening To?" goes into more detail.)

Words of Scripture
Since all of creation came from "God said," words are so powerful. Praying Scripture produces power and encouragement for the seeker. Words are containers and are weapons to speak and stand on. "Submit yourself and satan must flee" (James 4:7), or "Greater is He that is in me than he that is in the world" (1 John 4:4). When God created the world, He gave mankind dominion to rule over all His creations, but sin entered the perfect environment He created and mankind sold out that dominion to satan, who now is the god of this world. When Jesus came the first time to restore what mankind had lost, His precious Blood on the Cross was the ultimate sacrifice for sin. He cried out, "It is finished!" He came to restore mankind to an intimate relationship with God. Mankind could now fellowship directly to the Father through the Holy Spirit because Jesus Christ had paid the price for mankind's sin. After Jesus left the earth, His sent the Comforter (the Holy Spirit, the Paraclete) to be available to

His restored creation at any time, at any place. The believer is now a Priest after the Order of Melchizedek (Ps. 110:4). That means a believer who has accepted Jesus as Savior and Lord of his or her life can now go directly to Father God by way of Jesus Christ through the intimacy of the Holy Spirit. In the Old Testament, God set up a Priest to hear directly from God, and he would inform the people of God's Will and how to live. Now we can access God directly, anytime, anyplace, for He told us He would never leave us or forsake us (Deut. 31:6). If a person is not a practicing part of the Jewish religion, one does not have a clue what an awesome gift that was. In the Old Testament, sacrifices had to be brought to the temple, different types for different sins. All that type of sacrificing was eliminated when Jesus Christ came the first time to die for our sins and we were forgiven and restored fellowship with God. In Matthew 21:21, Jesus tells us, "Speak to the mountain [with faith and not doubt] and say to this mountain go, throw yourself into the sea, and it will be done!" Words are powerful combined with faith, without doubt. Start a notebook of your favorite scriptures, memorize them, speak them to your subconscious, and share with others when it is appropriate. Remember the Protection Psalm of 91. Read it and speak it often!

Gifts

From the Holy Spirit, the precious Bridegroom has given His Bride gifts already. The whole chapter 12 of 1 Corinthians explains gifts. Read the scripture and meditate on the gifts and determine what gift(s) you were given by the Lord to bless His Bride and further the Kingdom. The gifts are listed in verse 4. "Now there are varieties of gifts, but the same Spirit, and there are varieties of service, but the same Lord. By the same Spirit, there is the utterance of wisdom, the utterance of knowledge, to another faith, to another healing, to another the working of miracles, to another prophecy, to another to distinguish between spirits, to another various kinds of tongues, and to another the interpretation of tongues." The Scripture goes on to say, "For just as the body is one and has many members, and all the members of the body, though many, are one body, so it is with Christ." The Lord gives us these gifts to help us be overcomers in the fallen world. After Jesus left the earth, He sent the Comforter (the Holy Spirit, the Paraclete) to fill His restored creation, to be available at any time, at any place. The believer is now a Priest after the Order of Melchizedek (Ps. 110:4). That means a believer who has accepted Jesus as Savior and Lord of his or her life can now go directly to Father God by way of Jesus Christ through the intimacy of the Holy Spirit. In the Old Testament, God set up a Priest to hear directly from God, and he would inform the people of God's Will and how to live. Also, in the Old Testament, the Holy Spirit came upon the anointed ones God selected to do His Will. Now we can access God directly, anytime, anyplace, for He told us He would never leave us or forsake us (Deut. 31:6). Now, the direct connection to God is within us by way of the Holy Spirit, and we are directly linked to His Presence anytime we take the time to be there. Not being a practicing part of the Jewish religion, we do not have a clue what a gift that was. In the Old Testament, sacrifices had to be brought to the temple, different types for different sins, but all that was eliminated when Jesus Christ came the first time to die for our sins. From the Holy Spirit, the precious Bridegroom has given His Bride gifts already. The whole chapter 12 of 1 Corinthians explains gifts. Some say, "The gifts are not available since Jesus left the earth." I do not believe that; we need them now more than ever since Jesus left. We know a loving bridegroom never takes back his gifts from his bride.

Tithing
You may respond with, "How in the world can tithing be a weapon against the adversary?" Kevin Zadai, a guest on Sid Roth's program, stated that the adversary thinks all money in the world belongs to

him, and does not want Christians to have any money, even wages we earn or a penny picked up on the ground. Everything actually belongs to God, for He created it, and when we give the tithe of 10 percent or give to anything we do for the advancement of the Kingdom of God, we are exercising our Sonship and understanding God's covenant authority of man over satan, given before the fall. We are doing warfare against the devil and renewing our proper place in the Kingdom that Jesus had restored to us with His precious Blood on the Cross after the fall. Honoring God first by trusting Him with earthly things as important as money is to everyone on earth puts the adversary in his place.

Intimate Time with the Holy Spirit

The Lord gave us the precious gift of free will, which none of His other creations enjoy. With that gift, we are now responsible for choosing to spend quality time with the Lord through the Holy Spirit to determine what He has in mind for our lives. In the Old Testament, the people had God's chosen Priest to relay the Lord's messages, but now we have the freedom and responsibility to seek God's plan for each of us. He does have an individual plan for each of us. We seek the general plan through Scripture, then what He has for us individually through time spent in His Presence. He never goes against His Words to us but lovingly reaches out to inform us as we seek His Face. What a joy to hear that Still Small Voice and hear our Lord speak to our hearts to love us, guide us, and refine us through His Holy Spirit! Refinement is not always pleasant but necessary so our direct line with God can be free of the stumbling blocks we have directly or indirectly caused to be there. Prayer is exciting. Go on a treasure hunt with the Holy Spirit today and regain the enthusiasm for life and direction He desires for us. He has so many blessings and adventures to share with those whose seek Him. (More details are in the chapter "Ways to Develop Intimacy with the Holy Spirit.")

Put on Your Armor

"Finally, be strong in the Lord and in the strength of His might. Put on the whole armor of God, that you may be able to stand against the wiles of the devil. For we are not contending against flesh and blood, but against the principalities, against the powers, against the world rulers of this present darkness, against the spiritual hosts of wickedness in the heavenly places. Therefore take the whole armor of God, that you may be able to withstand in the evil day, and having done all, to STAND! Stand, therefore, having girded your loins with truth, and having put on the breastplate of righteousness, and having shod your feet with the equipment of the gospel of peace, above all taking the shield of faith, with which you can quench all the flaming darts of the evil one. And take the helmet of salvation, and sword of the Spirit, which is the Word of God. Pray at all times in the Spirit, with all prayer and supplication. To that end keep alert with all perseverance, making supplication for all the saints" (Eph. 6:10–18).

In olden times, warriors prepared for battle by putting on the armor before battle. We are told to prepare for our daily battles this way. Each piece of armor is for a specific type of battle. Defensive armor for protection includes the helmet (for the head); the girdle that supports daggers, swords, and other weapons; the breastplate to cover the chest and other vital organs, in two parts, extending down the legs; the brazen boots to protect the feet against rocks, thorns, etc.; and the shield to protect the body from blows and cuts. The offensive armor includes the sword, lance, etc. to overcome the enemy. Spiritually, we gird our loins with truth of the Scripture and God's Will. The breastplate of righteousness is willingly allowing the Lord to refine you to prepare you as a witness for spreading the gospel (good news). To shod your feet with the equipment of the gospel of peace means to prepare to take that gospel wherever the road takes you. Then above all, taking the shield of faith, in which you have been given a certain measure of faith when you became a believer, allowing it to grow as you grow closer to the Lord, knowing He has given you what you need to overcome the adversary, for you are able to quench the flaming darts of the evil one. Take the sword of the Spirit, which is the Word of God, that you are learning as you grow in your walk. Pray in the Spirit, praising the Lord and thanking Him for His many blessings. Keep alert and pray for yourself and others. Be a prayer warrior ready to stand on the Word and stand for the Lord against the adversary. The Lord prepares us for battle as we reach out to Him and allow Him to dress us in His Armor.

Prayers and Your Prayer Language

These are weapons as well. Prayers are essential to Christian growth for ourselves and the Body of Believers. It is something every one of us can do for ourselves. Jesus was asked by His disciples how to pray. In Matthew 6:5, Jesus tells us how to pray. Read through 15 for The Lord's Prayer and Jesus's comment about how important forgiveness is before praying. All through this book is help in praying. To understand Praying in the Spirit, read the chapter about Intimacy with the Holy Spirit, if you want to learn more about this prayer language. In the Scripture just quoted, in Ephesians 6:11, Paul tells us to pray at all times in the Spirit, with all prayer and supplication. In 2 Corinthians 12:7–10, Paul said he was given a thorn in the flesh, a messenger of satan. You can imagine he prayed in his prayer language when his human mind did not understand about that. The Lord told him that His grace was sufficient for him after Paul asked the Lord to remove the thorn three times. Most of us will not be asked to endure what Paul did for the sake of the gospel, but we need to see our hearts to know we are truly willing. So as a final note in warfare, we are so thankful that when we come to the end of what we can do, we can relax and allow the Lord to do what He does. We can rely on Him and trust Him for strength and guidance to bring us through any situation. Look at Paul's life (2 Timothy 3:11 refers to some of it). He was shipwrecked, was stoned and left for dead, was bitten by a deadly serpent and lived, had been in prison, was beaten five times with the forty lashes save one (the same type of scourging that Christ received before crucifixion), etc., until finally, later, he was decapitated. He fought and honored God with his trust, long-suffering, and faithfulness to the Lord. May we also learn from the example Paul set and be willing to enter into the Lord's suffering if He requires it from us to further the Kingdom of God. I do believe, as we can catch a glimpse of the eternal Kingdom, keeping our eyes fixed on the Lord, that vision can bring us through, knowing this suffering is for a short time but our life with God Almighty will flow through the rest of our existence. When we do not know how to pray, shut out the adversary, pray in the Spirit, for that dispatches the angels to read your Book in Heaven and come to your aid to help you do the Perfect Will of the Father. Praise God!

The Fruit of the Spirit
As the Lord gently and tenderly grows us up in Him, the fruit of the spirit is made manifest. "But the fruit of the Spirit is love, joy, peace, patience, kindness, goodness, faithfulness, gentleness, self-control; against such there is no law" (Gal. 5:22–23). As we become a new creation in Christ after we receive Jesus as our Savior and Lord (2 Cor. 5:17), we begin changing as the Lord refines us in His love. The old nature begins to pass away. We begin to die to our old ways, the old nature, and begin to take on the qualities of the Lord, our new nature from Christ. As He refines us, He starts removing the dross to make us the new creation that He desires us to become. How does this happen? As you learn to die to your old ways (self), you are able to replace that with an improved nature straight from the Lord. It happens slowly, like how fruit on a tree manifests as the tree matures to be able to hold on to the fruit. (I am learning to stop and ask what the Lord would do in a situation, then ask Him for His guidance and

submit to His Will instead of just reacting to a situation. Learn to be an actor, not a reactor.) Read the chapter titled "The Fruit of the Spirit" for more in-depth information.

Praise and Thanksgiving
All to God in everything. The first book of Thessalonians 5:18 says to us to rejoice always, pray constantly, give thanks in all circumstances, for this is the Will of God in Christ Jesus for you. When you are in His Will, there is power. There is also power in gratitude; it shows us we are not in control—God is! If we are engaged in praise and worship, we are directing our praise to God, focusing on Him, and the adversary is behind us. Ephesians 5:20 tells us to always and, for everything, give thanks in the name of our Lord Jesus Christ to God the Father.

John Ramirez, who was a devil worshiper for twenty-five years and came to the Lord quite a few years, said, "The devil has three steps to tormenting. Tormenting fear has three steps—worry, panic attacks, and then tormentings of fear. So the devil will start with the worry. Worry factor, worry this, worry that. Worry at your job, worry about your tomorrow, worry about your future, worry about your family, worry about your finances, worry about your career. And then it goes into panic attacks. And after panic attack, the devil put the nail in the coffin, which is he released the tormentors of fear upon you, upon your family. But I got good news. I know how to fight, dismantle, uproot, and destroy fear out of your life, once and for all. I had to know how to do it, because I was one of them. I was one of them that used to do, apply that kind of spiritual technique on people's lives for twenty-five years. I want to teach you how you can take that fear off, uproot it, and live in total freedom. I believe you have to make a decision. I always say, you have to make that decision. You have to step forward. You have to really say, 'What, fear? I renounced you. I rebuke you. Today is a day that you're leaving my life!'"

Know the truth and allow the Lord to set you free. Please never forget 2 Corinthians 10:3–5: "For though we walk in the flesh, we do not war after the flesh. For the weapons of our warfare are not carnal, but mighty through God to the pulling down of strongholds. Casting down imaginations, and every high thing that exalts itself against the knowledge of God, and bringing into captivity every thought to the obedience of Christ." Our imagination is a powerful thing. Used as a positive, it is hope. It is the ability to see with the heart what you are unable to see with your eyes now. As you visualize, you compel yourself to inspired action. Walk by faith, on God's Word, and see the finished product like God does, the end from the beginning. We visualize all the time in everything, so paint the correct, powerful picture in your mind and act upon it. Practice this in everything and take your worry, which is very negative, and exchange it for hope and action, to overcome the world and the adversary.

Thoughts to Loose the Good Spirits

*Spirit of Adoption.* "For you have not received the spirit of bondage again to fear, but have received the Spirit of adoption whereby we cry, 'Abba, Father'" (Rom. 8:15).

Spirit of Grace and Supplication cause them to look upon Jesus, who was pierced (Zech. 12:10).

*Ministering Spirits are* sent forth to them who shall be heirs of salvation (Heb. 1:13–14).

*Holy Spirit.* (A familiar spirit is a counterpart to the Holy Spirit.) Discern between the two by the known fruit. "Ye shall know them by their fruit...a corrupt tree brings forth evil fruit" (Matt. 7:16–17). The Holy Spirit shows us the truth and by it sets us free—a valuable Gift of the Holy Spirit is the discerning of spirits, by which this revelation was given. (I have seen people set free by the knowledge of spirits and the power of the Holy Spirit.)

Human beings are held captive of satan and cannot free

themselves from the invisible cells or bars. They are held captive in fear, disease, failure, bondage to sin, and evil habits that destroy the body, soul, and spirit (Acts 26:17–18; Mark 16:17). Only the power of the Holy Spirit can set a person free, because "greater is He that is within you than he that is in the world" (1 John 4:4), and no weapon formed against you shall prosper, and every tongue that shall rise against you in judgment, you shall condemn. "This is the heritage of the servants of the Lord, and their righteousness is from me, says the Lord" (Isa. 54:17). You are an overcomer (Rom. 8:37; 1 John 5:5).

God does not give us a spirit of fear and timidity, but of power, of love, and of a sound mind (2 Tim. 1:7).

# Crying Out to God
## And Some of God's Responses

*Crying Out in Scripture*
The following Hebrew and Greek words, their definitions, and the descriptions of how they are used in Scripture give a clear picture of what it means to cry out.

*A Cry of Deep Distress: Za'aq (Hebrew)*
God "didst see the affliction of our fathers in Egypt, and heardest their cry [za'aq] by the Red sea...and...didst divide the sea before them, so that they went through the midst of the sea on the dry land" (Neh. 9:9–11).

*To Cry Out for Help: Tsa'aq (Hebrew)*
When the Israelites could not find fresh water in the wilderness, Moses "cried [tsa'aq] unto the Lord; and the Lord showed him a tree, which when he had cast into the waters, the waters were made sweet" (Exod. 15:25).

*To Call with a Loud Sound: Qara' (Hebrew)*
"Jabez called [qara'] on the God of Israel, saying, Oh that thou wouldest bless me indeed....And God granted him that which he requested" (1 Chron. 4:10).

*To Shout a War Cry: Ruwa (Hebrew)*
"Then the men of Judah gave a shout [ruwa]: and as the men of Judah shouted, it came to pass, that God smote Jeroboam and all Israel" (2 Chron. 13:15).

*A Cry for Help: Shavah (Hebrew)*
"He will fulfill the desire of them that fear him: he also will hear their cry [shavah], and will save them" (Ps. 145:19).

*A Cry of Deep Distress: Tsaaqah (Hebrew)*
"He forgetteth not the cry [tsaaqah] of the humble" (Ps. 9:12).

*To Cry Out: Krazo (Greek)*
When the Apostle Peter walked out on the water at the invitation of Jesus, Peter was "afraid; and beginning to sink, he cried [krazo], saying, Lord, save me. And immediately Jesus stretched forth his hand, and caught him" (Matt. 14:30–31).

*To Implore with Strong Voice: Boao (Greek)*
A blind man in Jericho heard that Jesus was passing near him. "And he cried [boao], saying, Jesus, thou son of David, have mercy on me.... And Jesus said unto him, Receive thy sight: thy faith hath saved thee" (Luke 18:38–42).

*Characteristics of a Cry*
Crying out to God is an act of desperation and total concentration. It is a fervent expression of faith in God and trust in His goodness and power to act on your behalf. Crying out to God expresses the following traits:

*Genuine Humility*
It is hard for people to admit that they cannot solve a problem or overcome an obstacle, but it is true that we need God's help. He delights in a broken and contrite heart that humbly seeks His aid. "He forgetteth not the cry of the humble" (Ps. 9:12; also Ps. 10:17).

*Unconditional Surrender*
When a situation becomes so desperate that only God can deliver you, a cry represents total, unconditional surrender. Don't try to bargain with God—leave your life in His hands. "If I regard iniquity in my heart, the Lord will not hear me" (Ps. 66:18).

*A Plea for Mercy*
Apart from Christ, we have no value that merits God's favor. When driven to a point of despair or destruction, your unworthiness before God often becomes more apparent, and it can motivate you to cry out to Him for mercy. "It is of the Lord's mercies that we are not consumed, because his compassions fail not. They are new every morning: great is thy faithfulness" (Lam. 3:22–23).

*Personal Helplessness*
Do you tend to believe that you need God's help with only the really hard things? Remember, Jesus said, "Without me ye can do nothing" (John 15:5).

*Faith in God's Power and Resources*
Your cry to God acknowledges God's ability to do what no one else can do. During the storm on the Sea of Galilee, the disciples acknowledged Jesus's power to rescue them when they cried out, "Lord, save us: we perish" (Matt. 8:25.)

*Desperation*
Crying out to God is an admission of one's need for God. The psalmist declared, "In my distress I called upon the Lord, and cried unto my God: He heard my voice out of his temple, and my cry came before him, even into his ears" (Ps. 18:6).

*Examples of God's Response to Crying Out*
The Bible is filled with examples of times when God answered the cries of His people. Below are a few examples of occasions on which individuals cried out to God and God heard their cries and delivered them:

*Elijah Cried Out, and God Revived a Dead Child*
"He cried unto the Lord, and said, O Lord my God, hast thou also

brought evil upon the widow with whom I sojourn, by slaying her son? And he stretched himself upon the child three times, and cried unto the Lord, and said, O Lord my God, I pray thee, let this child's soul come into him again. And the Lord heard the voice of Elijah; and the soul of the child came into him again, and he revived" (1 Kings 17:20–22).

### Jehoshaphat Cried Out, and God Delivered Him from Death
"It came to pass, when the captains of the chariots saw Jehoshaphat, that they said, It is the king of Israel. Therefore they compassed about him to fight: but Jehoshaphat cried out, and the Lord helped him; and God moved them to depart from him" (2 Chron. 18:31).

### Hezekiah Cried Out, and God Gave Him Victory
"Hezekiah the king, and the prophet Isaiah the son of Amoz, prayed and cried to heaven. And the Lord sent an angel, which cut off all the mighty men of valor, and the leaders and captains in the camp of the king of Assyria. So he returned with shame of face to his own land" (2 Chron. 32:20–21).

### Jesus's Disciples Cried Out to Him in a Storm, and Jesus Calmed the Sea
"As they sailed he fell asleep: and there came down a storm of wind on the lake; and they were filled with water, and were in jeopardy. And they came to him, and awoke him, saying, Master, master, we perish. Then he arose, and rebuked the wind and the raging of the water: and they ceased, and there was a calm" (Luke 8:23–24).

### Blind Bartimaeus Called to Jesus, and He Restored His Sight
"And they came to Jericho. And as he was leaving Jericho with his disciples and a great crowd, Bartimaeus, a blind beggar, the son of Timaeus, was sitting by the roadside. And when he heard that it was Jesus of Nazareth, he began to cry out and say, 'Jesus, Son of David, have mercy on me!' And many rebuked him, telling him to be silent.

But he cried out all the more, 'Son of David, have mercy on me!' And Jesus stopped and said, 'Call him.' And they called the blind man, saying to him, 'Take heart. Get up; He is calling you.' And throwing off his cloak, he sprang up and came to Jesus. And Jesus said to him, 'What do you want me to do for you?' And the blind man said to him, 'Rabbi, let me recover my sight.' And Jesus said to him, 'Go your way; your faith has made you well.' And immediately he recovered his sight and followed him on the way" (Mark 10:46).

An Invitation from the Living God

Psalm 50:15 declares this Word from the Lord: "Call upon me in the day of trouble: I will deliver thee." We are children of the living God, and our Heavenly Father appeals to us to cry out to Him for deliverance. Let us be quick to cry out to Him with humility, sincerity, and faith. God "will fulfill the desire of them that fear him: he also will hear their cry, and will save them" (Ps. 145:19).

The following article is adapted from materials in the Anger Resolution Seminar.

Since God is no respecter of persons, He can talk to any believer through the "Still Small Voice within" if a believer will spend the quiet time with Him and desires His Presence. Psalm 138 says, "In the day when I cried out, you answered me, and made me bold with strength in my soul." In one of Dr. David Jeremiah's daily devotionals, he stated, "The amazing fact is that God has no limits. A key turning point in our lives comes the moment we recognize our weaknesses, and trust our lives to Him. When we stop pretending that we have god-like abilities and cry out to Him. This is one of the reasons Paul could write, 'When I am weak, then I Am strong' [2 Cor. 12:10]. The Bible promises that as you cry out, He is ready to answer and make you bold and strong in the Spirit!"

Our pastor Willie preached a sermon, "I Will Answer," and it really spoke to the congregation. He quoted this Scripture, Jeremiah 33:3, "Call to me and I will answer, and show you great and mighty

CRYING OUT TO GOD

things which you do not know." The RSV Bible says hidden things that I take to mean His mysteries. God desires an interchange with us, which is what fellowship is all about. Psalm 46 is an awesome Psalm. Please read the whole thing and get blessed with the comfort and peace it gives you. "God is our refuse and strength, a very present help in trouble." Keep reading down to verse 10, which keeps coming to my mind: "Be still and know I AM God." If you ever need to feel the Presence of the Lord and who He really is, read the whole Psalm out loud and bask in His glorious, magnificent Presence. Read this and fear will have to flee because there is no place in Him for fear, only peace, joy, and love with strength and power. Selah at the end of many Psalms and also in Habakkuk does not have a clear meaning. Some say it is used in music as a pause to catch the breath at the end of a line. Selah may have been used to "pause and calmly think about that" (what was just read), lifting up our hearts in praise to God for His great truths, His mercy, power, sustaining grace, and sufficiency. Our Pastor took us through Psalm 88, and if you have not read it, you should, for Heman cried out to God the whole Psalm with more things than most of us experience. Psalm 34:17 brings us back to God's mercy. He hears and delivers us out of our troubles, and verse 22 tells us, "The Lord redeems the soul of His servants: and none of them who trust in Him shall be desolate!" These are promises we can stand on and believe because God said them.

We can all relate to God's deliverance from storms in Psalms 107:19–21. When we cry out to the Lord in our trouble, "He saves us out of our distress. He sent His Word, and healed us, and delivered us from our destructions. Oh, that men would praise the Lord for His goodness and for His wonderful works to the children of men!" With grace and mercy the Lord saves us. This refers to Christ's work on the Cross for us (Rom. 8:2). Let us praise the Lord constantly for His mighty care of us.

182

A blind man in Jericho heard that Jesus was passing near him. "And he cried, saying, Jesus, thou son of David, have mercy on me.... And Jesus said unto him, Receive thy sight: thy faith hath saved thee" (Luke 18:38–42). There are references all through Scripture where man cries out to God and God listens and responds. God promises, "If you call on me, I will answer. I will show you great and mighty things. I am always available to you 24-7, anytime, anyplace!" His answer may not be what you want it to be, but listen to God. He will clearly direct your path. The power of prayer cannot be emphasized enough. That will be discussed more in the chapter about prayers.

Psalm 50:15 declares this Word from the Lord: "Call upon me in the day of trouble: I will deliver thee." We are children of the living God, and our Heavenly Father appeals to us to cry out to Him for deliverance. Let us be quick to cry out to Him with humility, sincerity, and faith. God "will fulfill the desire of them that fear him: he also will hear their cry, and will save them" (Ps. 145:19). Crying out to God is an act of desperation and total concentration. It is a fervent expression of faith in God and trust in His goodness and power to act on your behalf. Crying out to God expresses the following traits: genuine humility, unconditional surrender, a plea for mercy, personal helplessness, faith in God's power and resources, and desperation. I researched on Google "Crying Out to God." I was led to the Institute in Basic Life Principles, and their Anger Resolution Seminar had some great posting about it.

Examples of My Writings to the Lord: Crying Out to God
As I Spent Quiet Time with Him
I date my journaling because I can look back and remember what the Lord has brought me through during certain seasons of my life. Sometime the messages are just personal to my current needs or the general needs of our body of believers, and sometimes there

are messages that are designed to share with others. Sometimes it seems like it is Jesus talking to me, and sometimes God the Father, all through the Holy Spirit, which manifests personally through that Still Small Voice.

Learning the Wisdom of Lessons of Life
"God, we know you have our good in mind always, but sometimes it is wrapped in so much pain and suffering it is difficult to discern in this limited environment. You impressed on me years ago. I must enter into the 'suffering that is bound to come to us here on earth to value the suffering that our Lord did on the cross for us.' That is hard to fathom, but use my short comings to your glory, and as I die to self and truly surrender to your perfect will in my life, help me to trust and always praise you in everything with thanksgiving, offering up my life to you in your care to direct my path. Your ways are higher than my ways, and your thoughts are higher than my thoughts. Help me to learn my lessons quickly and allow you to work out the dross in exchange for gold." (January 28, 2015)

Here is an example of my crying out to God, and then His response at the same sitting. This is how personal the fellowship becomes as you honor God with your time and desire His intimacy.

"Lord, I am having difficulty sensing your Presence today. I need our time together and have been hungry for listening. Quieten my mind and allow me to hear that Still Small Voice that means so much to my life!"

"Child, I am here. Reach out and up, for I see your desire to meet me in your special worship place. I am here now for you. Sometimes nothing has to be said. We are merely together like dear friends who can sit next to each other and not say a word, just be next to each other, content in our just being together. You do this with your husband, so that should not seem strange to you. Know I am always here, dear one." (January 16, 2015)

What a comfort I received when my heart was troubled and I needed my Abba Father!

I noticed as I journaled more, longer messages were poured out for me. The images the Lord placed in my mind were glorious! I was mindful to check everything I received to make sure it was scripturally sound, for I only wanted to honor God with my intimacy, not add anything of my own. The comfort, encouragement, joy, and delight I received from those "Still Small Voice" visits were incredible. Anytime I needed quiet time with the Lord, He was available, no waiting, 24-7, always available to me anytime, day or night, as close as a breath, closer than a brother. He honored every effort on my part and poured out His mighty love every time. Some messages I felt led to title; the others I did not receive a title.

(God's Powerful Presence)
"My children need me more than ever at this time. The adversary is scheming and pouring out his vile now, but greater is my power within you than all he can conjure up. My power created all things perfect, and then he began his perversion—choose this day who you will follow, and I am here to walk with you every step of the way! Just put your foot forward, one step at a time, and I will never forsake you, for your God is by your side to love, comfort, and provide your needs, sometimes even before you know what they are. Even when you don't sense my Presence, I am here." (January 20, 2015)

God, you are more than enough! (My prayer to Him. This was written on January 20, 2015, and I posted it on Facebook to share with others.)

"Father, I come to you with all my troubled thoughts, and you give me peace. Father, I hurt physically, and you dry my tears and lift me up. Lord, I weep for the abuses I see in this world, and you comfort me so especially. My heart goes out to the needy and wanting in this world, and you give me a supernatural rest that touches my heart and lets me know you are still in control even though the world says otherwise. You remove the things from my life that do not glorify you even when I thought I needed them. You tell me to trust you, speak it, and in all things, surrender my will, praising and thanking you for all your mercies and grace. You are my God, my Savior, my King!"

## The Fruit of the Spirit
## So How Far Have You Come in Your Walk?

Galatians 5:22 tells us the fruit of the Spirit is love, joy, peace, patience, kindness, goodness, faithfulness, gentleness, and self-control. (Against such things there is no law.) Those who belong to Christ Jesus have crucified the sinful nature with its passions and desires. Since we live by the Spirit, let us keep in step with the Spirit. Let us not become conceited, provoking and envying each other.

Allow me to ask you a question, "What changes are you making in your life for those fruit of the Spirit to manifest?" Fruit grows as the tree matures. Are you reading and speaking your scriptures? Are you forgiving others and yourself as needed? All the garbage we collect from the world and the toxins we generate take up too much room in our bodies and mind for the Lord to fill us with more of the fruit. My biggest problem is me, since that is the only thing I can change and control. My suggestion is to try making different choices and see the results; it is not easy, but feeling the result is well worth the effort. We all have the same universal problem, self, and the adversary. Both want to rule, but God is the true ruler! We are happiest when we let Him rule and die to self and stand against the adversary with God's truth, the Word. Are we abiding in Him, and He in us? In John 15:4, the Lord tells us to "remain in Him, and He will remain in us. No branch can bear fruit unless you remain in me!"

Wow! If this is the criteria for a mature believer in the Lord Jesus Christ, where am I in my walk? Our Lord Jesus showed us on the earth how to display and live these attributes. It is humbling and encouraging to read these words as my journey shows me over and over the refinement possess of taking the dross out to make something beautiful of my life to glorify the Lord. No wonder one of my main prayers starts with, "Lord, I submit myself to you!" That is necessary continually for me, and I suspect you have trouble with that as well. In this process of dying to self and allowing the Lord to develop this new creation in Christ, He is constantly working, renewing the old nature into a thing of beauty that He purposes for us (1 Cor. 13).

The word *love* has certainly been used with everything, but concentrating on what a fruit of the Spirit would be should go past the Eros-type love, which refers to humanly love, and Philos, which means brotherly-type love, to Agape, which means God's kind of love. Since Jesus told us the greatest commandment is to love the Lord your God with all your heart and soul and mind, and your neighbor as yourself, then love must be the greatest fruit of the spirit!

Rick Warren defines *joy* as the settled assurance that God is in control of our life, the quiet confidence that ultimately everything is going to be all right, and the determined choice to praise God in every situation. My thought is that it is the harmony within us that comes through obeying God and reaping His blessings.

Peace must be the quiet strength one experiences when one is in complete harmony with the Father as we rest in Him, hiding Him in our heart. The definition from the internet suggests totality or completeness, wholeness, fulfillment, and security.

Patience—the internet defines the quality or virtue of patience as presented as either forbearance of endurance. In the former sense, it is a quality of self-restraint or of not giving way to anger, even in the face of provocation. It is attributed to both God and man and is closely related to mercy and compassion.

Kindness is manifested in the full salvation that comes through Christ. The way we treat others and oneself reflects this special quality that comes from the Lord.

If you think of the quality of goodness as not a mere passive quality but the deliberate preference of right to wrong, you would be correct. It is the firm and persistent resistance of all moral evil and the choosing and flowing of all moral good.

Faithfulness means lasting or enduring and can be applied to God's trustworthiness with truth and allowing us to be able to count on Him when needed.

Gentleness to me is an extreme example of kindness carried to the next level, where my dealing with a situation is the way the Lord would do it.

Self-control is simply saying no to something that does not please God or should be avoided. The dictionary says that it is simply that important, impressive, and nearly impossible practice of learning to maintain control of the beast of one's own sinful passions. It is being a master of your own domain not only when faced with trial or temptation—easier said than done.

The more fruit that is developed in your walk with the Lord, the closer you are in your fellowship with Him, because you are dying to self and allowing the nature of God to make you the New Creation (creature) in Him. The more your nature is like His, the more Mind of Christ you can operate in, and His Wisdom is poured out on you. Praise God! So often, my impatience and annoyances show the lack of my fruit growth, but it is an indicator to do something about it. We have choices, and I want to choose the better way, which is the Lord's way! My prayer is, "Lord, help me die to self and allow more of you in my nature so I can become more like you, Lord. Thank you and praise your name!" As you grow in your walk with the Lord, you see the fruit manifest in your life, and you have a choice to follow the Lord and grow in that fruit. You can develop that fruit and grow much like a muscle gets stronger and develops. Just strive to submit to the Lord and allow His perfect Will to manifest in your life. Developing the fruit of the spirit certainly helps one live in harmony with God's Will and function more in harmony with others. "Not my will, Lord, but Yours!" If you want to know more of the nature of God in all His Ways, spend more time with the Holy Spirit. Make the time!

The Spiritual Gifts of the Holy Spirit
Please do not confuse the Fruit of the Spirit with the Gifts of the Spirit. They are very different. The gifts are described in 1 Corinthians 11:2, Romans 12, and Ephesians 4; 1 Peter 4 also touches on the spiritual gifts. We need to remember there are diversities of gifts, but the same Spirit. There are differences of administration but the same Lord. There are diversities of operation, but the same God, which works all in all. As a believer, everyone has at least one gift. Some can have more than one, but as far as I know, no one operates in all of them. It is exciting to discover those gifts within oneself. The Spiritual Gifts manifest within you, and you either have them or not. Use them or lose them. Sometimes the Lord will allow you to operate in one that you do not normally operate in for a certain time or one time when needed. The Walk with the Lord is always exciting and eventful. Somewhat like a natural relationship. You learn to determine the Heart of the Lord and what pleases Him. These gifts are given to strengthen the Body and minister to the Body of Christ for all to profit.

There are three revelation gifts: word of wisdom, word of knowledge, and distinguishing between spirits.

There are three power gifts that do something: faith, gifts of healings, and miracles.

There are three utterance or inspirational gifts: prophecy, diverse kinds of tongues, and interpretation of tongues.

We have barely touched on the gifts here. For more detailed information, spend time with the book *The Holy Spirit and His Gifts* by Kenneth E. Hagin.

## About Prayers

Prayer is a mighty tool in God's Hand to bring us where He wants us to be. James 5:16 states, "The fervent prayer of a righteous person avails much." God wants us to pray for many reasons. We focus on our Lord when we pray, and we develop the fellowship He wants with us when we offer our prayers to Him. I believe prayer invites Him into our lives and situations to intervene with His Wisdom and solutions for our needs. He never goes against our will, for He gave us the greatest gift of free will, which no other thing in creation has. We are able to see His work in our lives to do well by us when we pray specific prayers and then see how He is able to provide when we truly give the problems to Him and allow Him to work.

When the disciples asked Jesus how to pray, in Matthew 6:9–13, He gave us what we call the Lord's Prayer. However, He told them many things before sharing the prayer that was important to prepare their hearts for this atmosphere of prayer. In chapter 5, He explained the beatitudes, which explain the core of the Ten Commandments in His Sermon on the Mount. Read the whole chapter to prepare for what the Lord's Prayer really means.

Some of my prayers are actual scriptures put together as one prayer. If I pray God's Word, then I know I am praying His Will for me and there is more power because His words created our universe and us, so I know how strong they are. All through Genesis, "He said," and it was done. The way we get to know the Will of God is through His Word, so seek Him through that Word and always follow the path He has planned for you before the foundation of the earth. It is personal and unique to you! He formed us from the womb (Isa. 49:5), and Matthew 10:30 tells us even the hairs on our head are numbered, so He has to know us moment by moment because that number changes constantly.

Make prayer personal, for it is just you and God! To get to know anyone, it is necessary to spend time with that person. Any time you carve out to be in God's Presence is awesome. He blesses it beyond your expectation. What a joy for His children to reach out and desire to be sitting at His Feet, learning, worshipping, praising, and exalting our Mighty God! Never feel guilty for relaxing in our Father's Presence and spending time with Him. He created us for that purpose. So you can feel fulfilled with the joy that falls on you during this very special time. Praise God!

Here are some scripture I pray, but bring your own to the Lord. Make them personal to you. You are unique to God.

Lord, I submit myself to you, and satan must flee, for greater is He that is in me than he that is in the world, and no weapon formed against me shall prosper (James 4:7; 1 John 4:4; Isa. 54:17). (Several scriptures together.)

But He was wounded for our transgressions. He was bruised, for our iniquities upon Him were the chastisement that made us whole, and with His Stripes (or wounds), I am healed (or someone I am praying for is healed) (Isa. 53:5).

Father, make me the head and not the tail. Bless my going out and my coming in (Deut. 28:13; Deut. 28:6).

Give me favor, Lord. All our needs are met in Christ Jesus according to His riches in glory (Phil. 4:19).

We are more than conquerors (Rom. 8:37).

The harvest is poured out to us, now! Satan, you must take your hand off it now! It is written, "All our needs are met according to His riches in glory" (Phil. 4:19). He owns everything, and we are His children and declare His abundance.

All scripture is made for reproof (2 Tim. 2:16).

The grass withers, the flower fades, but the Word of our God will stand forever (Isa. 40:8).

Blessings for a believer: "I will greatly rejoice in the Lord, my soul shall exult in my God; for He has clothed me with the garments of salvation, He has covered me with the robe of righteousness, as a bridegroom decks himself with a garland, and as a bride adorns herself with her jewels. For as the earth brings forth its shoots, and as a garden causes what is sown in it to spring up, so the Lord God will cause righteousness and praise to spring forth before all the nations" (Isa. 61:10–11).

My pastor in Waco, Texas, Richard Freeman, always said this prayer before bringing the good news of the Gospel from Psalms 19:14. "Let the words of my mouth and the meditations of my heart, be acceptable in thy sight, O Lord, my rock and my redeemer."

Prayers for Specific Times
On Memorial Day (or any specific day), celebration of our freedom, let us always remember our servicemen and servicewomen and the families of our veterans and the loved ones of those who died to give us the freedom we enjoy today and unfortunately so often take for granted.

Today, as I write this, we are battling the Coronavirus and practicing social distancing, which means we need to stay six to eight feet from each other. That means we are missing out on hugs! And if you are a hugger, you feel starved. So spend more time with your Heavenly Father and allow Him to hug you though the Holy Spirit, reaching out in kindness and love to others, as He puts in your heart to do. You can hear His Still Small Voice if you will try. He promises His flock can hear His Voice. How do we do that?

Below is taken from a piece written by Lillian Hunsberger on the internet, on a Bethany Global posting (and I have added notes):

1. Position your heart. Know Him. Remember the word *know* in the Scripture means intimate fellowship (what this book is all about). "Delight yourself in the Lord and He will give you the desires of your heart" (Ps. 37:4).

2. Prepare your mind. Is anything between us that keeps us from being in tune with each other? Sin, unforgiveness, fear, anger, hate, etc. Ask Him to help bring it to mind and give it to the Lord for you to free your mind and enter into His Peace.

3. Ponder the Word. Meditate and be absorbed into the Word. Find scriptures that speak to your spirit.

4. Praise with your soul, always. If you cannot think of things to say or a scripture, just praise. I find that works every time.

5. Present it to your mentors (not everyone; be selective). We lift one another up when we share. We were meant to fellowship. We are fashioned that way. Others help hone us, and often God helps get the dross out of us this way when we are on the same page with Him and are in peace with others.

6. Never stop learning, no matter how far we have come in our walk. There is still much to learn!

A Prayer During the Coronavirus Epidemic (Or Any Crisis)
*Read 2 Chronicles 7:14*

Dear Lord, continue to please bless our country, and thank you for all your many blessings to us. Lord, we ask your help to bring us back to a right relationship with you and our fellowmen. May we endeavor to know more of you and your nature and less of the world in and around us. Lord, forgive us and touch our hearts with your Holy Spirit to help us love you and others to become what you intended us to be. Help us seek your will, allowing you to have your will in our lives. We know we can trust you with our very lives since you are the one who created us and put your plan in our heart to become what you desire us to be. Let us be slow to anger and tender toward one another but stand against injustice, standing on your Word and spreading the Good News as you instructed us to. Let us be salt and light to a dim world that has lost its flavor. Thank you for being as close as our breath, so we may reach out to you at any moment, day or night, and you will never leave us or forsake us, as you promised. Thank you for giving your very own Son, Jesus, to save our souls and pour out the love you sent into the world to us through Him! Thank you for the Holy Spirit, which whom we can fellowship and from whom we learn your ways. Praise you, Lord. You are a Mighty God! You told us to speak to the mountain and command it to be removed and not to doubt in our heart, to believe in my heart without doubts what I say and it will come to pass. We command this horrible virus from hell to leave our world. In the name of Jesus of Nazareth, believe that will come to pass, knowing that when two or more are gathered in His Name, He will make it manifest. Praise you, God! We repent and stand on that scripture. Thank you, dear Lord! You told us we are overcomers, and greater is He that is within us than he that is in the world, and no weapon formed against us shall prosper, and every tongue that shall rise against us in judgment shall be condemned.

Bless you, dear reader, and may the Lord enrich our lives as we truly seek Him! Amen.

More Prayers

Prayer is a mighty tool in God's Hand to bring us where He wants us to be. James 5:16 states, "The fervent prayer of a righteous person avails much." God wants us to pray for many reasons. We focus on our Lord when we pray, and we develop the fellowship He wants with us when we offer our prayers to Him. I believe prayer invites Him into our lives and situations to intervene with His Wisdom and solutions for our needs. He never goes against our will, for He gave us the greatest gift of free will, which no other thing in creation has. We are able to see His work in our lives to do well by us when we pray specific prayers, then see how He is able to provide when we truly give the problems to Him and allow Him to work.

A Blessing for the Reader

As we journey on this road to intimacy with the Lord, allow me to ask Him to bless you by quickening your mind, giving you a hunger to know Him better every day, and healing your mind, body, and emotions by "restoring what the canker worm has stolen" (Joel 2:25). We serve such a mighty God that He satisfies your soul and brings you joy, peace, strength, and gladness like the manna He poured out daily on the children of Israel in the desert. He promises that as you seek Him, you will find Him. Do you long for adventure, joy, gladness, peace, strength, hope, prosperity, fellowship, and on and on? The Word offers you life! "You will seek me and find me when you seek me with all your heart" (Jer. 29:13). "But if from there you seek the Lord your God, you will find him if you seek him with all your heart and with all your soul" (Deut. 4:29). He meets us wherever we are at this moment and is always available, night or day, at a moment's notice, promising you that He "sticks closer than a brother" (Prov. 18:24). "Be strong and courageous. Do not be afraid or terrified because of them, for the Lord your God goes with you; He will never leave you nor forsake you" (Deut. 31:6).

Our moments are filled with choices. "For many are called, but few are chosen" (Matt. 22:14). "I call heaven and earth as witnesses against you that I have set before you like and death, blessings and curses. Now choose life, so that you and your children may live and that you may love the Lord your God, listen to His voice, and hold fast to Him. For the Lord is your life, and He will give you many years in the land He swore to give to your father" (Deut. 30:19).

Will you choose life and follow the Lord? What a journey you will have! Make your choices in life wisely with much prayer, for you live with them daily on your earth journey and some throughout eternity.

Prayer is a mighty tool in the hand of God to bring us to where he wants us to be!

# ABOUT PRAYERS

*****

I just added a Dake's Annotated Reference Bible to my collection and want to share this part with you about prayer: Sevenfold ways to pray to get prayers answered:

1. Pray to the Father (John 16:23)
2. In the Name of Jesus (John 14:12–15)
3. By the Holy Spirit (Rom. 8:26)
4. With full understanding of right and privileges (1 Cor. 14:1)
5. In harmony with the Word (John 15:7)
6. In faith, nothing doubting (James 1:6)
7. With praises for an answer (Phil. 4:6)

## Final Remarks

Here are some things I have learned from living eighty years on this planet and desire to share with you (not necessarily in any order):

- A person is about as happy as he or she makes up his or her mind to be.
- God is more interested in my reaction to what happens to me than what occurred. Because He can turn all things into good for those who love the Lord and are called to His purpose (Rom. 8:28).
- "The joy of the Lord is my strength" (Neh. 8:10). When I start my day with that scripture, the rest of the day follows suit.
- "I can do all things through Christ who strengthens me" (Phil. 4:13).
- God is able to use a balanced life more effectively.
- God wants to communicate with me through the Holy Spirit. "My sheep hear my Voice and I know them, and they follow me" (John 10:27). Luke 12:7 states, "And even the very hairs of your head are numbered."

A Blessing for the Reader

As we journey on this road to intimacy with the Lord, allow me to ask Him to bless you by quickening your mind, giving you a hunger to know Him better every day, and healing your mind, body, and emotions by "restoring what the canker worm has stolen" (Joel 2:25). We serve such a Mighty God that He satisfies your soul and brings you joy, peace, strength, and gladness like the manna He poured out daily on the children of Israel in the desert. He promises that as you seek Him, you will find Him. Do you long for adventure, joy, gladness, peace, strength, hope, prosperity, fellowship, and on and on? The Word offers you life! "You will seek me and find me when you seek me with all your heart" (Jer. 29:13). "But if from there you seek the Lord your God, you will find him if you seek him with all your heart and with all your soul" (Deut. 4:29). He meets us wherever we are at this moment and is always available, night or day, at a moment's notice, promising you that He "sticks closer than a brother" (Prov. 18:24). "Be strong and courageous. Do not be afraid or terrified because of them, for the Lord your God goes with you; He will never leave you nor forsake you" (Deut. 31:6). The first book of John 4:8 tells us that Perfect love casts out fear.

Our moments are filled with choices. "For many are called, but few are chosen" (Matt. 22:14). "I call heaven and earth as witnesses against you that I have set before you like and death, blessings and curses. Now choose life, so that you and your children may live and that you may love the Lord your God, listen to His voice, and hold fast to Him. For the Lord is your life, and He will give you many years in the land He swore to give to your father" (Deut. 30:19).

Will you choose life and follow the Lord? What a journey you will have! Make your choices in life wisely, with much prayer, for you live with them daily, and those around you do also on your earth journey, and some throughout eternity.

Remember, to know the Will of God, read the Bible! To be led by the Spirit, do the Will of God as much as you know!

God wants our most valuable asset, our time. Are you willing to give Him the time you need to know Him intimately?

An Encouragement

May I take a moment to encourage all of us a little? I do believe the Lord is doing a new thing in this new year in many of our lives to encourage us and to spread the gospel to the hurting. As this new year takes off, may we be mindful of the needs of others and reach out whenever possible to make another's life a little better and make the world around us, which we have a little control over, a kinder, more loving place. We all have needs and should appreciate the thoughtfulness of others, so let's try to take a moment to tell another when they go the extra mile how much we appreciate it. We are the family of God, and when one hurts, all feel the effects, like rings in a lake when a rock is thrown in. The circles form and flow out over the water and affect the stillness of the lake. Let us pray for one another and lift one another up and speak kindly to one another, for words are powerful and can heal or wound. May the words we speak be a blessing, not a curse in the lives of others. May the Lord bless all our deeds and be pleased with our efforts.

Donna Rigney, who was on Sid Roth's program *It's Supernatural,* said, "The most important thing for us to be doing is spending time in intimate fellowship with the Lord. That's what He's looking for. He told me in this end-time revival, He's only going to use those that spend time with Him, that know Him, that will sacrifice time in their lives to get to know Him, to talk to him, to listen to Him, and to do what He tells them. To hear his word, and not obey! That won't get you anywhere. We need to hear His Word. We have to obey it. We have to live holy lives set apart for Him. Live lives of intimate fellowship with Him. What He's done with me with intimacy, He wants to do with everybody."

I echo Donna's statement, thus my book, *Our Fellowship with His Holy Spirit,* fits right in here. I pray the Lord uses it to inspire you to seek Him. In Jeremiah 29:13, He tells us, "You will seek me and find me when you seek me with all your heart." Seek Him now, for the time is short. So many times I am impressed to look up. Your redemption draws nigh! Any day, any time, He could return to planet Earth. Are you ready to stand before Him and give an accounting of your life on earth? As your develop that intimacy with your Creator/ God, do you thank Him for the Gift of Life He has given you, and do you thank Him for every breath He gives as you need it? For without it, you cease to exist!

Is your name recorded in the Lamb's Book of Life so you can

spend eternity with Jesus? Nothing is as important as that! We are not assured of anything but this minute in time. God bless you!

One final scripture that has meant so much to me during my journey is Romans 5:1–5, especially verses 2 to 5. The RSV version speaks to me more on this scripture: "Therefore, since we are justified by faith, we have peace with God through our Lord Jesus Christ. Through Him we have obtained access to this grace in which we stand, and we rejoice in our hope of sharing the glory of God. More than that, we rejoice in our sufferings, knowing that suffering produces endurance, and endurance produces character, and character produces hope, and hope does not disappoint us because God's love has been poured into our hearts though the Holy Spirit which has been given to us."

## Extra Goodies

### A Collection of Inspirations to Uplift You
### (From Family and Friends)

The Invitation Letter
The letter I sent asking for others to share their testimony if they felt led to do it.

Dear family and Christian friends,

For years the Lord has been leading me to write a book about developing intimacy with Him through fellowship with His Holy Spirit, of course with the underlying theme of a salvation experience that leads to the Great Commission. He gave me the book title years ago, but I thought it was the name for a Bible Study, until I listened to that Still Small Voice and realized it was the title for this offering, a book from layman to layman about a spiritual journey during the refining process of walking with the Lord on a day-to-day basis. Over the years, writing for our church paper, newsletters, and materials for new members and articles has been a source of joy for me.

My reason for writing all of you is to tell you about the final chapter, of which I would like you to be a part, if you desire and feel led to do. This chapter is called "Extra Goodies," and is subtitled "A Collection of Inspirations to Uplift You (From Family and Friends)." A few of my Christian friends will be asked to contribute if they feel led to do so. This idea came from reading Austin's (my grandson's) posting on Facebook (which is included at the bottom). It touched my heart, and I asked him if I could include it in my book, and he told me yes! Your contribution need not be very long. Just ask the Lord what He wants you to write, keeping in mind we are offering the Word, spiritual experiences, inspiration, etc. to encourage, inform, and uplift the human spirit, directing it toward our Heavenly Father, to worship, praise, and thank Him for His many blessings. Sharing personally will allow others to see how the Lord deals with us in our individual walk with Him.

If you are excited, as I am, to spread the good news, please consider writing a page for the book. Pray about it, let the Holy Spirit lead you what to say, and e-mail or send me your thoughts as soon as you can get it to me. I have a desire to have all our names in the Lamb's Book of Life and to continue our existence in the glorious heaven that the Lord has prepared for all who believe in Him and ask Him into their hearts as Savior and Lord. Our family together can take a small step in being a part of bringing that about, by making sure we have had the Salvation experience and are working on making Him Lord of our lives. I am diligently working on this book because I feel an urgency to complete the task. God provided a publisher in an interesting way, so my part is to listen, record, and complete!

Years ago, in my early walk, the Lord impressed me to study His Word and fellowship with Him an hour a day. This was really difficult, but how rewarding that has been during my journey with Him! It formed a basis for what has developed with this focus, allowing me to have some amazing experiences while listening for His guiding. I awaken in the morning with thoughts and words flowing, sometimes almost faster than I can write them. This journey has been exciting, challenging, and a wonderful opportunity to learn more of the ways of the Lord. I pray each day that I can die more to self and allow more of the Holy Spirit to guide my thoughts and actions. Every day the Lord has a unique calling and purpose for our lives, and how exciting it is to learn more of His Will and purpose for us! Sharing our experiences with others benefits others as well as builds our testimony and faith.

Each of you has blessed my life through the years, and I am so thankful for you all! I continue to be blessed that the Lord gave Jim a vision to be part of this walk, to study and grow with me on a daily basis, to pray for the needs of others, to encourage me with my divine calling, and to allow me to be part of his walk!

May the Lord guide you daily as you obey His leading. Here are some thoughts to help you determine what He might lead you to write:

1. What place does God have in your life?
2. What are the actions you take to grow closer to Him?
3. What does your quiet time with Him look like?
4. Is there a specific illustration you experienced that brought you to a closer relationship with the Lord that could help another Christian build his or her faith or bring them to the Lord in a personal relationship? Etc.

I trust the Lord will be instructing you what to say if you decide to share in this endeavor.

Bless you all and feel my love,
Mom (Patti, etc.)

*****

Austin Roberson, my grandson, posted this on Facebook. It gave me the idea to share how the Lord works individually with us, and he said I could use it in the book.

A poem I wrote to God that I want to share with you, called "You Are My Opposite."

I am the nails that hold you to the cross. I am the voice that yells, "Crucify Him." I am Judas's kiss. I am Peter denying our relationship. I am a shaking fist and clenched teeth. I am the one pointing the finger and saying, "This is your fault." I am the runaway. I am the reason for your broken heart. I am the tears on your face. I am the weakness.

But you alone silence that with three words: "I love you." You are my healer. You are my peace. You are my forgiveness. You are my freedom. You are my embrace. You are my second chance. You are my clarity. You are the new smile on my face. You are my new beginning. I know that I am your choice. You are true love. You have always been my past even when I rejected you. You are my future. You are my comfort. You're incomparable. You are my opposite. You are God alone.

*****

Betty is a friend from Christ Centered Church and in Keenagers with us. She is a delight to know, and the gospel is evident in her life!

I have learned so much in my walk with my Savior. I found out early on that it's not about me, for He is my strength. Many years ago, my husband left me and five small children. I was so scared at what would happen to us. But then I remembered something my dad taught us early in life. With God first and family next in your life, you can do anything you need to for your family. This gave me peace. I was able to find jobs to support us. Life wasn't easy, but God kept my body healthy so I could work hard. I praise Him for that.

In 1999, my eldest daughter died from a drug overdose.

My church family prayed us through that, and God walked beside us. In 1986, one of my daughters was convicted of five counts of murder and put in prison for five life sentences. She has been there for thirty-two years now, and again, God is still holding my hand. In 2012, my youngest daughter died from a kidney and liver disease. Again, God never left me. I don't tell you this to make you feel sorry for me, because I don't need that. I have a living Savior that walks with me always, and He keeps my spirits high. My peace and joy come from Him alone. If you don't know my Savior, I pray that you seek Him with all your heart!

In Christ,
Betty

*****

"For He will command his angels concerning you to guard you in all your ways. On their hands they will bear you up, so that you will not dash your foot against a stone" (Ps. 91:11–12).

After the doctor told me I had cancer, He said something that changed my life. "People react to the news in all sorts of ways. And no matter what their attitude, some of them live and some of them die. But the ones who lie down and give up? They all die."

I resolved not to give up. I resolved to live. But treatment was hard. I lost all my teeth. Surgery disfigured my neck and shoulder. Chemo destroyed my immune system and caused deadly blood clots. Radiation burned my neck and throat so badly I could barely speak or swallow; I had to take my nutrition through a plastic tube hanging out my abdomen. My wife and mother fed me, transported me, medicated me, cleaned me, and wept for me.

I was so angry at God. When I told my mom that, her answer changed me yet again. "Well, my son, you just need to get over that. Because right now you need God's help more than ever." There was no way I was going to give up. Mom reminded me that there was no way God would give up either.

God sent many angels to help me that year: my wife, mother, friends, neighbors, doctors and nurses, technicians and counselors, colleagues, and strangers. They bore me up with prayer, meals, company, letters, envelopes with money to help us pay our bills. Their love bore me up. God loved me through them. Thanks to that love, I stumbled but did not fall.

My life has changed a lot since then. I became a personal trainer and fitness instructor at the YMCA. I help people living with cancer and other chronic diseases find their own strength and love for life. Cancer didn't change me. God did. I almost gave up, but God never did. When we need them the most, God sends angels to bear us up. What a glorious friend! What a holy opportunity! What a blessing!

—Bob Johnson

Here is my reply to him after reading his offering for this chapter.

Wow! What a testimony! The Lord led me to you, and I understand why! God bless you, Bob. Thank you for sharing your lifesaving testimony to others. It will certainly be helpful to others in their walk with the Lord. God can use our pain and challenges for the good of others, and thank you for your courage and commitment. It shows in your life. I am thankful He spared you for us, and the world. The joy and loving concern you exhibit to others is heartwarming and obvious. You are very important in the lives of many, and the Lord is using your talents daily. I am honored to call you friend and a Christian brother.

Note: Here is a man whose voice is critical as an actor as well as a trainer and YMCA instructor! (He leads the cancer survivors' group, called Live Strong.) Knowing his testimony and hearing the joy he brings to his classes, what a celebration it is and a tribute to the Lord's healing ability to return him to our classes with his singing voice intact and humor ever present! Thank you, Lord. His classes sense his caring and commitment to us and his appreciation for all the Lord has done for him. It shows in his work and his personal relationships. He just had his ten-year scan for cancer, and he is cancer free! Praise God!

*****

My maternal grandmother wrote this blessing (just before she died in 1948) to her children and grandchildren. Even though my grandfather was a preacher, his wife knew the value of a personal, intimate relationship with the Lord and was not hesitant to share the good news of the gospel with those who would open their heart to listen. My grandmother Martha Jane Stallard, who was a midwife in Virginia, delivered children all over the mountain area on horseback. She had ten children of her own. I am blessed to have this heritage! Her grammar was not the best, but her love of the Lord was pure and inspirational to all she met!

*****

This one is from June Tunstill, October 24, 2017. (She is my spiritual *mom*, a very close friend in the Lord who has gone to be with the Lord and her husband now.)

Seventy-five years ago, on the first Sunday in September 1942, I was baptized and became a member of Epworth Methodist Church in Lexington, Kentucky (several years later, it was Epworth United Methodist Church). I had given my life to Jesus Christ at a revival service the previous week. I was nineteen years of age.

The following years were filled with many experiences and opportunities for spiritual growth. I married a young man, and we were blessed with sixty-one years together. God was with us through it all. My husband was a volunteer into the Army Signal Corps during World War II and was overseas for two years. After the war was over and peace came, there was the time of getting jobs and establishing a home. Jay became a firefighter with the Lexington Fire Department, and I worked for the US Department of Agriculture for twelve years, followed by forty years as church secretary and homebound visitor.

There were times of illness, surgeries, loss of parents, along with other family members and friends. Through all the years, God kept His promise that "He would never leave or forsake us." He was always there, through the good and the not-so-good times. He gave us strength and courage to face every situation and gave us a long and happy life together. He was the head of our home, and still is, although I am now alone and in a retirement home. I am so thankful for the abiding Presence of His Holy Spirit and am thankful every day for His loving care and blessings.

*****

This is from June's nephew named Carl Chapman, with whom we had a business venture.

Although I had been a Christian for several years, my personal relationship with God, Jesus, and the Holy Spirit did not until I started reading the Bible every morning and talking with God several times a day. I start each day with twenty to thirty minutes reading the Bible and then telling God how grateful I am to him for all the good and not-so-good experiences.

I do know that a child of God, He knows what is best for me, and although I don't always understand it, I accept and follow in blind faith. I also know that everything that happens in my life does work out to be good.

Part of my daily prayer time with God includes giving me the wisdom to know what the Holy Spirit is communicating to me and giving me the courage and self-discipline to do it. I also give thanks on His sending Jesus to provide a means of restoring the broken relationship between mankind and God.

—Carl Chapman

*****

Written on September 27, 2017, below is a testimony from Coleen Trotter (a friend from classes at the YMCA).

God is my all, my everything. He is my breath. He is my joy. He is my light in darkness. He is my provider. He is my comfort in times of loneliness and sadness. He is my Savior! I will praise Him all the days of my life. Thank you, God the Father, God the Son, and God the Holy Spirit!

I lift my hands to you. No other help do I need. If you should leave me, where should I go? In my weakness you have made me strong.

I thank you for allowing me to attend daily Mass and Eucharistic Adoration. May I always be pleasing to you and do your holy will. Jesus, I trust in you!

*****

Below is the testimony of David Estep (My cousin, Christine's husband).

Being saved at an early age and being reared in a Christian home and environment, I took spiritual things for granted. There came a critical time in my life being weighed down with trying. I lifted my soul to God and cried, "O God, I've tried all my life to live the Christian life, and I've failed miserably. If I'm going to live this Christian life, you will have to live it through me. I am in total dependency and believe you will do this. Henceforth, I am going to trust you, Lord, to do so." What a weight was lifted! My life has not been the same since!

Knowing Jesus Christ is what life is all about; this is my testimony! When all else fails, God is faithful. Put Him to the test and trust Him fully—yes, fully! Tell Him to take your whole life even though you may not feel you deserve anything, and you will be blessed beyond belief. To say that God is good is an understatement. He is my all in all. Please come to Him only through His Son, Jesus Christ, for that is the only way!

Three of my first cousins are almost like sisters, and this is Christine's husband. David and I can sit and discuss spiritual things for hours, so you can see why after you read his testimony. We are on the same page!

*****

Below is "Driving by Faith" by Chris Roberson.

Knowing it is a three-and-a-half-hour drive from Idaho to the airport in Salt Lake City, Utah, I decided to hit the road early this morning. My eagerness to blaze an early trail put me in perfect alignment to the rising sun. Literally, it was centered in my line of sight! Add to this scenario a construction zone, other vehicles, and the corpses of numerous insects that had laid down their lives on my windshield, and I was truly flying blind!

I laughed in my spirit and said, "Lord, I am truly driving by faith, 'coz I can't see a stinking thing!"

Then I heard that unmistakable voice that said, "That is the way I want you to go through life, so blinded by my Son that you can't see your own way!"

Wow, Lord! You got my attention. Blind me to my own ways and light my path.

"Your word is a lamp to my feet ant a light to my path" (Ps. 119:105).

Chris is my son-in-law, Julie's husband. His relationship with the Lord has always touched my heart. He is a graphic designer, and I worked with him at a Business Express Press in Dallas before he became my son-in-law. I was touched by the spiritual growth I saw in him even as a young man. His father was a preacher (he died before I met Chris), and his mother lived her faith and was certainly an inspiration to him. Mother and I prayed for the man my daughter, Julie, would marry, and we have been blessed with His choice for her. His delightful humor is apparent in this offering.

*****

Have you ever thought about what you will do when you see Jesus? Dallas Holm and Praise sang a song, "I Saw the Lord," and the first time I heard it, I cannot explain how I reacted and how it touched my heart. It got me to thinking about that incredible experience.

My sweet sister in Christ Elaine said she thought when we see

God face-to-face, He would ask two questions, "What did you do with my Son, Jesus, and how did you treat your neighbor?" Sounds like the great commandment Jesus told the Pharisees when they tried to trick him about what is the greatest commandment of the ten.

This is a testimony from Elaine Wadlington, a dear friend, business and prayer partner when I lived in Dallas. She knows the answer to this for sure now, for she went to be with the Lord in 2001. Thank you, Elaine, for being such a willing prayer partner with me during such challenging times for both of us when we felt the Lord's Hand so strongly in our lives!

*****

This one is from Sandra O'Neal, a friend from our YMCA workouts.

After two and a half years of debilitating depression, my husband was in total despair, as was I.

Beginning in 2010, the two of us experienced the deaths of our fathers, the death of his brother, my cancer, forced retirement for both, moving from our beloved farm, my mother's spiral into dementia, and several other family crises. It seemed as though we were in an eddy of swirling sadness that had grabbed us and was pulling us under.

During the Christmas holiday of 2015, David became physically nauseated and emotionally withdrawn.

The ordinarily gregarious and talkative doctor lost twenty pounds in a month and became reluctant to move out of his favorite chair. Every physical test, scan, MRI, and scope was ordered—results were negative. Antidepressants were prescribed and changed, prescribed and changed. Prayers were offered. Social opportunities were offered and declined. Trips to the doctors twice a week became the norm. David went in the hospital for a week.

By March of 2017, I, too, was seeing a psychiatrist, on medication, and vacillating between planning David's next doctor visit or his funeral—all seemed to be lost. Friends came over occasionally to stay with David so I could get out of the house, but I was still emotionally and physically exhausted. One evening, I called my friend Mikal and just sobbed. She patiently told me I only needed to ask for help and that people wanted to help but did not know what to do. They needed specifics. Wait, what? That's it?

I called on neighbors, friends, and church family—they took David to his doctor appointments, came to visit, took him for rides, took me to the hospital to visit him, brought food. As the Alcoholics Anonymous book says, I "let go and let God." The same week I talked with Mikal, I received a phone call from Patti—she was crying but sounded joyous! She wanted to share the Word she had just received for David and me:

"When I intervene, I bring healing, power, and strength to my children. You are an overcomer in this fallen world, Sandra. I know your need, and I am pouring out exactly what is needed for David now!

(To me) "Praise me and thank me for my loving care for David and Sandra." (I felt the Lord had special plans for you, and He said, "You are right, I have mighty plans for Sandra's life, which has been revealed to her and will soon be made manifest. Praise me together and expect a financial harvest now! You are the messenger!)"

The Lord says, "I am here with you, Sandra!"

The next week, David began to improve. He is scheduled only for quarterly check-ups with his doctors. He is exercising, eating, seeing friends, going out, verbally engaging, and we have actually planned a trip. [At this writing, the Lord has

been faithful, and David and Sandra are doing well.]
    I am not in control—God is. Just ask.

—Sandra Park O'Neal

*****

I have always felt that I have had good faith in the Lord, but it wasn't until January 2012 that my faith went to a greater level. This is just a small moment in my life where God left a huge impact on my life. My high school sweetheart, ex-husband, and father of my son was in a tragic car accident in 2009. His name was Jimmy. This accident left him a quadriplegic, on a breathing machine, for almost a year. I was still very close with his sister, and she included me on every decision that she had to make for him. We decided it was time to start weaning him off the ventilator after almost a year. We left it in God's hands. The more Jimmy was weaned off the ventilator, the more alert he became, but he still couldn't talk. Over the next two years, he started talking again but could never walk. In December of 2011, the nursing home where Jimmy lived selected a resident to go home on Christmas Day, and this year they selected Jimmy. We were so excited because quadriplegics don't generally ever leave a nursing home and, better yet, go back home, and especially on Christmas Day. After talking with his sister, we decided he would come to my house on Christmas morning. The ambulance picked him up from the nursing home and drove him to Richmond, where I lived at that time, dropped him off to spend the day with us. We made the necessary changes to the house to accommodate his Geri chair. The whole family was there, including my dad, whom I hadn't spoken to in almost five years—mostly my family, because Jimmy and his sister don't have a lot of family. We cooked dinner, opened gifts, and just enjoyed what felt like the perfect Christmas. Most importantly, my son got to have his dad home for Christmas. I remember pushing Jimmy into the kitchen, where he closed his eyes and smelled the aroma of Christmas dinner in the oven. We had a spectacular day. The ambulance came back to get him that Christmas afternoon. We all walked out as they put him in the ambulance and said our goodbyes. I remember Jimmy looked at my son and said, "Take care of your mama."

About two weeks later, I went back to visit him at the nursing home. His eyes were closed, and he wouldn't wake up for anything. I asked the staff what was going on, and they said he hadn't been feeling well. So I left, not giving it a second thought. One thing about Jimmy is that I met him when I was fourteen years old. I had shared more than half of my life with him, whether it was as girlfriend, wife, mother of our son, or friend; we had been through a lot since 1987. He never forgot my birthday for thirty-seven years, even when he could barely talk after the accident. I remember the nurse calling me for Jimmy, holding the phone for him so he could wish me a happy birthday. So a few weeks went by, and I received a call from the nursing home that said Jimmy had gone out to the hospital and they didn't think he would make it. I immediately went to the hospital, called my son and his sister to tell them to come to the hospital. We spent the entire next twenty-four hours with him until he took his last breath on January 26, my birthday. That year, I received the greatest gift: Jimmy got to go home and be with the Lord, see his nanny and papa, his mom and dad. He could walk again and run free in Heaven.

That was the moment in time where I knew I've always believed in God, but to watch God work a miracle bringing

Jimmy home on Christmas Day because he knew a month and a day later Jimmy would be called to his real home and on my birthday. I had a moment that will never leave me where I said only God can make something like this happen. My faith and life will forever be different.

—Susan Neville

Susan is a sweet friend we met at one of our senior events at the Willows in Lexington a few years ago. We bonded immediately and have seen each other as much as our busy schedules allowed. She loves the Lord, and I see His work in the life of her and her family.

*****

Below is Laura's testimony. (Another dear friend I met at the YMCA years ago).

I have been active in the Methodist Church since I was a small child. I am the granddaughter and cousin of Methodist ministers. I sang in the Choir, was active in a youth group, and attended faithfully. As I grew older and had a family and a career, I was not as active in the church as I had been when I was younger. I was filled with longing to be a part of that fellowship again.

I was seriously injured in February of this year. I was broken and in so much pain. I was sitting in the hospital one day, so full of despair and fear. I opened the drawer next to my bed, and there was a Bible. I started to read and pray daily. It calmed me, and I felt that I had been spiritually reborn.

This past spring, I was rebaptized as a result of my spiritual awakening. I recently joined that church where I was baptized, and for the first time in a long time, I felt like I was home.

I am grateful to God for His blessings and His love. God is good, and His grace fills me with peace.

I have watched my dear friend Laura grow in leaps and bounds as the Lord has become so personal to her through the many broken bones she had endured the last few years and how she is an overcomer!

*****

This one is from Lois Carter. (Another sister in Christ from our YMCA classes).

Surely, during this life, we have all had doubts and fears. We have doubted our ability to accomplish, to exceed, and to excel. We have been fearful of trying new things and venturing out to do what we have only dreamed of doing. The Bible says that God never gave us a spirit of fear. As a matter of fact, the Bible says specifically and numerous times, "Fear not!" We need to stop and take some time to revitalize our thinking. The only things we can't do are the things that we choose not to do.

I remember the theme song that preceded every Walt Disney show on Sunday nights that said, "A dream is a wish your heart makes when you're fast asleep." Have you dreamed of doing something that you've put off for one reason or another? You didn't have the time, no money, house repairs, kids or grandkids, or just whatever? I pray that you would revisit those dreams that came straight from your heart and make them a reality. Don't be plagued by the "I wish I hads!" Just get up and do, get up and go, because believe it or not, our time on this earth is quickly winding down. We certainly don't have time for regrets.

Have you ever shared those dreams with your family or your friends? Please do, because they could very well be the ones to help you bring those dreams into fruition, just by mentioning them or reminding you. Not pursuing your dreams or even having the impetus to do so is a mark of immaturity. I pray that we have all reached our pinnacle of maturation in every way—physically, emotionally, socially—every way, but spiritually, that should be perpetual.

Let me share the story of a lady I have known for a very long time. She was blessed to have both parents in her life. She was a good girl, so to speak, though she did do some very childish things. She was adventurous, was outspoken, and had a mind of her own. As she progressed and excelled in school, her doggedness stifled her thinking. She couldn't wait to graduate high school—and almost didn't—doing things her way. College was not on her agenda, but to please her parents, she went, but not for long. What she wanted and had always dreamed about was having a big house, or any house, for that matter. She had the kids, but not many, just enough to quickly find out that having babies required money, honey! She found jobs, but none that required any special skills. She only had to have sense enough to do repetitive-action work. She finally realized that if she wanted a job that actually required some thinking, furthering her education was the answer. But lo and behold, it was indeed too late for her, because now it would have to come out of her pocket for a higher education. Once again, she would have to put her dreams on the back burner, because money was as scarce as hen's teeth, and there were children to feed and clothe. Not only that, but the children were now school age, and their education was very important to her. All the meager earnings she had made went for the care and upkeep of those children, and there was nothing left for her. She continued to keep that dream alive in her heart, and she continued to live life. That's what some of us do: we live humdrum, so-so, everyday lives.

She raised her children, took care of ailing siblings and her aged parents, and her spouse's too, until they had all passed away. It was then that she asked herself, "What now?"

She always knew that God was looking down on her, because she was His child. She loved Him and knew that she couldn't put a number to the countless ways or times that she had been blessed. When she turned the corner to her sixties, she once again dreamed of going back to school. She needed that hankering that she had kept pushed down for so long to be fulfilled. She talked to God about it, and He gave her the desire of her heart. Off she went to pursue her dream. She attended school, completed her course with perfect attendance, and graduated magna cum laude. Her spouse and her children encouraged her all along the way, from the beginning to the very end. The only thing else that she felt God required during that time was that she counsel the young ones so that they, hopefully, wouldn't waste life's limited time drifting like she had. So through it all, she knew that she had to keep a positive outlook, wear a smile, and be a beacon of light for others. That was why she was also awarded the inspiration award. I tell this story because the subject is me.

My dream was to be qualified to do something. God, in His infinite wisdom, allowed me to fulfill that dream that had lingered in my heart for a very long time, and He will do the same for you. Just have a little talk with Jesus and tell Him all about your dreams. He will hear your faintest cry, and He will answer by and by. All that is required as you are going through is to encourage someone else along the way.

Pray with them, pray for them, then dream and hold tight! Nothing is impossible with God, and it is never too late to walk confidently into your dreams.

Lois just had a stroke last month, and her testimony is positive as it was before. God is faithful and able, and she is speaking her healing and displaying the overcomer she is!

*****

Lord, I'm coming home!

Just last Sunday, the morning speaker we happened to be listening to was assuring each of us that in times like these, we each need to find our Voice in the Storm. And what a storm we currently have upon us in COVID-19! As the speaker pointed out to us in 1 Thessalonians 5:4–5, "We are sons [and daughters] of light and not of darkness." Just as the Lord's voice said in Mark 4:39, "Peace be still!" I have continued to hear God's voice throughout these last four weeks, along with the reassuring voice of my partner for fifty-one years, Bennie. And I pray that my testimony will be a voice in the storm, saying, "God is in control. Peace, be still!"

Unbeknownst to me or Bennie, in the weeks before his home going, God was preparing both me and Bennie. The Sunday-morning sermon Ben had prepared for March 15 was about God's message to the small church at Ephesus. This message was one of hope and optimism. God's commendation was that they had not grown weary (Rev. 2:3). Yet His condemnation was that they had left their first love. And His recommendation was that they remember and repent (verse 5). In preparing this sermon, Ben had spoken to me several times about its timeliness and of God's speaking to him through this sermon. Little did either of us know that

Ben would not preach this sermon from Cramer's pulpit. Church was canceled on the fifteenth, and Ben went home to be with the Lord on the seventeenth.

And on that Sunday, the fifteenth, Ben and I had our own church service in our living room. After eating a big breakfast together, we sat in our recliners and watched several TV preachers—James Kennedy, Charles Stanley, and David Jeremiah. The final speaker was Jon Weiss, a minister here in Lexington. His message was taken from the Song of Solomon. We heard God's plan from His Word for a man and a woman to enjoy the oneness and intimacy that God intended. Ben had prayer, praying especially for America as President Trump had declared that Sunday a Day of Prayer. Ben then joked about me doing the work of a deacon as I prepared and served him communion. And after the service, for our noon meal, we headed to one of our favorite restaurants, Applebee's, and, as always, got the two-for-$20 special.

That night, Ben shared with me his letter to his Cramer family, as he said these were his random thoughts, just simply what was on his mind, and he wasn't sure about mailing the letter. I assured him that, yes, he needed to mail it since we hadn't met that day. And of course, as his favorite editor, I did point out only one error—the absence of a comma. In his letter, he mentioned the word weary twice, and his admonition and prayer to his Cramer family was that "we remain strong, healthy, and positive in the upcoming weeks and months." He further stated, "Perhaps we'll be able to meet this weekend if the coast is clear." Yes, God cleared the coast two days later, as He parted the clouds and received Ben's spirit. And yes, we, his Cramer family, were able to meet that very weekend at his memorial service. Had he died a week or so later, COVID-19 could have prevented the Cramer family from joining his immediate family at the service.

It was just eleven days after his death that Ben was scheduled to speak in Louisiana. His topic was on "We the Victors in a War Defeated by Love." He began his sermon by saying "We" in the title is us who are a holy people (1 Pet. 1:15), a chosen people (1 Pet. 2:1–10), a suffering people (1 Pet. 4:12–19), a faithful people (2 Pet. 1:9), a hopeful people (2 Pet. 3:10–13), and a prayerful people (1 Thess. 5:17). Yes, his sermon declared that we are the victors. And how sweet it was for me to see at the bottom of the first page, in all caps, bold, and highlighted, "Married my biggest prayer warrior of all time—Adele." He went on to speak of the war going on today, describing our enemy, satan. His final point was from Ephesians 3:16–19. By the way, I counted over thirty scriptural references that he quoted in his five-page sermon. In the Ephesians passage, Paul prayed that the Ephesians would be strengthened with might through the Spirit in the inner man. He also desired that Christ dwell in their hearts and that they know how wide, how long, how deep, and how tall God's love is. By knowing love, they would be filled with all the fullness of God. Even though Ben never preached this sermon, I pray that his outline can be distributed, so many can hear his voice in the storm and be prayer warriors arming themselves with both prayer and love.

How beautifully God prepared me for Ben's home going! It was no coincidence that our last meeting at the corner of Cramer and Hanover was Sunday, March 8. This year on this day, we celebrated Cramer's 105th anniversary (along with Hagan Page's twenty-second birthday). The fellowship room was decorated with golden balloons and golden centerpieces. That day was also my namesake Mary Adele Rutherford's birthday. She and my grandfather Homer Neely Rutherford had ministered at Cramer for thirty-eight years before Ben and I came in 1975. Little did we know that day would be Ben's last time to stand behind the pulpit and preach and also to enjoy his last church fellowship meal.

St. Patrick's Day, March 17, the day began as always. Ben usually left around eight o'clock and waited at the kitchen counter for his Community or Keurig Newman's coffee to fill his cup. As I approached him, he bent his head forward to receive my kiss on his forehead. He definitely was not a morning person and would enjoy a bowl of cereal later in the morning at church. This day I went to Carolyn's to look through her last year's Easter stash that didn't sell. She had asked me to come and get whatever I wanted for my grandkids, who were still young enough to enjoy baskets. Arriving home around two o'clock, I wondered if Ben was home yet but saw no car as the garage door opened. We usually ate around four o'clock since Ben had not eaten lunch. In planning for supper, I had decided on a steak dinner, which was our special biweekly or monthly treat. At four thirty, I called his cell, laughing and leaving the message, "Come home, come home. It's suppertime." By five thirty, I called again, getting no answer. I decided to head to the church to see if he was still there.

As usual, fellowship doors were locked. But I was surprised that his office doors were also locked. Going back downstairs, I noticed hall lights were still on and the hallway was flooded. My thought was, "He's here mopping," and I called for him but got no answer. Turning to the restrooms, I walked to the men's room and, looking in, saw his shoes and blue jeans on the floor with his head at the commode. This time my thought was, "He's fixing the plumbing." But it soon changed to "No, he's fallen and is unconscious." I went to him and, holding his hand, felt the coldness. I then ran for my phone and called 911. The dispatcher switched me to someone who kept me on the phone, taking down information as I continued to cry out, "I can't believe it, I can't believe it." He encouraged me to give Ben CPR. I tried pulling on his legs to get him flat but couldn't move him. It was then that I heard the emergency sirens and ran to the fellowship doors to open them for the paramedics.

Finding Bennie was such a shock. But in the midst of the horror, I saw such a peace in his demeanor as well as his position. His eyes were closed, with his chin resting on his chest. He was lying on his back, with his shoulders resting on the broken toilet tank. His hands were resting on his stomach, and his legs were extended toward the restroom door. He was lying on his cane. And water was flowing from the top of the tank onto him. The first horrible thought was quickly replaced with a peace I couldn't understand. And my thoughts went to Bible verses of "fountain of living waters" (Jer. 2:13) and "water springing up into everlasting life" (John 4:14), as well as "Come take of the water of life freely" (Rev. 22:17) and "I will pour water on Him who is thirsty" (Isa. 44:3). The assurance of a peaceful home going was reinforced later when the coroner said that the fall did not cause his death. Rather, his heart stopped and he was dead before he fell. There was a deep gash behind his ear, but very little blood, proving that his heart had stopped pumping before he fell. I saw no blood when I found him. And how similar to Ben's brother Steve's death; he had a gash behind his ear as he had fallen in a parking lot, hitting his head on a concrete slab and succumbing to a heart attack—Steve at fifty-seven, Ben at seventy-four, and their dad at fifty-four.

Julie and Greg came immediately to the church, soon followed by Alicia and Tim and family arriving from Shelbyville. The neighbors had also gathered outside in the church yard—Warren from behind the fellowship building, Mike and Kim from across Cramer, and Nancy from down Hanover, giving out condolences and hugs as we waited for the coroner. And as I saw the coroner bringing Bennie out of the fellowship doors amid the golden balloons and centerpiece, I was reminded of New Jerusalem's golden city and streets awaiting Ben in heaven.

Jenny arrived from South Florida the next morning. Sherry and Mike drove in later that morning from Ohio. How thankful I was that all four daughters, along with Tim, Alicia's husband, accompanied me to Kerr Brothers to make the arrangements for Ben's service and burial. And how familiar we were with this funeral home, just a few blocks from the church, where so many times we gathered to say goodbye to loved ones and church members as Bennie presided over the service. Even in the midst of COVID-19, which prevented us from having a large service at Cramer, every detail was orchestrated by God. The viewing and service ended up being sixty-two people strong. The next morning at the cemetery, thirty-one were present. When Ben and I discussed who would do his funeral service, Ben's response was always, "My sons-in-law!" And my response was, "No, they are not preachers, nor are they Church of Christ!" But the four of them did his service, and what a beautiful service it was! Ringing in my ears was Ben's response, "I told you so!"

Not only did God show Himself to me in all that occurred the days before Bennie's death as well as at the time of his death, but also in the days following his death. In 2011, we had taken out small insurance policies that would cover our funeral service and burial. After meeting with Kerr Brothers and the Lexington Cemetery, I realized that the policy covered everything, with less than $1,000 left over. And since his death, I have received three checks. The first two came the night he died and were $50 less than the amount Ben deposited weekly from his salary. Since we hadn't met Sunday, I assumed Ben hadn't received his check from the church, yet God provided that amount. Later that week, I gave the treasurer our church offering, covering two Sundays we hadn't met. And again we received, this time in the mail, a check for $25 more than our offering. God always provides!

My last story is about cash stashed in the underwear drawer. Ever since I can remember, Ben had always stashed cash in his underwear drawer. It was his gas money, date night money when we ate out, vacation money, paying for gas and food, birthday, anniversary, and Christmas money for his sweetheart, four daughters, and twenty-one grandkids. A few years back, I decided to do the same, so I, too, had stashed cash in my underwear drawer. And because of COVID-19 and banks closing, etc., I had decided to withdraw some money ($4,000) from our savings account. A day or two after Ben's death, both our air conditioner and garbage disposal stopped working, our bed fell under the weight of too many granddaughters, the riding lawn mower refused to start, and the brake light on Ben's car was out. I had added up our cash on hand, coming up with about $7,000. And I began to put aside money—the amount needed to finish paying for gravestone, the amount needed to fix air conditioner. And very soon the cash on hand was down to nothing. I was surprised at how fast it had disappeared. When I decided to keep Ben's newer and larger RAV4, I said, "Okay, Lord, how can I do this? Trade in my Camry and pay off the RAV4? I need $4,000."

The next morning, I decided to look behind Ben's underwear drawer. Maybe cash or a money envelope had gotten stuck or fallen behind the drawer. As I pulled it out, I noticed that his stashed wallet looked fat. And when I looked inside, guess what I found? His stashed cash—$3,300! I had assumed I moved it to my underwear drawer but hadn't. With my checking and savings account, I could handle $700. But God took care of even that! I received a letter and check from Tim, Cramer's treasurer, saying he had spoken with several of the men and they had agreed to continue to pay Bennie's checks to me for now. Guess what the amount of the check is? Yes, $714! Does God provide? You better believe it! God's voice in the storm is very loud and clear!

Did I say above was last story? Can I indulge you for a final, short one? Funeral director had given me Ben's wedding band in a red velvet pouch. Jenny had said I could put it on a chain. I had put the pouch in my jewelry armoire. Several days ago, I thought, "Why don't I try his ring on?" Thanks to Arthur, my knuckles are larger and my finger size is a 10. Yes, the ring fit, and I have one more constant reminder of the nearness of my sweetheart. Is God good? Absolutely! Am I covered? Always and forever! And I do have a Voice in the Storm!

Adele Hill is the wife of Bennie Hill, a pastor who just passed away, and works out with me at the YMCA. She was a student of my husband, Jim's first teaching class at Bryan Station. We have become good friends.

*****

## Eye Shadow Blessing

Just like a stone thrown into the water creates a ripple effect across the surface, so it is that two people meeting can start a sequence of events. Along the same line is my motto, "When God does one thing, He does a thousand."

I met Suzanne, a European-born senior citizen, when my office was relocated. She seemed critical and negative. Each week, Suzanne and her friends arrived early for their exercise class so they could get their favorite chairs and equipment, but mostly it was so that they could socialize. They talked freely, as if I couldn't hear them, but as they chatted right outside my door, I heard the stories of their lives. I learned about Suzanne's remarkable story of how she escaped war-ravaged Europe and her journey over many years to the United States.

After several weeks, the ladies began to greet me and include me in their conversation. If I was away from the office, they asked about me. One day, Suzanne came to me with a complaint. For months every time I saw her, she would bring it up. So I listened and tried to resolve the issue. It took a year or so, but somehow she seemed satisfied she had been heard and her problem had been solved. As a result, she trusted me and began to ask me health-related questions, and I would answer.

Suzanne and I had more and more interaction, and we found some things in common; I look back and see that God's hand was weaving our relationship together. One day I was wearing yellow, a color we both happen to like a lot. She beamed as she told me it reminded her that she had something that she wanted to give me. "When will you be in next?" she asked me. We arranged a time to meet, but we kept missing each other and weeks went by.

In the meantime, with a new season, I wanted to change my eye shadow. Daily I looked at magazines, television, and people around me without much success with what new makeup colors might work for me. Such a small thing, but it was important to me.

Finally, I saw Suzanne again. As our paths crossed, her face brightened as she told me that she just happened to have the item with her. "I'll get it from my car and meet you after class," she said. I watched the clock so I wouldn't miss her like I had so many times before.

When she was done, we walked together into the cold, sunny air. "Wait here. I'll go to my car." I waited several minutes, wishing I had grabbed my coat. I was very cold. People greeted me with comments: "Where's your coat? It's cold out here." One lady said to another, "Oh, she's young. She doesn't need a coat."

Suzanne had parked a considerable distance from the door but finally drove up. She rolled down the window and tossed a casual yellow bag to me. It was an open reversible summer bag, which I thought was very special, because Suzanne had given it to me. She barely gave me time to say thanks as she drove quickly away. It was so like her to give a gift and not want a fuss made over her generosity.

When I opened the bag at home later that night, I noticed a makeup purse inside. When I picked it up, it had more weight than I had expected. Inside was a three-by-five-inch case of eye makeup of the higher-price variety filled with colors that I wouldn't normally consider buying. I started to play with them then and there. The new colors were perfect!

Nancy is a nurse at the YMCA. Jim and I have become good friends with her.

# Extra Goodies

*****

## Naomi's Testimony

As I think of words to write about my longtime friend Patti, so many come to mind. I may have to enter a whole chapter. God placed Patti in my life just at the right time. I didn't know it at that time, but I firmly believe it now. They say hindsight is twenty-twenty. She didn't know me from Adam or Eve, but she embraced me anyway. From church member acquaintance to mentor to friend, she has been a bridge when I was in troubled waters, a link to God, always pointing me in His direction. I know that whatever is written in this book, it will always point you in the direction of God, no matter your issue, and I mean no matter—she will always urge you to seek God first and then be still and listen.

My dear friend Patti, you have no idea how you have helped me take a closer walk with Jesus and seek His will, not mine.

—Naomi R.

In 2004, Naomi and I met when I worked at Calvary Baptist Church in Danville. I took pictures of new members when they joined the church, and I met her at that time. Later, I was facilitating a divorce care class, and she enrolled. From there, we traveled through our journeys, touching each other's lives as the Lord worked at getting the dross out of both of our lives. We learned so much from the class and became better acquainted as we double-dated with our present husbands and married a month apart. We celebrated our anniversaries together for several years. We are dear friends; even though we live in different cities, we try to schedule time together whenever possible.

*****

I have been in church since a very young age and accepted Christ and was baptized at age twelve. Even though being involved with youth groups and choir, I did not truly understand about the Holy Spirit. Later in life, through being with Christian friends in a prayer group, participating in the "I Found It Campaign," headed by Bill Bright, and through Bible Study Fellowship, I came to have a personal relationship with the Lord. Before this, I felt uncomfortable talking about or saying the name Jesus, but that all changed. The Holy Spirit started opening up areas in my spiritual being. God's Word was easier to understand and meant much more.

Ephesians 2:18 says that we have access to the Father through One Spirit. It is amazing that God has blessed me and all believers with the power of the Holy Spirit that can help me know Him more and more. I pray that this wonderful Holy Spirit continue to lead and guide me and I will be more like Him until I see Him face-to-face!

—Pam J.

Pam is a friend I have known for years. She was a friend of my mother and daddy. We have attended the same church together for fifteen years.

*****

September 2020, Richard Rice goes to church with me and was our art teacher. When I was ill, he sent this picture on a get-well card with bluebonnets on it to cheer me up. I loved to paint on rocks and birdhouses made from gourds I grew and painted on. He teased me and called them bluebells. They gave me much joy to look at, and I remember our painting classes (acrylic) with other friends at the church on Wednesdays. This shows a little of the talent God blessed him with to minister to us.

WISHING YOU A
SPEEDY RECOVERY.

Richard
&
Jean

*****

Eulavene Preston's Testimony, October 20, 2017

I have always known about God, as I was raised up in a Christian home. My father was a preacher. I went to church while growing up but never accepted God until I was in my sixties. Thank God I did before it was too late. I have been married sixty years and had five children and worked all my married life. I retired at age seventy-five, am now eighty. When I retired, I took up art class and am still painting. I love painting. I think God made me wait for this time to do what I love to do, and I will paint until I can't anymore. But God has His eye on this sparrow!

Eula and I attend church and a seniors' group called Keenagers at Christ Centered Church. We also painted together, and I asked her to show some of the talents the Lord gave her by painting a picture, "His Eye Is on the Sparrow."

Picture of "His Eye Is on the Sparrow" by Eula.

236

*****

This one is from Rosa Floyd. (Another friend from the YMCA Class who moved to Ohio).

Everyone has a story, and since I have lived eighty-six years on this earth, I have many. I was born to a poor, uneducated family from Kentucky as the Great Depression was ending, which was an event in itself. My dad needed work and was told he could get a job over the state line into Ohio and he could stay with the family who invited him. Mother and Dad went with hope and dreams of a better life. Mother was to deliver me any day, and after I was delivered, two ladies that lived there named me. Unfortunately, work did not come for Dad, and I am sure the family who invited us were glad to send the now family of three back to Kentucky! I feel I was kissed by God at birth, and this was the first of many proofs of His love over my life. I became a Christian at age twelve, and God has guided me ever since. My parents' marriage ended, but my mother saw that I receive a high school education, and God blessed me with ambition to do better.

As a Christian from age twelve, I was determined to marry a Christian boy. My only friends in high school were Christians, and one of my girlfriends had a twin brother who was in our class. After graduation, we were married, and that marriage was blessed by the devil. The boy was mentally ill, and as a young girl, I didn't know what to do. He would start an argument, and if I didn't argue, I was accused of being all puffed up and mad. He abused me in every way possible. He told me I was to submit to my husband and that I was ugly and dumb. I worked outside the home and kept a spotless home, thinking he would love me and not be mad at me. In those days, there were no resources to help, and my mother told me that marriage was forever. I prayed to God to take this burden away and help me be a better person. God did bless me with a beautiful little girl. Oh, the joy that filled my soul! But her daddy abused her too. Once, when she was training to eat with a spoon, she had spoon in one hand but picked up food with the other hand, and he took the handle of his dinner knife and hit her on the head. She was no more than a year old. When she started to cry, he jumped up from his chair and started shaking her, yelling at her to shut up. I ran to the bathroom, crying also. He came in the bathroom and shoved my head under the water until it was my last breath. Only God saved me that day. He took up with another woman a couple of years later and finally left me by telling me it was my fault and how inadequate I was. I had no skills, no job, and a child to support. I was devastated, and God was all I had. I cried and begged God to not let this happen, but it turned out to be the most wonderful gift that God ever gave me. Within two years, I had a wonderful job, met a kind, gentle, humble man who loved me and my child. We had comforts, prosperity, a wonderful church, and I could give my child a good education, huge wedding, and a new car as a gift. Life has been wonderful ever since, and all I need to do is get quiet and talk to Jesus, and He makes everything all right.

My husband's father was a church elder. One sister was married to a church deacon, and one sister married a preacher. My husband was raised in the church, and the family members were all devout protestant Christians. He died in 2007 at age seventy-five, never finding peace, which proves going to church does not make one a Christian. He had the upbringing but was too sick for it to help him.

Looking back, I know it was God who blessed me to graduate business school and with an opportunity to take additional classes at the University of Kentucky. I worked for a Fortune 500 company and was a secretary for every level of management up to vice president. God blessed me with a beautiful child that went to Bible college, and her daughter followed, graduating from Bible college also. My son-in-law and grandson are also strong believers that God is our foundation and protector, and we know we will see His face when we have finished the job on earth He has for us to do. I am comforted that my entire family members are strong believers, and I will be joined in heaven as they finish the task God has given them to do.

*****

This is from Jim Shifflett, my husband of fifteen years.

My earliest experience with church was largely uneventful—sporadic attendance at a large Baptist church in a large city with an older brother and sister when I was seven to nine years old. My second experience with church was while living on a tobacco farm and attending a small country Methodist church for almost six years with my brother, sister, and mother. My father had been raised by his father doing farmwork and had no life of church and seldom attended. I was sprinkled at age ten and. with Jesus and my mother, was put on the right course.

As I entered my teen years, my family moved to Lexington and began attending the Christian church and was soon baptized by immersion. This was the time I confessed my sins to Jesus and accepted Him as my Savior. I became highly involved in Bible school, the youth group, and soon became a Junior Deacon, participating in church rituals and programs.

After entering college at the University of Kentucky, I

lived in my parents' home and worked off-hours as part-time custodian at the church, helping with my college finances and keeping close to the Lord. In my second year of college, I considered going into the ministry, but after much thought and prayer, I remained with my original thought of becoming a teacher.

During my early teaching years, I attended a couple of different churches, usually going as a single man with a female friend. All along during these still-maturing years, I kept Jesus as my focal point and Lord.

As I continued in my profession of teaching and in my personal life, I found that my belief in the Lord was needed more and more, particularly in dealing with school problems with students, parents, and even other teachers; many times I asked the Lord to guide me in my decisions.

In my retirement years, particularly the past sixteen years, my wife, Patti, and I have become very active in the programs of our church; we participate in the Senior's Group, Keenagers, Bible Study Classes, Prayer room during services, heading the Prayer Chain on the internet, and biographical articles for the Church Newsletters. During the many challenges of this time (i.e., health issues—stroke, heart attack, etc.) and other personal issues, we have prayed and asked the Lord for His help and guidance. I will always look toward Jesus as my Savior.

*****

## What Is Prayer in My Life? (Communicating with God Throughout the Entire Day)

### by Jan Falwell

I have always been taught and thought it was just the meditative, down-on-the-knees, asking God to heal something or someone or myself. Growing up, citing memorized prayers did not mean much at all to me because they were not from my heart, just spoken words from memory. But in recent years, I have come to know it is a 24-7 thing. Or at least it should be. And I know God wants others to see Jesus in us and in what we do all day long. All our thoughts and actions should revolve around "What would Jesus do?" And it isn't during some quiet moments in the morning or the evening when we pray that we are getting credit for praying.

I think payer is a way of relating, being present and in the moment, and learning to be ourselves. It should involve a relationship with God, with who we are in our heart, and also to those around us and who we come in contact with. I do feel the quiet moments just talking to Him are of utmost importance to start off our day and to end it also. If something tragic happens during the day to take our attention back to our knees, then definitely go back to Him immediately. When Jesus did things, like His healings, it was not always done on His knees or stopping to ask His Father for a favor. He did it because it was from His heart and His foundational love for the individual He was healing or talking with.

I also believe it should represent the way we carry on our daily activities and interact with everyone we come in contact with. It should be our way of displaying who we are to others and doing things like Jesus did so that maybe, if they do not believe, they will see Jesus in us and want to be more like Him through us and the example we display. Hopefully, it will make any situation we are involved in better.

I also feel that if we have strong faith in Him, as we should, with all the things He has promised, then we should be busy 24-7 (or at least the waking hours) in thanking Him for allowing us to live one more day, to do the things He has put us here on earth to do. This would then have to include everything at work, at home, being a family member, a grocery shopper, and even making meals. I feel like I communicate in the kitchen through my ability to cook and the like, because it came from Him. Even with my health, I have used my condition to pass on what I have experienced to help others. I have gained this ability to teach from Him and only Him.

Maybe my definition or prayer is different from yours, but I believe God wants us to "communicate with Him" in every action and thought we have, and that would have to include more than just morning and night, on our knees, asking Him for something we feel we need or want. So why should prayer be limited to just when you are in a quiet place, on your knees, or with folded hands? I surely don't do it, and therefore why should you? It is basically an earnest wish or request, whether for someone to drive safely or to have a great day. He has my back even when in the kitchen, preparing food for myself or others I love, especially when I give so much of it away. The food is blessed through the whole process of its preparation and eating, like we do when we say the blessing. If we have faith in God, then the activities of the day should point to making something better, thanks to Him. Praying without ceasing (1 Thess. 5:17; Eph. 6:18). Pray on all occasions / all kinds of requests, on all occasions. (Drive safely, have a great day, prepare meal, in His name.)

Jan said she received this idea from something on the internet about the definition of prayer. She loved the definition. What is *prayer?* Prayer does not just happen when we kneel or put our hands together and focus, expecting things from God. Thinking positive and wishing good for others is a prayer. When you hug a friend, that's a prayer. When you cook something to nourish a family and friends, that's a prayer. When we send off our near and dear ones with "Drive safely" or "Be safe," that is a prayer. When you are helping someone by giving your time and energy, you are praying. When you forgive someone in your heart, that's a prayer. Prayer is a vibration, a feeling, a thought. Prayer is the voice of love, friendship, genuine relationships. Prayer is an expression of your silent being. "Keep praying always."

Jan is my friend from a workout class from the YMCA. She and her husband socialize with us and share spiritual growth, health information, prayers, and friendship in the Lord. When I read her testimony, it reminded me of Brother Lawrence from the little book from the 1600s called *Practicing the Presence of God,* where Brother Lawrence washed dishes so much, and when he did, he worshipped God and spent quality time with God whatever he did.

*****

Bob and Linda's Testimony

> We all have a story to testify of God's sustaining grace and power in our lives, and this is our God story. In June 2012, Bob received a medical diagnosis of pulmonary fibrosis, a terminal lung disease that requires a lung transplant to survive. He had been active, experiencing a chronic cough with slight shortness of breath, so this diagnosis was unexpected and overwhelming. His disease progressed rapidly, and within two months, the doctors gave Bob

two weeks to live, were arranging Hospice care, and were unwilling to list him for a transplant in Colorado, where we lived for many years close to family and friends. God had another plan, and through prayer and miraculous intervention, God opened a door for us to move to Kentucky, where Bob was accepted into a transplant program and put on the waiting list for a donor. Our life was flipped upside down, and everything that was familiar to us was taken away. It felt like Abraham leaving home for a foreign country.

Trust becomes challenging when the unknown is ahead of you. Hope grew dim at times, but God always gave us a promise from His Word or worked through the prayers and support of family and friends. We've had many prayer warriors standing with us. When our faith wavered, God was always faithful. We've been on the mountaintop and walked through the valleys, but Jesus brought us through it all, never leaving or forsaking us.

Bob was experiencing many complications posttransplant. I was exhausted, weary, and the Lord knew I needed a word from Him. If we listen closely, we can hear the Still Small Voice of God. He spoke to me through His creation. Driving to the hospital one spring morning, I heard these words: "As I bring new life to my creation after a winter season, I will bring new life to Bob through this transplant. My children, you have been through the winter season. Now it is time to breathe in newness of life." Psalm 27:14 became an encouragement in my weariness, reminding me to wait for the Lord. We trusted God with our finances and continued to give in to His kingdom as we did before Bob's illness. We had many medical expenses but never lacked for anything. God supplied all our needs (Phil. 4:19). We saw God's miraculous hand at work with physical healing the doctors had no explanation for and complications that only God could have brought us through.

After he had been listed for eighteen months and three dry runs, Bob's health was declining and we knew he needed a transplant soon. The Lord gave him Psalm 118:17 at this time: "I will not die but live and tell of the works of the Lord." Shortly after he was given this verse, Bob was given the gift of life with a double lung transplant. We would never have chosen this journey, but what we do know and have experienced is God's love, faithfulness, provision, and power in our lives at a depth we've never experienced before. His grace is sufficient, and His strength is made perfect in our weakness. We've grown and matured in our walk with the Lord because of the trials we have experienced. Praise Him!

Dear Patti,

Bob and I felt led to write our contribution to your book together.

An interesting tidbit to share with you. In March of 2015, we got a call from an acquaintance (a friend of a dear friend of ours) in Colorado. This acquaintance had been praying for us and felt God told her to contact the local paper in Greeley, Colorado, and the Guidepost magazine about our story and journey of transplant. We had been seeking the Lord about opening doors to share our story and hadn't been in contact with this lady. I journaled this and wrote, "So how you work, Lord. In mysterious ways we wait for you." As far as we know, neither of the above happened, or if it did, we didn't hear from either source. But now you have asked us to share some of our journey to be published in your book, which the Lord has laid in your heart. God's timing and His will!

September 1, 2014
A word for Bob and Linda Thomas After prayer and during their journey.

"Encouragement to My People
Beloved children of mine, I know your struggles are many. Look up. I am ever present, available, and will never leave you! Hope, prayer, and faith draw me ever so near for you to see my manifestations. I AM that I AM! Speak out loud. I trust you, Lord. Through all your struggles for words, make my power manifest to you, children! Your good is ever on my mind. Your Father cares about your every need. I am here! I am here! Listening closely to your prayers, only a heartbeat away, my children, caring, loving, and ministering to your needs. Agape love is with you now, blessing you all."

Bob and Linda came to the altar to have the spiritual elders lay hands on him and pray for his healing, as described in James 5:13–16 by Pastor Willie. The Holy Spirit impressed on me Psalms 118:17, that Bob would live and not die. I told her that after we finished the prayer, and she said that was the exact scripture the Lord gave him when he was diagnosed with the lung disease. We were on the same page with the Holy Spirit. Bob and Linda are friends of ours, attended church with us until recently, and we were in small groups together.

*****

## What If I Had One Month to Live

### by Grace Cox

To get the news that I had one month to live would be devastating to me. Say, for the last fifty-six years, I had lived a godly life and hope that I have set an example for my family, friends, and whoever I met.

1. I would make sure my heart was right with God by asking for forgiveness and repentance of any sins. I would ask God to create in me a pure heart, making sure my life was in order, and I would have no regrets. I would pray that God would help me endure whatever I am facing. You see, I have been a caregiver the biggest part of my life, helping others to cope, but for me that's a different story.

2. Then, I would witness to all my family and friends, testifying what the Lord has done for me, and that I am not afraid of dying but wanted to make sure they were saved. I would tell them, "God loves you. He offers you a full and meaningful life."

In this the love of God was manifested toward us, that God has sent His only begotten Son into the world, that we might live through Him.

But we must put our trust and faith that He is God's only Son; through Him you can have eternal life. You are a sinner by nature. You remain a sinner by choice.

To receive Jesus Christ as your Savior, you must...

Confess with your mouth that Jesus is Lord and believe in your heart that God raised Him from the dead, you will be saved, and live eternally with Jesus (1 John 1:9). Salvation is a free gift of God! It is yours for the taking. For whosoever shall call upon the Name of the Lord shall be saved (Rom. 10:13).

Amazing Grace! He took me through many dangers, toils, and snares. I have already come. 'Twas Grace that brought me safe thus far, and Grace will lead me home.

In my final farewell, that I have finished my service on

earth and will take residency in Heaven...forever...and God would say, "Well done, good and faithful servant!"

Faith makes a Christian.

Life proves a Christian.

Trials confirm a Christian.

Death crowns a Christian.

Grace is a neighbor and fellow church member who is an inspiration to all of us. She is a little older than I, and I can see her wisdom in her story and who is at the center of her life!

\*\*\*\*\*

Yvonne Worthington

Every Christian has a testimony. Mine certainly is not earth-shattering. Having grown up in a loving Christian home, I have been immeasurably blessed over the years in numerous ways with a wonderful husband of fifty three years, precious children, and friends wherever an Air Force career took us. Each of us encounters ups and downs in life, but I have always known that God has been close, on whom I could trust and lean for help and comfort. Psalm 105:4 says, "Look to the Lord and his strength; seek his face always." Truly, he has cared for me and mine. During the past few years, my husband passed away from this earth following a lengthy illness. Not once did either of us doubt God's loving comfort and decision. And now, I, too, am facing life-changing illness, but as always, God, along with doctors, family, and friends, is present for strength, comfort, and peace. I have known that "God is our refuge and strength; an ever present help in trouble" (Ps. 46:1).

None of us can predict our future, but we can be assured of his love, grace, comfort, and peace in whatever life offers, if only we trust and accept him. My prayer is that I will make decisions pleasing to God, knowing that he is my hope and that "Nothing is impossible with God" (Luke 1:37). I will attempt to live the rest of my life by Colossians 4:2, "Devote yourselves to prayer, being watchful and always thankful."

I sincerely endorse this book. Knowing Patti, having observed her endless dedication not only to God but also to her writings using God's Word, I know this will be inspirational to anyone reading them.

Yvonne Nicholls Worthington is my dear, longtime friend and roommate from University of Kentucky in 1958.

*****

Judith Courtney-Young

"In my distress I called upon the Lord, And cried out to my God; He heard my voice from His temple, And my cry came before Him, even to His ears" (Ps. 18:6).

At the age of eight years old, living in a world of alcoholism, abuse, and fear, I had God as my shelter from the pain I endured. I am so thankful for a grandmother who taught me about God, took me to church, and most of all, taught me to pray. There were many nights of watching my father beat my mother, abuse me and my brother. I knew that if I reached out to God through prayer, he would hear my cries and come to protect us. I had faith that God would stop the abuse, and to my knees in prayer I fell each time life became unbearable.

You may ask, "Did he help you? Did God hear you? Oh, yes, He did, every time." At that young age, I believed there was a Father in heaven that loved me, a Father who was good and kind, a Father I could call on at any time or anywhere when I needed love, protection, or help. He kept me strong in all my weak moments, and He carried me when I could not fight anymore. God was there then in my life, and He is still here in my life.

He can be in your life too. Just pray and ask His Son, Jesus Christ, into your heart, and He will never leave or forsake you. God Bless!

—Judith Courtney-Young

Judith wrote the following song:

Are You Ready?

The Bible tells us to be ready, ready for the coming of the Lord.
The Bible teaches us love and kindness, the Bible tells us how to live.
The Bible gives us direction, for our walk with Him.
Are you listening, are you ready, are you prepared?
For Jesus is coming.
Yes, Jesus is coming.
He says He's coming very soon.
He'll come on the clouds from Heaven above.

Will you be ready?
Will your name be written in the Book of Life
Or will God turn his eyes away?
Because you weren't ready, you weren't ready, you weren't ready.

The Bible teaches of his wonderful grace, it tells us to always have faith.
The Bible tells us whatever is noble, whatever is true, we're supposed to do.

Are you listening, are you ready, are you prepared?
For Jesus is coming.
Yes, Jesus is coming.
He says He's coming very soon.
He'll come on the clouds from Heaven above.

Will you be ready?
Will your name be written in the Book of Life
Or will God turn his eyes away?
Because you weren't ready, you weren't ready, you weren't ready.

Revelations 22:12 tells us, "Behold, I am coming soon."
So get ready!

written and composed by Judith Courtney
Sister for Christ
All rights reserved. Copyrighted 2012.

Judith uses her talent in an inspiring music ministry, and I wanted to leave you with the words of the song Judith wrote as the last thought of the book. Just reach out to the Lord and allow Him to bless your life. Patti

*****

My Son Greg's Post on Facebook

"But they that wait on the Lord shall renew their strength, they shall mount up with wings as eagles; they shall run and not be weary, and they shall walk, and not faint." (Isa. 40:31)

The word wait in the Hebrew is *qavah* and means to bring together by twisting. The sense is that if we delay waiting upon the Lord, we will be constantly seeking His face, and bound together with Him, we will be desirous of carrying out His Will. The Holy Spirit uses eagles as an example. Eagles do not stay perpetually young but do, in fact, periodically take on a luster on their wings that gives them a perpetual youthful appearance. Such is intended here. God promises to give strength for the journey in order that we may run and not be weary.

A few years ago, God burdened me to begin a discipleship group called Disciple of God. I did not heed that calling right away. It was revealed to me that I had forgotten about the letter C. I knew my ABCs but had forgotten about the Great Commission. "Go ye therefore to teach all nations, baptizing them in the name of the Father, the Son, and the Holy Ghost: Teaching them to observe all things whatsoever I have commanded you: and lo, I am with you always, even unto the end of the world. Amen" (Matt. 28:19–20). Without Christ (the letter *c*), I was serving my own purpose with the Great Omission. If you look at that phrase close enough, you will see that by relying on that *o*, which stood for zero, I was on a zero mission for our Lord and Savior.

I had become like the "lifeless church" in Revelation 3:2, "Be watchful, and strengthen the things which remain, that are ready to die: for I have not found they works perfect before God." I was overcome with the realization that I had a spiritual act of worship that I had better follow in Romans 12:2, "And be not conformed to this world; but be ye transformed by the renewing of your mind, that ye may prove what is that good, and acceptable and perfect will of God."

Oh, God, how can you use me? I am a forty-two-year-old man who was saved in the fifth grade and simply existed on a daily basis. What have I ever done to further your Kingdom? His promise to the Israelites in the Old Testament was a comfort to me. "And thou shall remember all the way which the Lord thy God led thee these 40 years in the wilderness, to humble thee, and to prove thee to know what was in thine heart, whether thou wouldest keep His commandments, or no. And He humbled thee, and suffered thee to hunger, and fed thee with manna, which thou knewest not, neither did thou Fathers know; that He might make thee know that man does not live by bread alone but every word that proceedeth out of the mouth of the Lord doth man live. Thy raiment waxed not upon thee, neither did they foot swell, these forty years. Thou shall also consider in thine heart, that as a man chasteneth his son, so the Lord thy God chasteneth thee. Therefore thou shall keep the commandments of the Lord thy God, to walk in His ways, and to fear Him" (Deut. 8:2–6).

God was preparing me these forty years for just such a time as this. He had never forgotten me or forsaken me. He had carried me through the struggles of life and used them to strengthen me. I must be thankful for the blessings in my life as well as the struggles that keep me on God's anointed path. "Therefore being justified by faith, we have peace with god through our Lord Jesus: By whom also we have access by faith into His grace wherein we stand, and rejoice in the hope of the glory of God. And not only so, but we glory in tribulations also: knowing that tribulation worketh patience; and patience, experience, and experience, hope; And hope maketh not ashamed; because the love of God is shed abroad in our hearts by the Holy Spirit which is given to us" (Rom. 5:1–5). How can I do less than serve Him completely? "For I long to see you, that I may impart unto you some spiritual gift, to the end ye might be established; That is, that I may be comforted together with you by the mutual faith of you and me" (Rom. 1:11–12).

Please pray for this new ministry, Disciple of God, that the Lord has begun. Pray that I can die to self each morning and serve my Holy Father in Heaven for the appointed time He has given me here on this earth. Please pray that I can be a witness to others, that my light would not go out and my salt would not become bitter. Should you want daily meditations as God leads me, please respond to me and let me know how I can pray for you today.

—Greg Millspaugh

As I was typing this for the manuscript, I realized God gave me, and also for my children, the scripture in Deuteronomy 8 that He gave Greg when I was in my forties as well! Also, the scripture in Romans got me through the challenging times when I was single. God is so faithful!